For Bo and John Strohbehn,

Who will be sorely missed in the Dartmouth community (and we know sorely needed by the locals at Duke). We hope to bridge the needs of both communities when we see you at Duke.

With our warmest best wishes,

Don Pease and Pat McKee

CRAIG CLAIBORNE'S SOUTHERN COOKING

CRAIG CLAIBORNE'S

Southern Cooking

WINGS BOOKS
NEW YORK • AVENEL, NEW JERSEY

This 1992 edition is published by Wings Books,
distributed by Outlet Book Company, Inc., a Random House Company,
40 Engelhard Avenue, Avenel, New Jersey 07001, by arrangement with Times Books.

In preparing a recipe for your family or guests, you should of course find out whether
anyone has an allergy to any food. If someone does have a sensitivity to an ingredient, it
should be avoided, even in small amounts.

Printed and bound in the United States of America

Library of Congress Cataloging-in-Publication Data

Claiborne, Craig.
[Southern cooking]
Craig Claiborne's Southern cooking.
p.   cm.
Originally published: New York : Times Books, 1987.
Includes index.
ISBN 0-517-07757-4
1. Cookery, American—Southern style.   I. Title.
[TX715.2.S68C53   1992]
641.5975—dc20   92-5038
                                                                CIP

To my sister,
Augusta Claiborne Barnwell

Acknowledgments

Many of the recipes in this book were sent to me over the years or demonstrated for me in my kitchen by both amateur and professional cooks. To all I am grateful.

Sybil Arant
Lee Barnes
Ruth Adams Brown
Dip's Country Kitchen
Dean Fearing
Margaret Field
Billye Hanan
Valerie Hart
Eleanor Hempstead
Gene Hovis
Carolyn Knutsen
Tom Leeper
Edna Lewis
Zarela Martinez

Sandy Miller
Bill Neal
Patrick O'Connell
Marina Polvany
Paul Prudhomme
Stephan Pyles
Laura Sandifer
Ann Seranne
Albert Stoddard
Charlie Swayze, Sr.
Elizabeth Terry
Dorothy Ann Webb
Karen and Chris Weihs
Emily Winburn

Contents

Introduction

In countless interviews for *The New York Times* over the past thirty years, I have learned that nothing can equal the universal appeal of the food of one's childhood and early youth. It may be avgolemono, the lemon-and-egg soup, for the exiled Greek. It may be a bowl of soba—buckwheat noodles—in a piping hot broth for a transplanted Japanese; a breakfast dish of congee, a kind of rice porridge with chicken or beef balls, for a displaced resident of Peking or Shanghai; or cha gio, the crisp and tasty spring roll (to be dipped into a fiery fish sauce with hot spices) for a Vietnamese away from the family hearth.

Nothing rekindles my spirits, gives comfort to my heart and mind, more than a visit to Mississippi and environs, to sit down to a dinner (the meal, as any Southerner knows, taken at midday) and be regaled, as I often have been, with a platter of fried chicken, field peas, collard greens, fresh corn on the cob, sliced tomatoes with French dressing (that's what we call a vinaigrette sauce), and to top it all off with a wedge of freshly baked pecan pie. With vanilla ice cream or without. The beverage for that meal being, more likely than not, sweetened iced tea.

I am inclined, because of the nature of my work for the last three decades, to eat sparingly so as to avoid, as I have been accused of doing, "excavating my grave with my teeth." But faced with that crisp-coated freshly fried chicken, collard greens, and all the rest, I throw caution to the wind; tomorrow be damned.

And each time I lift my fork, a thousand recollections of things past filter through my mind. I have mentioned much of this in an autobiography I wrote several years ago, the basics of it dating back to my cradle days in Sunflower, Mississippi. Since those days, I have had almost total recall of the sights and smells of home cooking.

In the very beginning, I had a black nurse named Aunt Catherine who was, in fact, my surrogate mother. For better or for worse, Southern-style in those unreconstructed days, I never knew or wondered about her last name. But it was she to whom I ran if I stumbled, if I bruised my knee, if I bled, if I cried when my feelings were wounded. She would pick me up, put me in her lap (she always wore a long, generally patterned or black dress, and apron) and rock me to comfort or sleep. I don't believe Aunt Catherine ever cooked, but she did go through one ritual of food preparation that is indelibly engraved on my mind. We owned cows that provided us with fresh, sweet milk that was stored in churns—tall earthenware urns. When left to remain overnight, the milk would "clabber," or become like yogurt, semisolid and lightly soured, the thickened golden cream rising to the top. The churn was covered with a round wooden cover with a hole in the middle. To produce butter and buttermilk, you would insert a round wooden pole in the center hole and at the base of the pole was a cross-shaped flat paddle. If you maneuvered the paddle up and down, the clabber would break down into a smooth-textured liquid with golden butter-flecks floating throughout. Aunt Catherine, me in her lap, would spend an hour churning with that paddle to make that buttermilk, which was, and is, pure manna to my taste.

Or, perhaps, she would use the raw, solid snow-white clabber to make cottage cheese. She would line a round earthenware crock with cheese-cloth, empty the clabber into it, and bring up the corners of the cloth. These she would tie together to make a bag for hanging. The bag would be suspended in a cool place on the porch, a bowl placed beneath, and at the end of a cool night it would be lifted down and opened. And there would be the purest cottage cheese that any palate could hope for.

Of those taking-the-first-step days, I have a few more solid recollections of food and feasting. When I was born, my father was a fairly well-off landowner and vice-president of the local bank. He was a handsome, modest but friendly gentleman who loved barbecues. On the wooded acreage next to our house, he would have long, deep trenches dug and the servants, or hired hands, would fill these slits with firewood. The wood would be ignited and allowed to burn for many hours until a white ash formed. The trenches would be covered with fence wire and on this, split chickens, goats, and other meats would be placed and lathered with a ketchup-based basting sauce. An hour or so later, family and guests would sit on benches at outdoor tables and dine on barbecued chicken, corn on the cob, sliced tomatoes, homemade bread, and a dozen or so desserts, including midsummer peach ice cream that had been turned laboriously by hand.

I also recall with fond memories the outings the family made in those years with neighbors and friends to Four Mile Lake, a watering spot near my small hometown. Gliding about on the water were small pleasure craft, many of whose passengers dangled fishing lines from cane poles, hoping a catfish would nibble. In the crystal-clear water, the lines could be seen all the way to the bottom. Many of the men wore white linen suits and black string ties and some wore white straw hats or boaters with wide brims. Some of the women carried parasols to guard their skin against that burning Mississippi sun.

Once a sufficient batch of catfish had been hauled aboard the various craft, they were carried ashore and cleaned with hunting knives. There were wide vats of hot oil near the shore and picnic tables not far away. The catfish would be dredged in a large tub of cornmeal and cooked in the hot fat until crisp without and succulent within. The catfish would be eaten with bottled ketchup, a little Worcestershire sauce, a little Tabasco sauce, and lemon wedges. And sweetened iced tea.

My mother, a Southern belle if ever there was one, loved beaten biscuits and served them often when she had friends over for afternoon coffee or "tea." Beaten biscuits, as any Southerner knows, are one of the most arduously made of all foods known to man. You combine flour with butter or butter and lard plus cold water and possibly milk to make a dough. You knead this well, turn it out onto a solid surface, and beat it by hand with a mallet or rolling pin for twenty minutes or longer until the dough "blisters." It is then rolled out, cut into small rounds, and baked until crisp without browning. Mother always served them split in half and with thin slices of Smithfield ham sandwiched between.

Outside the room in which I slept there was the sawed-off, wide circular stump of a walnut tree, and it was there, early in the morning, that I could hear the beating of that biscuit dough, whack after whack after whack.

One other remembrance of those days was my father's smokehouse in the backyard behind the kitchen. It was there that he smoked his own sausage, bacon, and ham.

When I was about four years old, my father's world collapsed, financially. A depression hit our area and he lost all his holdings. Literally. The land holdings, the bank funds, the house—everything except his family and spiritual faith, which was strong.

Shortly thereafter, I do not know when, it was decided that my mother would open a rooming and boardinghouse, a logical move since in those days it was one of the few paths a properly raised and "aristocratic" young Southern woman could pursue while holding her chin up and maintaining her prestige. Besides which, she was a magnificent cook, from appetizers through desserts. In order for this venture to succeed, it was necessary that we move to a larger town. We moved to Indianola, Mississippi, the county seat of Sunflower County, population about 3,500 at the time.

Within a few weeks of the opening, the boardinghouse was a notable success. The clients included the mayor of the town, numerous outstanding businessmen, schoolteachers, and so on. The dining room boasted an oval walnut dining table, large enough to seat twelve comfortably. It was invariably set with my mother's monogrammed wedding silver with a silver water goblet at each setting. Water or iced tea was poured from a sterling silver pitcher. The napkins and tablecloths were of linen.

Although our finances had reached a nadir, we still had numerous servants in the kitchen, all of them black. And that kitchen is where I spent my childhood. The servants—Joe and Blanche and Sally and Hugh —were my friends and playmates.

Blanche was the chief cook and she made the best fried chicken in the world. I had "picking" privileges. I was allowed to break off crisp bits of the outer coating of the chicken as it came hot from the skillet.

My mother had a fantastic palate, and I think that where Southern food is concerned, I lived in the best of all possible worlds. My mother had an incredible ability to reproduce any flavor, to analyze the ingredients of any dish she sampled. She could visit the restaurants of New Orleans and come back to re-create in her own kitchen such foods as eggs Nouvelle Orleans, oysters Rockefeller, shrimp rémoulade, and so forth.

Perhaps the most prized possession in my reference library (it contains numerous first editions of French classics such as the Alexandre Dumas *Grand Dictionnaire de Cuisine,* 1873) is the manuscript notebook compiled for me by my mother when I returned from the Navy in 1946 and rented an apartment in Chicago. It is filled with her favorite recipes, including her "famous" creation, chicken spaghetti, with its mushrooms and cubed chicken in a garlic-tinged tomato-and-meat sauce; "heirloom" recipes for a family Wedding Punch, which she notes is two hundred years old; many Cajun and Creole recipes; biscuits, corn muffins, hush puppies, and spoonbread; a recipe for crumpets, "a recipe from the most famous crumpet maker in all of England"; and a pasted-in recipe for ravioli Italiana made with "a dozen eggs, one peck or two bunches of spinach, one set of brains," plus instructions for making the pasta dough and the "gravy." The recipes are contained in a twenty-five-cent composition book with a cardboard binder in mottled black and white.

One of my favorite recollections of my mother's boardinghouse was her annual chitlin suppers, which always occurred during hog-killing time. The chitlins (or chitterlings, if you prefer) were always served with vinegar and hot pepper flakes plus turnip greens and lots of corn bread. Prior to that annual feast, she would give the boarders ample notice that it was about to happen, and if they didn't like it they could simply dine elsewhere.

When I was about twelve or thirteen years old I conceived my first "original" dish. For some reason unfathomable to me, I decided I would like to sample creamed chicken livers, and I mentioned this to Joe, the second in command of that boardinghouse kitchen. And prepare it he did to my great delight. It consisted simply of sautéed chicken livers served in a light cream sauce, heavily spiced with black pepper.

Another of my youthful inventions in that kitchen was a dish that (long before I became a professional food writer) stood me in good stead, Sunday after Sunday, when I entertained at lunch in my bachelor quarters in Chicago. My mother would, at times, serve eggs Benedict (a distinctly Yankee creation) for special occasions. I decided to create or have created my own version of that dish. I asked Joe to make me sliced ham on toast triangles with a poached egg and a cheese sauce spooned on top. He did, and it was a great success.

I have always been fascinated to think that my mother, who never had a cooking lesson in her life and who never set foot on European soil, cooked numerous French dishes, mainly desserts. Principal among them was charlotte russe, my favorite childhood celebration food. In my innocence I thought of it as the most glorious and Southern of dishes. My mother derived a good deal of her non-Southern cooking knowledge from a first edition of *The Boston Cooking-School Cook Book,* which was, in a sense, her culinary bible.

Herbs and spices were not well-varied and not in great demand in the Southern kitchens with which I was familiar in my youth. The principal green herb was fresh parsley, which was used ubiquitously either chopped or as a leaf for garnish. Celery, garlic, sweet green peppers (more often than not referred to as bell peppers because of their shape), and onions were much in use principally for Cajun and Creole dishes. Bay leaves were fairly common and black pepper was used in generous amounts. Tabasco sauce and Worcestershire (almost universally referred to as Lea & Perrins in my mother's manuscript book) were used in liberal amounts. Sage, nutmeg, and cayenne were in relatively frequent use. When my mother referred to "shallots," she invariably meant green onions or scallions. This is also true in much of the cooking of Louisiana.

It is not a question of chauvinism, but I have always averred that Southern cooking is by far the vastest and most varied of all traditional regional cooking in this country. I do not wish to demean the other regional cooking of the nation, but it is far more limited in scope. Consider West Coast or California cooking. And by that I do not mean the "new" cooking, which has not yet been altogether codified. The three regional dishes that come most readily to my mind are cioppino, a fish stew that is not universally known, crab with Louis dressing, and Caesar salad. When I think of New England cooking I consider various clam chowders and red flannel hash made with corned beef and cubed beets, and when I think of Northeast cooking, I think mostly of deli foods, things like corned beef sandwiches and pastrami. There is, of course, Pennsylvania Dutch cooking and Shaker cooking, but compared to the overall cooking of the South, they both have their well-defined parameters.

Southern cooking, on the other hand, embraces soul food, which is a blend of primarily African and American Indian; Creole, which is a marriage of innocent Spanish and, to a degree, bastardized French; the Cajun, which is the creation of hardscrabble whites (they had to live in Louisiana on what they were able to forage from the land and rivers and sea) with French overtones; the cooking of the Southwest (Tex-Mex) with its strong Mexican overtones—a basic blend of cornmeal and hot chilies; and barbecues, which are to be found in one aspect or another in all Southern states, using either vinegar and/or ketchup as a primary ingredient for its basting sauce. (Foods that are not cooked with a basting sauce are not, as is presumed in much of the North, barbecued; they are grilled, broiled, spit-roasted, or spit-turned.)

Complete volumes could and have been written about each of these elements of Southern cooking—Creole, Cajun, Tex-Mex, soul food, and barbecues. An encyclopedic, exhaustive study of all Southern dishes would, of necessity, demand a number of books sufficient to fill a library shelf and more.

This book, in brief, is a very personal compendium of recipes that reflect the food of the traditional South—such obvious, delectable, inescapable entities as fried chicken, country ham, black-eyed peas, and collard greens —to recent creations from the minds and stoves of some of the great new Southern chefs, dishes such as Black-eyed Peas Vinaigrette, Yellow Bell Pepper and Serrano Chili Soup, and Halibut Fillets with Mango and Basil Sauce. It incorporates many ingredients—herbs mostly—that were unknown or unused many years ago by my mother. Her treasures are scattered throughout. I have also included many recipes from the Southwest, which, to my mind, is one of the most interesting and yeasty sections of the South overall. I hope that this book is a testament to the cooking of the American South as it exists today.

Craig Claiborne
East Hampton, New York

CRAIG CLAIBORNE'S SOUTHERN COOKING

*Appetizers &
First Courses*

CHEESE STRAWS

Since my earliest childhood, I have had what amounts to a passion for cheese straws, particularly those with a tangy bite that comes not only from the cheese but from a touch or more of cayenne. The source of the recipe given here for those straws is Charlie Swayze, Sr., a family friend of many years from Greenwood, Mississippi.

8 tablespoons butter
½ pound sharp Cheddar or blue cheese
1 ¾ cups flour

Salt to taste, if desired
Cayenne pepper to taste (see note)
1 teaspoon Worcestershire sauce

1. Preheat the oven to 300 degrees.

2. Put the butter and cheese in the container of a food processor. Add the flour, salt, cayenne, and Worcestershire. Cover and blend thoroughly. If a food processor is not used, put the flour, salt, and cayenne in a bowl. Add the butter, cheese, and Worcestershire, and using two knives or a pastry blender, blend thoroughly.

3. Use a cookie press outfitted with a houndstooth or star dispenser. Push the dough out onto an ungreased baking sheet to make individual straws. Or, if desired, roll the dough out to ⅛-inch thickness and cut it into individual strips, which can be twisted if desired, or other shapes. Arrange the pieces on 1 or 2 ungreased baking sheets.

4. Place the baking sheet or sheets in the oven and bake 20 to 25 minutes, or until the straws are crisp and lightly browned. If you wish a darker color, let them cook longer. Remove and let cool.

YIELD: ABOUT 6 DOZEN.

NOTE: *The original recipe calls for a minimum of 1/2 teaspoon cayenne, but this may be increased or decreased according to taste.*

FRESH TOMATO ASPIC

This was one of my mother's so-called party dishes. It appeared quite often as the first course of a Sunday dinner (dinner is the midday meal in the South; the evening meal is supper), molded perhaps, or cut into squares and served in a lettuce leaf (often referred to as a "lettuce cup") and with a small dab of mayonnaise on top. If she did not make the aspic with fresh tomatoes, she used bottled tomato juice.

3 or 4 ripe tomatoes (about 1 1/2
pounds), cored and peeled
1 envelope granular gelatin
Salt to taste, if desired
Freshly ground pepper to taste

Juice of 1/2 lemon
1/2 teaspoon Worcestershire sauce
1/4 cup finely chopped parsley, optional
1 tablespoon finely chopped celery
leaves, optional

1. Do not chop the tomatoes or blend them. Rather, push them down in a measuring cup. There should be exactly 2 cups.
2. Add half the tomatoes to a saucepan. Pour off about 2 tablespoons of the natural tomato juice into a small bowl. Add the gelatin and stir to soften. Spoon and scrape this into the saucepan and stir. Bring just to the boil, stirring until the gelatin is dissolved. Add the remaining 1 cup tomatoes.
3. Add the salt, pepper, lemon juice, Worcestershire, parsley, and celery.
4. Pour the mixture into a small, rectangular loaf pan and place in the refrigerator. Let stand several hours or overnight, until set.
5. Serve sliced with a dab of mayonnaise on each slice.

YIELD: 4 TO 6 SERVINGS.

MOCK HEADCHEESE

Although headcheese is prepared in many parts of America, it is reminiscent of my Mississippi childhood. My father raised numerous animals, including chickens, cows, and hogs, and the heads of the latter were turned into hog's-head cheese. The preparation of the dish with actual hog's heads is a trifle difficult in this day and age. You can prepare a highly acceptable mock version of the dish using pigs' knuckles and pigs' feet.

2 1/2 pounds pork knuckles
1 1/2 pounds pigs' feet
12 cups water
2 small carrots
1 celery rib, quartered
1 onion stuck with 2 cloves
2 whole allspice
1 bay leaf
Salt to taste, if desired
6 peppercorns, crushed

2 garlic cloves, unpeeled but lightly flattened
2 sprigs fresh thyme, or 1/2 teaspoon dried
1 pound cooked ham steak
1 hot red pepper
2 tablespoons white wine vinegar
1/8 teaspoon ground nutmeg
1/4 cup chopped parsley

1. Put the knuckles and pigs' feet in a small kettle and add water to cover. Bring to the boil and simmer about 1 minute. Drain well.

2. Return the knuckles and pigs' feet to a clean kettle and add the water, carrots, celery, onion, allspice, bay leaf, salt, peppercorns, garlic, and thyme. Bring to the boil and simmer 3 hours, skimming the surface as necessary. Remove from the heat and let cool.

3. Remove the knuckles and pigs' feet. Remove and reserve all meat and skin. There should be about 4 cups. Discard the bones. Strain the liquid. There should be about 3 1/2 cups.

4. Combine the meat, skin, and liquid. Cut the ham into 1/2-inch cubes and add it. Add the red pepper, vinegar, nutmeg, and salt and bring to the boil. Cook down about 30 minutes and remove from the heat. Remove the hot red pepper and stir in the chopped parsley.

5. Pour the mixture into a 9½ × 5¼ × 2-inch loaf pan and let stand until cool. Refrigerate overnight. Unmold and slice.

YIELD: 8 TO 12 SERVINGS.

HEADCHEESE VINAIGRETTE

My mother had a great fondness for many dishes that are ultimately of French origin, several of which I have adapted for this book. She did not use olive oil to a great degree, and she certainly did not have access in my Mississippi home to Dijon-style or Düsseldorf mustard. She used a very ordinary brand of store-bought vinegar, mostly white, the only kind available to her in the small town of my childhood. Her favorite and most used cookbook, incidentally, was Fannie Farmer's, which did offer recipes for numerous well-researched French dishes.

1 pound headcheese, homemade or
* purchased*
6 tablespoons finely chopped onion
1 teaspoon finely chopped garlic
¼ cup finely chopped parsley
2 tablespoons prepared mustard,
* preferably Dijon or Düsseldorf*

2 tablespoons red wine vinegar
6 tablespoons olive oil
Salt to taste, if desired
Freshly ground pepper to taste

1. Cut the headcheese into bite-size morsels and place them in a mixing bowl.
2. Add the remaining ingredients and toss.
3. Serve with crusty bread or toast.

YIELD: 4 OR MORE SERVINGS.

PIMIENTO CHEESE SPREAD

*1/2 pound mild yellow Cheddar or
  longhorn cheese*
*1/2 pound white aged sharp Cheddar
  cheese*
1 can (7 ounces) pimientos
*1 cup chopped scallions, including
  green part*

1/2 cup mayonnaise
2 teaspoons lemon juice
1 teaspoon finely minced garlic
2 tablespoons Worcestershire sauce
6 drops Tabasco sauce
1/2 teaspoon freshly ground pepper

1. Use a meat grinder, if possible, to grate the cheeses, using the cutter with large holes. Otherwise, use the coarse side of a cheese grater. Put the grated cheese in a mixing bowl and add half the juice from the canned pimientos. Dice the drained pimientos and add them along with the scallions.

2. Combine the mayonnaise, lemon juice, and garlic and add to the cheese mixture. Add the Worcestershire, Tabasco, and pepper and blend well.

3. Serve at room temperature as a spread for crisp crackers and raw vegetables or use as a sandwich spread.

YIELD: 8 TO 12 SERVINGS.

NOTE: *Unused pimiento cheese may be tightly sealed and kept for several days in the refrigerator.*

LIVER PUDDING

This is a Southern version of an easily and well-made pâté. It is the creation of my good friend Edna Lewis, a native of Virginia and one of the best cooks I know.

*1 1/2 pounds pork liver, preferably in
   one piece (see note)*
*1 1/2 pounds fresh pork jowl (see note),
   or 1 1/2 pounds fresh unsalted pork
   belly or uncured bacon*

1 onion (about 1/2 pound), peeled
Salt to taste, if desired
Freshly ground pepper to taste
*1 teaspoon finely chopped fresh sage, or
   1/2 teaspoon dried*

1. Put the liver and pork in a kettle and add the onion and water to cover. Bring to the boil. Cover and cook about 2 hours.

2. Preheat the oven to 275 degrees.

3. Remove the meats and onion from the kettle. There should be 2 cups of broth. If there is more, skim off the clearest top portion, discarding the bottom portion with its meat residue.

4. Cut the meats into small chunks. Using a meat grinder or food processor, coarsely grind the meats and onion. Spoon and scrape into a mixing bowl. Stir in the 2 cups reserved broth. The mixture will be quite thin.

5. Stir in the salt, pepper, and sage. Mix well and pour into a heavy tin loaf pan or 2-quart casserole. Place in the oven and bake 2½ hours. The long cooking helps to develop the flavor of the pudding and makes it easy to slice. When cool, place in a cold place or in the refrigerator.

6. Serve sliced with buttered toast.

YIELD: 6 TO 8 SERVINGS.

NOTE: *Fresh pork liver and pork jowl are available in many pork stores and on request from many butchers.*

INDIVIDUAL WILD MUSHROOM PIES

³/₄ pound pastry (see following recipe)
4 tablespoons butter, plus melted butter
  for molds
1 ¹/₂ pounds assorted wild mushrooms
  such as shiitake, oyster mushrooms,
  chanterelles, hedgehog, white or
  black trumpet mushrooms, or others
  (see note)

1 cup finely chopped scallions, both
  white and green parts
1 ¹/₂ teaspoons finely chopped fresh
  thyme leaves, or half the amount
  dried
¹/₂ cup finely diced country ham
1 tablespoon dry sherry
1 ¹/₂ cups heavy cream

1. Preheat the oven to 475 degrees.

2. Let the pastry stand briefly outside the refrigerator.

3. Use 8 heart-shaped or round metal or ovenproof molds, each with a capacity of ²/₃ cup, and brush inside each with a little melted butter.

4. Lay a 16 × 16-inch square of clear plastic wrap on a flat surface and place 1 pastry patty in the center. Cover with a second square of clear plastic wrap. Roll out the round of pastry into a large circle ¹/₈ inch thick. Cut the circle into quarters. Repeat with the other pastry patty. Lay one portion of dough on top of each individual mold, lightly pressing the dough inside to fill the mold. Leave the outside edges overhanging and trim around the bottom of the edges. Bake about 10 minutes and let cool.

5. Slice the mushrooms into bite-size pieces. There should be about 2 quarts loosely packed.

6. Heat the 4 tablespoons butter in a heavy skillet and add the scallions, thyme, and ham. Cook briefly until the ham starts to take on color. Add the mushrooms and sherry. Bring to the boil and cover closely. Cook over moderate heat about 2 minutes and add the cream. Uncover and continue cooking over high heat 5 to 7 minutes.

7. Remove the pastry shells from the molds. Heap the mushroom mixture inside the pastry shells and serve.

YIELD: 8 SERVINGS.

NOTE: *If desired, you might use half the volume of wild mushrooms called for in this recipe and add an equal amount of commercial mushrooms.*

PASTRY

2 cups flour
1 teaspoon salt, optional
½ cup solid white vegetable shortening

4 tablespoons cold butter, cut into
* small cubes*
2 to 3 tablespoons ice water

1. Combine the flour, salt, shortening, and butter in a mixing bowl and refrigerate until thoroughly chilled.

2. Using the fingers, quickly blend the ingredients until they have the consistency of coarse cornmeal.

3. Add the water a little at a time, tossing the mixture with the tines of a fork. Take care to add only enough water so that the pastry can be gathered into 2 cohesive balls. Shape each ball into a flat patty, each about ¾ inch thick. Wrap each in clear plastic wrap and refrigerate 1 hour or longer.

YIELD: ABOUT ¾ POUND PASTRY.

MARINATED SEAFOOD COCKTAIL

24 littleneck clams
½ pound shrimp, peeled and deveined
Salt to taste, if desired
1 bay leaf
1 dried hot red pepper
20 small mussels, well scrubbed
3 tablespoons dry white wine
½ cup chopped ripe tomatoes
½ cup finely chopped onion

1 tablespoon finely minced garlic
1 ½ cups cubed avocado
¼ cup fresh lime juice
1 cup tomato juice
2 teaspoons crushed dried coriander
* seeds*
¼ teaspoon dried hot red pepper flakes
2 teaspoons chopped fresh coriander,
* optional, or parsley*

1. Open and save the clams and their liquid. There should be about ½ cup clams and 1 cup liquid.

2. Place the shrimp in a saucepan and add water to cover, salt, bay leaf, and hot red pepper. Bring to the boil. Remove from the heat and let cool. Drain and cut the shrimp into cubes. Set aside.

3. Put the mussels in a saucepan with the wine. Cover closely and bring to the boil. Cook 4 or 5 minutes, until the mussels open. Drain. Remove the mussels from their shells. Remove and discard the rubber band–like strand that surrounds each mussel.

4. Put the clams and their liquid in a mixing bowl. Add the shrimp and mussels, tomatoes, onion, garlic, avocado, lime juice, tomato juice, coriander seeds, red pepper flakes, and coriander or parsley. Cover and refrigerate several hours until ready to serve.

YIELD: 8 OR MORE SERVINGS.

CRAB BAYOU TECHE

This recipe was sent to me years ago by a reader who lived in New Iberia, Louisiana, most famed as the home of Tabasco sauce. New Iberia was founded by the Spanish inhabitants of this country on the banks of a bayou called Teche, which, according to some sources, is an American Indian word for snake.

6 tablespoons butter, at room
    temperature
3 hard-cooked egg yolks
½ teaspoon dry mustard
¼ teaspoon curry powder (do not add
    more)
¼ cup dry white wine
¾ cup heavy cream

3 tablespoons chopped chives
1 pound lump crabmeat, picked over
    well, or cooked lobster, cubed
Salt to taste, if desired
Freshly ground pepper to taste
1 garlic clove, peeled
½ cup bread crumbs

1. Preheat the oven to 350 degrees.

2. Put 4 tablespoons butter in a mixing bowl. Put the egg yolks through a fine sieve and add them to the butter. Stir to blend.

3. Combine the mustard and curry powder with the wine and stir to blend. Beat this into the butter mixture. Beat in the cream. If the mixture looks a bit curdled, do not be concerned. Stir in the chives and fold in the crabmeat. Add salt and pepper to taste. Stir gently so as not to break up the crab any more than necessary.

4. Rub 8 individual ramekins or scallop shells with the garlic clove and fill them with equal amounts of the crab mixture.

5. Heat the remaining 2 tablespoons butter in a small frying pan and add the bread crumbs. Stir until the crumbs are coated. Spoon equal amounts of crumbs over the crab.

6. Bake 20 minutes, or until it is bubbling hot and the tops are browned. To brown further, run the ramekins quickly under the broiler.

YIELD: 8 FIRST-COURSE SERVINGS.

CAJUN POPCORN (BATTER-FRIED CRAWFISH)

This is a recipe, one of several, given to me by my friend of many years, Paul Prudhomme, the finest Creole and Cajun chef. One taste of these and you can't stop popping the tiny deep-fried crawfish into your mouth. That shrimp-shaped critter, incidentally, is always referred to as crawfish in the South. Crayfish to a Southern ear sounds pretentious, as though you are putting on airs.

2 eggs, well beaten
1 1/4 cups milk
1/2 cup corn flour (see note)
1/2 cup all-purpose flour
1 teaspoon sugar
Salt to taste, if desired
1 teaspoon plus 1 tablespoon finely
*   chopped garlic*
1 teaspoon finely chopped onion
1 teaspoon finely ground white pepper

1/8 teaspoon finely ground black pepper
1/2 teaspoon cayenne pepper
1/4 teaspoon dried thyme
1/8 teaspoon pulverized bay leaf
1 cup Mayonnaise (page 263)
Tabasco sauce
Oil for deep-frying
2 pounds crawfish tails, peeled, or very
*   small shrimp, peeled and deveined*

1. Blend the eggs and milk; beat well.

2. In a large bowl, combine the corn flour, all-purpose flour, sugar, salt, 1 teaspoon garlic, onion, peppers, thyme, and bay leaf. Blend well. Gradually add the milk mixture, stirring well with a whisk. Let stand 1 hour at room temperature.

3. Combine the 1 tablespoon finely chopped garlic with the mayonnaise and Tabasco to taste.

4. Heat 1 inch of oil in a black iron skillet, or use a deep-fat fryer. It is important that the oil be heated to a temperature as close to 370 degrees as possible. Coat a few pieces of seafood with batter and drop them into the hot fat. Cook, stirring occasionally, until golden brown all over, about 2 minutes.

5. As the coated seafood is cooked, drain well on paper towels. Continue with the remaining seafood.

6. Serve with garlic mayonnaise on the side.

YIELD: 4 TO 8 SERVINGS.

NOTE: *Corn flour is available at many health-food stores. If not available, increase the all-purpose flour to 1 cup.*

SHRIMP RÉMOULADE

French cuisine underwent numerous alterations in the professional kitchens of New Orleans. One of the most obvious examples of that, to my mind, is in the dishes named *rémoulade.* Classically, in France, this is nothing more than a mayonnaise to which chopped capers, those small sour pickles known as cornichons, chopped herbs including parsley, tarragon, chervil, and chives, plus anchovy paste, are added. The New Orleans version is more elaborate and contains horseradish, finely chopped celery, and scallions, among other things. This also brings to mind the thought that when New Orleans recipes call for shallots—one of the most widely used seasonings in classic and home kitchens—they generally mean scallions or green onions. Apparently, genuine shallots were not available to the early French settlers—chefs—in New Orleans and green onions were used as a substitute. To make a genuine shrimp rémoulade, New Orleans style, it is also *imperative* that you use Creole mustard, not ballpark American or Dijon-style.

THE SHRIMP:

2 pounds fresh shrimp in the shell
16 whole allspice
1 large garlic clove, peeled and crushed

12 peppercorns, crushed
Salt to taste, if desired

THE RÉMOULADE SAUCE:

2 tablespoons Creole mustard (see note)
1 tablespoon tarragon wine vinegar
Salt to taste, if desired
Freshly ground pepper to taste
1 cup olive oil
1 tablespoon paprika
1/2 cup finely chopped celery
1 cup chopped scallions

1 teaspoon chopped garlic
1/2 cup chopped parsley
2 tablespoons horseradish, preferably freshly grated
2 tablespoons anchovy paste
1/8 teaspoon cayenne pepper
2 tablespoons lemon juice
Tabasco sauce to taste

THE GARNISH:

Shredded romaine lettuce
Lemon wedges

1. Put the shrimp in a saucepan and add water to cover. Add the allspice, garlic clove, peppercorns, and salt. Bring gradually to the boil. Simmer about 1 minute and remove from the heat. Let stand until cool. Peel and devein the shrimp. There should be about 4 cups.

2. For the sauce, put the mustard and vinegar in a mixing bowl and add salt and pepper to taste. Beat with a wire whisk and gradually add the oil, stirring constantly. If you beat briskly enough, the oil should blend in smoothly without separating.

3. Stir in the remaining ingredients for the sauce.

4. Put about ½ cup shredded romaine on each of 8 salad plates. Arrange an equal number of shrimp on the lettuce. Spoon the sauce over to cover the shrimp completely. Serve with lemon wedges.

YIELD: 8 SERVINGS.

NOTE: *Zatarain's Creole mustard is available in many shops specializing in fine foods.*

OYSTERS BIENVILLE

Oysters Bienville were named for Jean-Baptiste Le Moyne, sieur de Bienville. He was born in 1680 in Montreal, Canada, and was the second colonial governor of Louisiana. He died in New Orleans in 1768. I was fascinated to read in the *Encyclopaedia Britannica* that when Bienville first came to New Orleans, the village was "a place of a hundred wretched hovels in a malarious wet thicket of willows and dwarf palmettos, infested by serpents and alligators." The oyster dish named in his honor is an elegant dish, with oysters baked in a cream sauce with crabmeat or shrimp.

36 oysters
¾ cup Fish Stock (page 274) or
  bottled clam juice, approximately
4 tablespoons butter
¼ pound finely chopped mushrooms
  (about 1 cup)
¼ cup finely chopped scallions,
  including green part
2 tablespoons finely minced sweet green
  pepper
1 teaspoon finely minced garlic
2 tablespoons dry white wine
3 tablespoons flour

3 eggs, lightly beaten
½ cup heavy cream
⅛ teaspoon freshly grated nutmeg
Pinch of cayenne pepper
Salt to taste, if desired
Freshly ground pepper to taste,
  preferably white
1 cup finely chopped cooked shrimp or
  shredded crabmeat
2 tablespoons dry sherry
½ cup fine fresh bread crumbs
½ cup freshly grated Romano,
  Gruyère, or Parmesan cheese

1. Preheat the oven to 500 degrees.

2. Shuck the oysters or have them shucked. Reserve half the shells, all the oysters, and ¼ cup of the liquid.

3. Add enough fish stock or clam juice to the oyster liquor to make 1 cup.

4. Heat the butter in a saucepan and add the mushrooms, scallions, green pepper, and garlic. Cook, stirring, until the mushrooms are wilted. Add the wine and cook until all the liquid evaporates. Do not burn the vegetables.

5. Sprinkle the mixture with flour, stirring with a wire whisk. Quickly add the oyster-liquor mixture, stirring rapidly with the whisk.

6. When the sauce has thickened, blend the eggs with the cream and add to the sauce. Cook, stirring constantly, about 10 seconds and remove from the heat. Add the nutmeg, cayenne, salt, and pepper to taste. Stir in the shrimp and sherry.

7. Rinse the oyster shells and pat them dry.

8. Traditionally, the shells are arranged on a bed of rock salt in 2 to 4 ovenproof baking dishes. It is easier, however, to use a baking sheet and arrange the shells, hollow side up, over it. Place 1 drained oyster in each shell. Spoon equal portions of the sauce over the oysters.

9. Blend the bread crumbs and cheese, and sprinkle equal amounts of this over each oyster in the half shell. Place in the oven and bake 15 to 20 minutes, or until the sauce is piping hot and lightly browned on top.

YIELD: 4 TO 6 SERVINGS.

OYSTERS ROCKEFELLER

The owners of Antoine's restaurant in New Orleans lay claim to the "invention" of this dish. It is credited to the original owner, Jules Alciatore, and is said to have been created around the turn of the century. It was named Rockefeller, not necessarily in tribute to John D., who may or may not have been a customer of the restaurant. He was simply one of the wealthiest men in America and the dish was dubbed with his family name because of the richness of the dish and the abundance of "green stuff" that topped the oysters.

36 oysters

2 pounds (or 2 10-ounce packages)
  fresh spinach

1 cup finely chopped scallions

1/2 cup finely chopped celery

1/2 cup finely chopped parsley

1 garlic clove, finely minced

1 can (2 ounces) anchovies, drained

8 tablespoons butter

1 tablespoon flour

1/2 cup heavy cream

Tabasco sauce to taste

1 or 2 tablespoons Pernod, Ricard, or
  other anise-flavored liqueur

1/3 cup grated Parmesan cheese

1. Preheat the oven to 450 degrees.

2. Open the oysters, leaving them on the half shell and reserving the oyster liquor.

3. Pick over the spinach and remove any tough stems and blemished leaves. Rinse well and put in a saucepan. Cover and cook, stirring, until spinach is wilted. Drain well and squeeze to remove excess moisture. Blend or put through a food grinder. There should be about 2 cups.

4. Put the scallions, celery, and parsley into the container of a food processor or an electric blender and blend. There should be about 1 cup.

5. Chop the garlic and anchovies together.

6. Heat 4 tablespoons butter in a skillet and add the scallion mixture. Stir about 1 minute and add the anchovy mixture. Cook, stirring, for about 1 minute and add the spinach. Stir to blend.

7. Heat the remaining 4 tablespoons butter in a saucepan and add the flour. Blend, stirring with a wire whisk, and add the oyster liquor, stirring vigorously with the whisk. Stir in the cream. Season with Tabasco. Do not add salt. Add the spinach mixture and Pernod. Let cool.

8. Spoon equal portions of the mixture on top of the oysters and smooth over the tops. Sprinkle with Parmesan cheese. Bake for about 25 minutes, or until piping hot.

YIELD: 6 SERVINGS.

OYSTERS CASINO

60 oysters on the half shell
60 squares (1 inch each) of lean bacon
10 tablespoons butter, melted

1 tablespoon lemon juice
1/2 cup finely chopped parsley

1. Preheat the broiler to high.
2. Each oyster should be loosened but left on the half shell.
3. Spread a layer of rock salt over a baking sheet. Arrange the oysters, shell side down, on the rock salt. Cover each oyster with a square of bacon. Place the baking sheet under the broiler and cook briefly, until the bacon curls and becomes slightly crisp, about 2 minutes.
4. Meanwhile, blend the butter, lemon juice, and parsley. Spoon equal amounts of this mixture onto each oyster. Run the baking sheet as quickly as possible under the broiler and cook just until butter is heated.

YIELD: 12 SERVINGS.

SEVICHE

Seviche has over the past decade or longer become very much a part of America's culinary culture. It is also sometimes spelled ceviche, and the name derives from the Spanish word *cebollo,* which means onions. I believe chopped onion was essential to the original preparation. There are countless versions of this fish-marinated-in-lime-juice preparation. This is the one that I prefer.

1 pound skinless, boneless fillets of fish,
   such as bluefish, red snapper,
   mackerel, or seafood, such as bay
   scallops
7 tablespoons lime juice
1 cup peeled, seeded, cubed, and
   drained ripe tomatoes
4 or more canned serrano chilies,
   drained and chopped
1/2 cup finely chopped red onion

1 tablespoon olive oil
2 teaspoons finely chopped fresh
   coriander
1/2 teaspoon crumbled dried oregano
Salt to taste, if desired
Freshly ground pepper to taste
1/2 cup diced avocado
1/4 cup finely diced heart of celery
1/4 cup ketchup
Grated rind of 1 lime

1. Cut the fish into 1/2-inch cubes. If bay scallops are used, cut them into quarters. Put the pieces in a bowl and add the lime juice. Cover and refrigerate, stirring occasionally, 12 hours or longer.

2. Add the remaining ingredients and chill until ready to serve.

YIELD: 6 TO 8 SERVINGS.

GUACAMOLE

Guacamole is a staple of many meals served in the American Southwest. It is, of course, a mashed avocado dip and the name derives from an Indian Nahuatl word, *ahuacatl,* meaning avocado, and *molli,* meaning a blend or concoction.

2 ripe, unblemished, not-too-soft
   avocados (about 3/4 pound each)
2 tablespoons lime juice
1/2 cup finely chopped onion
1 tablespoon olive oil

1/2 cup finely chopped fresh coriander
2 canned serrano chilies, drained,
   stems removed, and chopped
3/4 cup cubed, drained ripe tomatoes
Salt to taste, if desired

1. Cut the avocados in half and discard the pits. Remove the peel and put the avocado halves in a mixing bowl. Using a fork and knife scissors-fashion, cut the avocado roughly into 1/2-inch pieces. Sprinkle with lime juice and stir. There should be about 2 cups.

2. Put half the chopped avocado into the container of a food processor or electric blender and add ¼ cup onion, the olive oil, and ¼ cup coriander. Blend thoroughly. Add this to the remaining chopped avocado. Add the chilies. Stir in the remaining onion and coriander and the tomatoes. Add salt to taste.

YIELD: ABOUT 3 CUPS.

SAUSAGE-CHEESE BISCUITS

This is one of the finest cocktail snacks I have ever sampled. It is insidiously good, like peanuts or popcorn, and consists of well-spiced sausage baked into a roll and cut into rounds. It is a recipe given to me by my sister in Greenwood, Mississippi, one Christmas past.

1 ½ cups sifted flour
1 teaspoon baking powder
½ teaspoon baking soda
½ teaspoon salt, if desired
2 tablespoons solid white vegetable
*   shortening*

2 tablespoons cultured buttermilk
*   powder (see note)*
½ pound sharp Cheddar cheese, grated
1 pound homemade Spiced Sausage
*   (page 166)*

1. Preheat the oven to 425 degrees.
2. Set aside 1 tablespoon flour for kneading the dough.
3. Combine the remaining flour, baking powder, baking soda, and salt in a mixing bowl. Blend well. Add the shortening and cut it in with a pastry cutter. Add the buttermilk powder and blend well with the fingers.
4. Add the cheese and uncooked sausage and blend thoroughly. Turn the dough out onto a lightly floured board and knead briefly. Shape the mixture into balls about 1 inch in diameter, rolling between the palms of the hands. As the balls are shaped, arrange them on a baking sheet. (The biscuits may be frozen and baked later after thawing.)
5. Place in the oven and bake 15 to 20 minutes.

YIELD: ABOUT 5 DOZEN.

NOTE: *Cultured buttermilk powder is available in many supermarkets and health-food stores.*

BENNE WAFERS

There is a cocktail wafer that seems a vital part of the culture of Charleston, South Carolina, and that is called the benne wafer. *Benne* is the local word for sesame seeds, and few people seem to know that its use in the South, particularly South Carolina, dates from the days of slavery. The seeds were brought into the country from Africa aboard the slave ships, perhaps in the pockets of the hapless passengers. The word derives from the word *bĕne* from the language of the people of the upper Niger River Valley in Western Africa.

¹/₄ cup sesame seeds　　　*3 tablespoons butter*
1 cup flour　　　*1 egg yolk*
¹/₄ teaspoon salt, if desired　　　*Ice water*
Pinch of cayenne pepper

1. Toast the sesame seeds in a skillet over low heat, stirring frequently, or in a 300-degree oven for 15 minutes. Cool.
2. Preheat the oven to 350 degrees.
3. Place the flour, salt, and cayenne in a bowl. Work in the butter with the fingertips, until the mixture resembles coarse oatmeal. Add the cooled sesame seeds, the egg yolk, and enough ice water to make a dough.
4. Roll out the dough on a floured board and cut into 2-inch rounds. Place on an ungreased cookie sheet and bake 15 minutes, or until lightly golden. Cool on a rack.

YIELD: ABOUT 18 WAFERS.

SPICED COCKTAIL PECANS

6 tablespoons butter
1/2 teaspoon Tabasco sauce
1 teaspoon Worcestershire sauce

1 garlic clove, finely minced, optional
1 pound shelled pecans

1. Preheat the oven to 325 degrees.
2. Melt the butter and add the Tabasco, Worcestershire, and garlic. Heat briefly.
3. Scatter the pecans in one layer on a jelly-roll pan, and spoon the seasoned butter over them. Place in the oven and bake 20 to 30 minutes, shaking the pan and stirring the pecans often. Serve hot or cold.

YIELD: 1 POUND.

BAKED PECANS, GEORGIA STYLE

1 pound unbroken pecan halves
4 tablespoons butter
Salt to taste

1. Preheat the oven to 225 degrees.
2. Arrange the nuts over the bottom of a roasting pan large enough to hold them in one layer.
3. Cut the butter into small pieces and scatter it over the pecans. Bake 45 minutes to 1 1/2 hours, shaking the pan often and stirring the nuts about every 10 minutes.

4. After 45 minutes, test the nuts. Break a pecan meat in half: If it is white in the center, continue cooking. Cook until broken nut meats are light brown all the way through.

5. Scoop the nuts into a brown paper bag. Add salt to taste and shake well to coat.

YIELD: 1 POUND.

Eggs & Luncheon Dishes

HAM-STUFFED EGGS

Stuffed eggs were part and parcel of my Mississippi upbringing. The fillings varied from occasion to occasion, but if we ate out of doors, which was often—picnics, barbecues, catfish fries—stuffed eggs almost invariably were part of the food hamper that went along with us.

1 ounce boiled ham
4 Hard-Cooked Eggs (see following instructions)
1 tablespoon imported mustard, preferably Dijon or Düsseldorf
2 tablespoons butter, at room temperature

¼ teaspoon Worcestershire sauce
2 teaspoons mayonnaise
Salt to taste, if desired
Freshly ground pepper to taste
1 tablespoon finely chopped chives
Cutouts of black or green olives, pimientos, or pickles

1. Cut the ham into very fine dice and chop. Combine the sieved yolks and ham in a mixing bowl. Add the mustard and butter. Stir to blend.

2. Add the Worcestershire, mayonnaise, salt, pepper, and chives. Blend thoroughly. Equip a pastry bag with a star tube (No. 4). Fill the bag with the ham mixture and pipe it into the egg-white hollows. Garnish the top of each egg with a small slice of black or green olive or other cutout.

YIELD: 8 EGG HALVES.

HARD-COOKED EGGS

Place any given number of eggs in a saucepan or casserole and add warm water to cover. Add a little salt, if desired, to facilitate later peeling. Bring slowly to the boil and simmer about 12 minutes. Drain immediately under cold running water. Peel. To prepare the eggs for stuffing, slice them in half, put the yolks in a sieve, and press through with the fingers.

SARDINE-STUFFED EGGS

1 can (3 ¾ ounces) skinless and
   boneless sardines
4 Hard-Cooked Eggs (see preceding
   instructions)
2 teaspoons cider vinegar
1 tablespoon mayonnaise
2 tablespoons butter, at room
   temperature

1 tablespoon finely chopped parsley or
   dill, or a combination of both
Salt to taste, if desired
Freshly ground pepper to taste
Cutouts of black or green olives,
   pimientos, or pickles

1. Drain the sardines and put them in a bowl. Press with the back of a fork until smooth. Add the sieved egg yolks, vinegar, mayonnaise, butter, parsley, and salt and pepper to taste. Blend.

2. Equip a pastry bag with a star tube (No. 4). Fill the bag with the sardine mixture and pipe it into the egg-white hollows. Garnish the top of each stuffed egg with a small slice of black or green olive or other cutout.

YIELD: 8 EGG HALVES.

PICKLED EGGS

12 Hard-Cooked Eggs (page 26)
3 cups cider vinegar, or enough to
  cover the eggs
Salt to taste, if desired
3 small dried hot red peppers
10 whole allspice

2 blades mace, optional
6 whole cloves
12 coriander seeds
2 bay leaves
1 tablespoon sugar

1. Peel the eggs and pack them in sterilized jars.
2. Combine the remaining ingredients in a saucepan and simmer 5 minutes. Pour the vinegar mixture over the eggs and seal tight. Store for a week or more before serving.

YIELD: 1 DOZEN.

EGGS NOUVELLE ORLEANS

1 pound fresh lump crabmeat
5 tablespoons butter
2 tablespoons flour
1 1/4 cups milk
1/4 cup heavy cream
Salt to taste, if desired

Freshly ground pepper to taste
1/8 teaspoon freshly grated nutmeg
2 tablespoons Cognac
1/4 cup white vinegar
8 eggs
Paprika for garnish

1. Carefully pick over the crabmeat to remove any cartilage or shells. Leave the crab pieces in the largest lumps possible. Set aside.
2. Heat 1 tablespoon butter in a saucepan and add the flour, stirring with a wire whisk. When blended, add the milk, stirring rapidly with the whisk. When thickened and smooth, stir in the cream. Add salt, pepper, and nutmeg. Stir in the Cognac.

3. Meanwhile, in another saucepan, heat the remaining 4 tablespoons butter over low heat and add the crab. Gently fold the crabmeat in the butter until it is hot throughout. Do not cook the crab, simply heat it through.

4. Bring about 1½ inches of water to the simmer in a skillet, preferably a nonstick skillet. Add the vinegar.

5. Carefully break the eggs into the simmering water and cook until the whites are firm and the yolks are still liquid (2½ to 3 minutes). Using a slotted spoon, carefully scoop out the eggs and let them drain on paper towels.

6. Place about one-eighth of the crabmeat in each of 4 preheated gratin dishes or small, individual casseroles. Top each serving with 2 poached eggs. Spoon equal portions of the remaining crabmeat over the poached eggs, and spoon equal portions of the hot cream sauce over each serving. Sprinkle lightly with paprika. Serve hot.

YIELD: 4 SERVINGS.

BAKED EGGS MARYLAND

1 tablespoon butter
¼ cup finely chopped onion
½ teaspoon finely chopped garlic
¾ cup finely chopped mushrooms,
    including stems
¼ cup crabmeat, preferably lump or
    backfin
3 tablespoons heavy cream

8 Hard-Cooked Eggs (page 26)
1 tablespoon finely chopped parsley
Salt to taste, if desired
Freshly ground pepper to taste
⅛ teaspoon grated nutmeg
2¼ cups Basic Cream Sauce (page
    268)
¼ cup grated Parmesan cheese

1. Preheat the oven to 400 degrees.

2. Heat the butter in a saucepan and add the onion and garlic. Cook briefly until the onion is wilted. Add the mushrooms and cook until wilted. Add the crabmeat, cream, sieved yolks, parsley, salt, pepper, and nutmeg. Stir briefly to blend.

3. Stuff the egg whites with the crab mixture. Arrange the eggs neatly on a heatproof serving dish. Spoon the cream sauce over them and sprinkle with cheese. Bake briefly until heated through. If desired, run the eggs under the broiler to glaze lightly. Serve hot as a first course.

YIELD: 8 SERVINGS.

EGGS HUSSARDE

One of the most famous and delectable of breakfast or luncheon dishes in the restaurants of New Orleans is an egg dish called Eggs Hussarde, or à la Hussarde. The origin of this dish has, to my knowledge, never been recorded, but it is an American dish with obvious French overtones. It is made, for example, with a marchand de vin sauce and a hollandaise, both of which are classically French. The name derives from the word *hussarde*, which in English is *hussar,* a fifteenth-century horseman of the Hungarian light cavalry. The name is said to mean "eggs in a cavalier fashion."

3/4 cup Hollandaise Sauce (page 265)
1 3/4 cups Marchand de Vin Sauce (see
  following recipe)
8 broiled tomato halves (page 218)
8 thin slices cooked ham (about 1/2
  pound)

3 tablespoons butter, melted
8 Poached Eggs (page 31)
8 slices white bread, trimmed, English
  muffins, split, or Dutch (Holland)
  rusks

1. Prepare the hollandaise and the marchand de vin sauces and have them ready to spoon over the foods. Preheat the broiler.

2. Prepare the grilled tomato halves and set aside. Keep warm. Let the broiler remain heated.

3. Brush the ham slices with melted butter. Arrange the slices in one layer on a rack. Place the slices under the broiler and heat briefly, turning once. Keep warm.

4. Poach the eggs and set aside.

5. Toast the bread, muffins, or rusks, and arrange 2 slices on each of 4 plates.

6. Top each slice with a piece of ham. Spoon equal portions of marchand de vin sauce over the ham. Top each with a poached egg. Spoon equal amounts of hollandaise sauce over each egg. Garnish each serving with a grilled tomato half placed on the side.

YIELD: 4 SERVINGS.

MARCHAND DE VIN SAUCE

1 pound bony chicken parts, such as backs, necks, and wings

1 tablespoon corn, peanut, or vegetable oil

1/3 cup finely chopped onion

1/4 cup finely chopped shallots

1/4 cup finely chopped celery

1/4 cup finely chopped carrots

1/2 teaspoon finely minced garlic

3 tablespoons flour

2 cups dry red wine

1 1/2 cups beef broth

1/4 teaspoon dried thyme

1 bay leaf

4 sprigs fresh parsley

Salt to taste, if desired

12 peppercorns, crushed

2 tablespoons butter

1. Chop the chicken parts into 2-inch pieces.

2. Heat the oil in a heavy kettle. Add the chicken pieces and cook, stirring, about 20 minutes, or until thoroughly browned.

3. Add the onion, shallots, celery, carrots, and garlic. Stir. Sprinkle with flour and stir to blend evenly.

4. Add the wine and stir. Add the broth, thyme, bay leaf, parsley, salt, and peppercorns. Bring to the boil and cook, uncovered, skimming the surface often, about 1¼ hours.

5. Line a saucepan with a sieve and pour the sauce, solids and all, into the sieve. Strain, pushing to extract as much liquid as possible from the solids. Discard the solids.

6. Bring the sauce to the simmer and swirl in the butter.

YIELD: ABOUT 1¾ CUPS.

POACHED EGGS

4 cups water
3 tablespoons distilled white vinegar
8 eggs

1. Put the water in a fairly wide nonstick skillet. Add the vinegar and bring to the simmer.

2. As gently as possible, break the eggs into the water, taking care that they are spaced apart so that the whites do not touch. The water should be barely simmering. Cook until the whites are set and the yolks remain runny, 2½ to 3 minutes. Using a slotted spoon, drain the eggs on paper towels, handling them as carefully as possible to prevent the yolks from breaking.

YIELD: 8 POACHED EGGS.

EGGS AND HAM ON TOAST
WITH CHEESE SAUCE

I have noted in the introduction to this book that my mother used to serve eggs Benedict, which is of Yankee origin, on special occasions to the guests in her boardinghouse or to guests at her frequent bridge foursomes. I asked one of the kitchen staff in my mother's kitchen to prepare this dish, but to substitute a simple well-seasoned cheese sauce for the traditional hollandaise. This he did and I have served the dish often—with great success during my early bachelor days in Chicago. It has always seemed to me distinctly Southern.

2 slices buttered toast or toasted
   English muffin halves
2 thin slices boiled ham
2 Poached Eggs (see preceding recipe)
1 1/2 cups Cheese Sauce (see following
   recipe)

1/2 teaspoon paprika
2 small parsley sprigs
4 ripe tomato slices
Salt to taste, if desired
Freshly ground pepper
2 teaspoons coarsely chopped fresh basil

1. Arrange 1 slice of toast on each of 2 plates. Top each slice with a folded-over ham slice. Top the ham with the eggs. Spoon the cheese sauce over.

2. Sprinkle each serving with a little paprika and garnish with a small parsley sprig. Serve with tomato slices seasoned with salt and pepper to taste and garnished with chopped basil.

YIELD: 2 SERVINGS.

CHEESE SAUCE

1 1/2 tablespoons butter
1 1/2 tablespoons flour
1 cup milk
1/4 cup heavy cream
1/2 teaspoon grated nutmeg

Dash of cayenne
Salt to taste, if desired
Freshly ground pepper to taste
1 cup grated Cheddar cheese

1. Melt the butter in a small saucepan and add the flour, stirring with a wire whisk. When blended, add the milk, stirring vigorously with the whisk.

2. Add the cream, nutmeg, cayenne, salt, and pepper. If the sauce seems too thick, add a little more milk or cream. Bring to the boil and remove from the heat. Immediately add the cheese, stirring until it melts. Reheat but do not boil.

YIELD: ABOUT 1 1/2 CUPS.

EGGS SARDOU

This poached egg dish, a specialty of the restaurants of New Orleans, is named for the French playwright Victorien Sardou (1831–1908), who is best known as the author of *La Tosca,* the play on which Puccini's opera was based. It is a lesser-known fact that Sardou traveled in America and wrote a satire on the country entitled *L'Oncle Sam.* Presumably, it was during these travels that he visited New Orleans and was entertained at Antoine's restaurant. The owner, Antoine Alciatore, created the egg dish in his honor.

Eggs Sardou is a dish remembered from my childhood, and I rate it, along with eggs Benedict, as one of America's finest creations. It consists of poached eggs served in artichoke bottoms crossed with anchovy fillets. The eggs are then served with a bit of hollandaise sauce spooned on top, along with a garnish of truffles and/or finely chopped ham. Some recipes, including this one, call for creamed spinach as a base on which to place the artichokes; a nice idea, but not, I believe, a part of the original.

2 cups hot Creamed Spinach (see following recipe)	*8 tablespoons Hollandaise Sauce (page 265)*
8 Cooked Artichoke Bottoms (page 34)	*8 tablespoons finely chopped cooked ham and/or 8 thin black truffle slices*
8 flat anchovy fillets	
8 Poached Eggs (page 31)	

1. Put ½ cup creamed spinach on each of 4 heated plates. Smooth it over. Place 2 artichoke bottoms on top of the spinach, cut side up.

2. Arrange 2 flat anchovy fillets, crossed, over the 2 artichoke bottoms. Place 1 poached egg in the center of each artichoke bottom. Spoon 1 tablespoon hollandaise sauce over each egg.

3. Quickly heat the ham in a skillet and garnish the top of each egg with 1 tablespoon chopped ham and/or 1 truffle slice.

YIELD: 4 SERVINGS.

CREAMED SPINACH

1¼ pounds spinach in bulk, or 1½ packages (10 ounces each) spinach in plastic	1 cup milk
	Salt to taste, if desired
	Freshly ground black pepper to taste
2 tablespoons butter	Pinch of freshly grated nutmeg
1½ tablespoons flour	Pinch of cayenne pepper

1. Pick over the spinach and discard any tough stems or blemished leaves. Rinse well and drain.

2. Bring about 4 cups water to the boil in a saucepan and add the spinach. Let it cook about 2 minutes and drain, pressing or squeezing to extract as much liquid as possible from the leaves.

3. Heat 1 tablespoon butter in a saucepan and add the flour, stirring with a wire whisk. When blended, add the milk, stirring vigorously with the whisk. Add the salt, pepper, nutmeg, and cayenne pepper. Cook, stirring, until the mixture is thickened and smooth.

4. Put the spinach into the container of a food processor or electric blender and blend thoroughly, stirring down as necessary. There should be about 1 cup.

5. Put the spinach in the sauce and stir to blend. Bring to the simmer and swirl in the remaining 1 tablespoon butter.

YIELD: ABOUT 2 CUPS.

COOKED ARTICHOKE BOTTOMS

Cut off the stems of the artichokes, using a sharp knife to produce a neat, flat base. Rub any cut surfaces with lemon to prevent discoloration. Trim all around the sides and base until the base is smooth and white, with the green exterior pared away.

Place the artichoke on its side on a flat surface. Slice off the top, leaving a base about 1½ inches deep. Using a paring knife, trim around the sides and bottom to remove the green exterior that remains. Don't remove the fuzzy choke yet; it comes out easily when the artichokes are cooked.

They are now ready to be cooked in a *blanc légume,* or vegetable whitener, a blend of water and flour. Use enough to barely cover the artichoke bottoms. For each 6 cups of water use ¼ cup of flour.

Place a sieve over the saucepan in which the artichokes will be cooked. Add the flour. Pour cold water over the flour, rubbing to dissolve it. Add salt to taste. Add the artichoke bottoms and bring to a boil. Cover the pot closely and cook for about 25 minutes, or until the bottoms are tender. Remove the pot from the heat.

If the artichokes are not to be used immediately, let them rest in the cooking liquid. Before using, drain the artichoke bottoms and pull or scrape out the chokes.

OMELET WITH HOT CHILI SAUCE AND CHEESE

One of the best breakfasts I have ever dined on was an early-morning meal in San Antonio. My hostess had served an assortment of Tex-Mex foods at a buffet the evening before and there were a few leftovers, among them her version of what is called in the Southwest a *pico de gallo*, a fiery hot side dish of chopped chilies with tomato and avocado. I made omelets and used the *pico de gallo* (the actual translation is "rooster's beak," which picks at the palate) as a filling. I blended it with grated sharp Cheddar cheese.

4 eggs
Salt to taste, if desired
Freshly ground pepper to taste
4 teaspoons unsalted butter

2 to 4 tablespoons Hot Chili Sauce
　　with Avocado (see following recipe)
4 tablespoons packed, grated Gruyère,
　　Swiss, or Cheddar cheese

1. Make 1 omelet at a time. Break 2 eggs into each of 2 small bowls. Add salt and pepper and beat until thoroughly blended.

2. Heat a small, well-cured omelet pan or use a nonstick pan.

3. Heat 2 teaspoons butter in the pan. When it is sizzling, add 2 beaten eggs. Cook over high heat, shaking the pan and stirring rapidly with a fork held parallel to the bottom of the pan. When the eggs start to set, tilt the omelet pan and tap it against the stove burner. This should make the omelet slide about 1 inch away from the hand, curving the omelet.

4. Spoon 1 or 2 tablespoons of the hot chili sauce and 2 tablespoons of the cheese in the center of the omelet. With a fork, carefully and neatly fold the omelet into thirds to enclose the filling and give the omelet a neat, oval shape with pointed ends. Slide the omelet, seam side down, onto a heated plate. Serve immediately.

5. Use the remaining ingredients to make another omelet.

YIELD: 2 SERVINGS.

HOT CHILI SAUCE WITH AVOCADO

¼ cup finely chopped fresh or bottled
   jalapeño peppers
¼ cup seeded, finely diced tomatoes
¼ cup finely diced red onion
¼ cup diced avocado
2 tablespoons finely chopped fresh
   coriander

1 tablespoon freshly squeezed lime juice
Salt to taste, if desired
Freshly ground pepper to taste
1 teaspoon olive oil

Combine all the ingredients in a mixing bowl and serve at room temperature.

YIELD: ABOUT 1¼ CUPS.

CURRIED CORN AND CHEESE SOUFFLÉ

The spice rack in my family home throughout the 1920s and 1930s was by no means elaborate. It was an era when curried dishes were considered exotic throughout America. My mother used a great deal of curry powder, and she used it in this very good soufflé.

6 to 8 cooked ears of corn
1/4 pound sharp Cheddar cheese
3 tablespoons butter
3 tablespoons flour
2 tablespoons curry powder
1 1/2 cups milk

Salt to taste, if desired
Freshly ground pepper to taste
2 teaspoons cornstarch
1 tablespoon water
6 eggs, separated
1/4 cup grated Parmesan cheese

1. Preheat the oven to 400 degrees.

2. Using a knife, cut the kernels from the corn. There should be about 2 cups.

3. Grate the Cheddar cheese. There should be about 1½ cups loosely packed.

4. Melt 2 tablespoons butter in a saucepan and add the flour and curry powder, stirring with a wire whisk. When blended and smooth, add the milk, stirring rapidly with the whisk. Blend until thickened and smooth and add salt and pepper. Blend the cornstarch and water and stir it in.

5. Add the egg yolks, stirring constantly. Cook only until the mixture boils; remove it from the heat. Let cool. Add the Cheddar cheese and fold in the corn.

6. Rub the inside of a 1½-quart soufflé dish with the remaining 1 tablespoon butter. Add the Parmesan cheese and shake the cheese around until the bottom and sides are lightly coated. Shake out the excess cheese. Place the dish in the freezer until ready to use.

7. Beat the egg whites until stiff. Add half the whites to the soufflé mixture, stirring rapidly. Fold in the remaining whites. Spoon the mixture into the prepared soufflé dish. Place in the oven and immediately lower the oven heat to 375 degrees. Bake 25 to 35 minutes, depending on whether you wish a soufflé with a moist or firm center. Serve immediately.

YIELD: 4 TO 6 SERVINGS.

GRITS AND CHEESE SOUFFLÉ

1 cup quick-cooking or regular grits
2 cups milk
2 cups water
Salt to taste, if desired
Freshly ground pepper to taste

¼ teaspoon grated nutmeg
½ teaspoon Tabasco sauce, or to taste
⅓ pound sharp Cheddar cheese, grated
(about 1¾ cups)
6 large eggs, separated

1. Generously butter a 2-quart soufflé dish and place it in the freezer until ready to use.

2. Cook the grits in the milk and water according to package directions. Add salt to taste.

3. As the grits cook, preheat the oven to 425 degrees.

4. When the grits are cooked, scrape them into a mixing bowl. Add pepper, nutmeg, and Tabasco. Stir in all but ½ cup grated cheese.

5. Let cool slightly and add the egg yolks, stirring until well blended. Beat the whites until stiff. Add half the whites to the grits mixture and beat them in. Fold in the remaining whites, using a rubber spatula.

6. Spoon the mixture into the prepared soufflé dish and smooth over the top. Sprinkle with the remaining ½ cup cheese. Place in the oven and bake 25 minutes, or to the desired degree of doneness. Serve immediately.

YIELD: 6 SERVINGS.

EGG SALAD SANDWICHES

When I was younger and feasted on egg salad sandwiches, I felt pretty close to paradise. They were always made with fresh mayonnaise and store-bought white bread, which was, to tell the truth, gummy in texture. Years later, I learned how far superior they were when the salad was spread on slices of protein bread. I also added a bit of fresh basil from my garden.

4 eggs, at room temperature
3 tablespoons homemade Mayonnaise
  (page 263)
¼ cup finely chopped red onion or
  chives

Salt to taste, if desired
Freshly ground pepper to taste
8 slices white bread, preferably protein
  bread

1. Put the eggs in a saucepan, add cold water to cover, and bring to the boil. Simmer 12 to 15 minutes, depending on the size of the eggs. Drain and immediately run cold water over them to chill well.

2. Drain and peel the eggs. Put them through a sieve or ricer into a mixing bowl. There should be about 1½ cups.

3. Add the mayonnaise, onion, salt, and pepper and blend well.

4. Spread equal portions of the mixture on 4 slices of bread. Cover with the second slice of bread, trim crusts, cut diagonally into triangles, and serve.

YIELD: 4 SANDWICHES.

WATERCRESS SANDWICHES

I am not certain I ever dined on watercress during my childhood in Mississippi. I do recall that when I graduated from the University of Mississippi in the early 1940s, my family came to pick me up and drive me home. We passed a gushing falls called Big Springs, and the cold water was alive with tall, healthy sprigs of watercress. We gathered it by bunches and carried it back home, and never having heard of cream of watercress soup or other uses for the peppery green, we converted it into sandwiches. Perhaps the creation is not Southern. Except in my memory.

1 bunch watercress
2 to 3 tablespoons mayonnaise
Lemon juice to taste

Salt to taste, if desired
Freshly ground pepper to taste
8 thin slices white sandwich bread

1. Pat the watercress to remove excess moisture. Coarsely chop the watercress using a knife, blender, or food processor. Do not chop it too fine.

2. Add the mayonnaise, a little at a time, stirring to blend after each addition. The problem with a mayonnaise-and-watercress filling is generally an excess of mayonnaise; the filling becomes too liquid. Add just enough so that the filling holds together. Two tablespoons should be enough. Add the lemon juice, salt, and pepper.

3. Spoon equal portions of the filling onto 4 slices of bread. Top with the remaining 4 slices. Neatly trim the crusts from the bread. Cut the sandwiches as desired, into finger sandwiches, rectangular halves, or triangular halves or quarters.

YIELD: 4 TO 6 SERVINGS.

NEW ORLEANS OYSTER LOAF

One of my fondest memories of childhood came about on my first visit to New Orleans (the saying was that when a good Mississippian died, his soul went to New Orleans forever). It was then that I ate a New Orleans oyster loaf. It consisted of Italian bread sliced through the center and filled with crisp, cornmeal-covered oysters, deep-fried, with mayonnaise smeared on the oysters and Tabasco (mother's milk, it was laughingly referred to) sprinkled on according to taste.

1 loaf crusty French or Italian bread,
preferably 10 or 12 inches long
2 to 4 tablespoons butter, melted
24 Oysters Fried in Cornmeal (page
97)

2 to 4 tablespoons mayonnaise
Tabasco sauce to taste

1. Preheat the oven to 400 degrees.
2. Split the loaf in half lengthwise. Wrap it in foil and bake about 10 minutes.

3. Preheat the broiler. Brush each half of the bread on the split sides with melted butter and toast until golden on the split sides.

4. Pile the oysters on one half of the bread. Spoon the mayonnaise on top, and add a few dashes of Tabasco sauce. Cover with the second half of the bread. Cut the loaf in half crosswise, and serve.

YIELD: 2 SERVINGS.

PO' BOY SANDWICH

If I liked the New Orleans oyster loaf, I had an almost equal fondness for a po' boy sandwich. That is dialect, of course, for "poor boy." It consists of assorted salamis and cheese plus pepperoncini, lettuce, and other good things served on an open sandwich, the filling to be doused with olive oil and vinegar according to taste. Other places use other names such as "heroes" or "submarines," but they are to my mind inferior to the New Orleans original.

1 long crusty loaf Italian or French
   bread
1/4 cup olive oil
1 garlic clove, crushed
2 tablespoons grated Parmesan cheese
1/4 pound or less thinly sliced salami
1/4 pound or less thinly sliced
   prosciutto
1/4 pound or less thinly sliced
   mortadella
1/4 pound or less thinly sliced capicola
1/4 pound or less thinly sliced
   provolone or Fontina cheese

6 to 8 Tuscan peppers (pepperoncini)
3 roasted sweet peppers, preferably red
   (see note)
5 or 6 crisp lettuce leaves
1 ripe tomato, cored and sliced,
   optional
Salt to taste, if desired
Freshly ground pepper to taste, if
   desired
Additional olive oil, optional
2 teaspoons red wine vinegar, optional
Imported black olives, optional

1. Preheat the broiler.

2. Slice the bread lengthwise. Combine the olive oil and crushed garlic. Stir briefly. Brush the split halves of the bread with the oil and garlic. Sprinkle each half with Parmesan cheese. Run the bread under the broiler, split side up, until cheese is golden.

3. Arrange layers of salami, prosciutto, mortadella, capicola, provolone, Tuscan peppers, sweet peppers, lettuce, and tomatoes on one of the bread halves. Sprinkle, if desired, with salt and pepper. Sprinkle, if desired, with more oil and vinegar. Cover with the remaining bread half and slice into serving portions. Serve with black olives, if desired.

YIELD: 4 TO 6 SERVINGS.

NOTE: *To roast peppers, place them under a hot broiler and cook, turning often, until the skin is shriveled and partly blackened. Remove and put the peppers in a paper bag and let stand until cool enough to handle. Peel off the skins.*

CRABMEAT SALAD

1 egg yolk
Salt to taste, if desired
Freshly ground pepper to taste
1 tablespoon imported mustard
1 teaspoon vinegar
1/4 teaspoon Worcestershire sauce

Dash of Tabasco sauce
1 cup peanut oil
3 tablespoons water
*3/4 cup flaked crabmeat, picked over to
    remove any trace of shell or cartilage*

1. Put the yolk, salt, pepper, mustard, vinegar, Worcestershire, and Tabasco in a mixing bowl. Start beating with a wire whisk.

2. Gradually add the oil, beating vigorously until all the oil is added. Thin the sauce a bit with the water.

3. Add the crabmeat and stir to combine.

YIELD: 2 TO 4 SERVINGS.

AVOCADO WITH CRABMEAT

⅓ cup sour cream	¾ pound fresh crabmeat, preferably
⅓ cup Mayonnaise (page 263)	lump or backfin, picked over to
3 tablespoons lemon juice	remove all trace of shell and
¼ teaspoon paprika	cartilage
Salt to taste, if desired	2 or 3 ripe, unblemished avocados,
Freshly ground pepper to taste	split in half and seeded

1. Combine the sour cream and mayonnaise in a mixing bowl. Stir in the lemon juice, paprika, salt, and pepper.

2. Fold in the crabmeat, stirring as little as possible so as not to break up the lumps. Fill the avocado halves with the mixture and serve.

YIELD: 4 TO 6 SERVINGS.

TUNA WITH MEXICAN TABLE SAUCE

One of my favorite side dishes for Tex-Mex food and one that appears often on my table is a Mexican table sauce known as *salsa*. It is excellent when kept tightly sealed overnight. It makes a first-rate luncheon dish when served with canned tuna and a wedge of lemon on the side.

4 cans (7 ounces each) tuna	Mexican Table Sauce (page 272)
packed in oil	Toast
4 lemon halves, seeded	

1. Open the cans of tuna and drain off the oil. Serve the contents of each on a plate with a lemon half on the side.

2. Serve the table sauce on the side to be added according to individual taste. Serve with toast.

YIELD: 4 SERVINGS.

MUSHROOMS STUFFED WITH CRABMEAT

*1 pound mushrooms, preferably large
    ones (about 12 to a pound)*
3 tablespoons butter
1 tablespoon flour
½ cup milk
Salt to taste, if desired
Freshly ground pepper to taste

½ cup finely chopped scallions
⅓ pound crabmeat
1 tablespoon Cognac
1 egg yolk
Tabasco sauce
3 tablespoons butter, melted
¼ cup grated Parmesan cheese

1. Preheat the oven to 400 degrees.
2. Remove the stems and reserve the caps from the mushrooms. Chop the stems. There should be about 1 cup.
3. Melt 1 tablespoon butter in a saucepan and add the flour, stirring with a wire whisk. When blended, add the milk, stirring rapidly with the whisk. When blended and smooth, add salt and pepper to taste.
4. In another saucepan, heat the remaining 2 tablespoons butter and add the scallions and chopped mushroom stems. Cook, stirring, 4 minutes. Add the crabmeat, stir to blend, and add the Cognac. Add the white sauce and salt and pepper to taste. Blend. Add the egg yolk and Tabasco sauce to taste.
5. Place the mushrooms, hollow side down, in a buttered baking dish. Brush with half the melted butter and place in the oven for 10 minutes. Remove. Let cool.
6. Stuff the cavity of each mushroom with the crab mixture, heaping it up and smoothing it over. Arrange the mushrooms in the baking dish and sprinkle with Parmesan cheese and the remaining melted butter. Place in the oven and bake 20 minutes.

YIELD: 6 SERVINGS.

COLD PASTA NEW ORLEANS STYLE

It fascinates me that cold pasta salads have become a fashionable dish sold commercially and made at home. When I was very young, my sister, an excellent cook, was famous for her cold pasta "New Orleans style." I have always believed that she created the dish and she has never denied it. To make it, you cook thin strands of spaghetti, such as vermicelli or spaghettini, to the desired degree of doneness and marinate it with a well-seasoned vinaigrette sauce with garlic. Chill overnight, and add assorted vegetables, such as mushrooms, artichoke hearts, avocado, and cherry tomatoes. The following is my adaptation of her recipe, using mushrooms à la grecque.

½ pound pasta, preferably vermicelli or spaghettini

Salt, if desired

1 cup Salad Dressing with Garlic (page 269)

1 Chicken Cooked in Broth (about 3 pounds) (see following recipe)

1 cup homemade Mayonnaise (page 263)

Mushrooms à la Grecque (page 46), for garnish

12 small whole cooked beets, for garnish

1 package (9 ounces) frozen artichoke hearts, cooked according to package directions

1 avocado, seeded, peeled, and cut into 16 wedges

12 cherry tomatoes, or an equal number of tomato wedges

Chopped scallions for garnish, optional

Chopped parsley for garnish, optional

1. Drop the pasta into boiling salted water and cook to the desired degree of doneness. Do not overcook or the pasta will become mushy. Drain well.

2. Put the drained pasta into a mixing bowl while still warm and pour one-third of the salad dressing over it. Toss well. Let it cool. Cover with plastic wrap and refrigerate several hours or overnight.

3. Remove the chicken meat from the bones. Discard the bones and skin. Cut the meat into bite-size pieces.

4. Add the chicken to the pasta. Add the mayonnaise and gently toss to blend the ingredients.

5. Serve the pasta in a mound on a round plate. Garnish as follows: Arrange the mushrooms around the chicken or serve separately. Put the beets, artichoke hearts, and avocado wedges in separate bowls. Add equal parts of the remaining salad dressing to each bowl. Stir each to coat. Arrange these, and the tomatoes, around the pasta. Sprinkle with chopped scallions and parsley, if desired.

YIELD: 6 TO 8 SERVINGS.

CHICKEN COOKED IN BROTH

1 chicken (3 pounds cleaned weight)   3 sprigs fresh parsley
7 cups water   1/2 cup chopped celery
Salt, if desired   1 onion stuck with 2 cloves
12 peppercorns, crushed   1 carrot, trimmed and scraped
1 bay leaf
2 sprigs fresh thyme, or 1/2 teaspoon
    dried

Put the chicken in a kettle and add the remaining ingredients. Bring to the boil and simmer about 20 minutes. Let cool.

YIELD: ONE CHICKEN (ABOUT 3 CUPS DICED MEAT).

MUSHROOMS À LA GRECQUE

1/2 pound small mushrooms, preferably   1 small garlic clove, crushed and peeled
    button mushrooms   Salt to taste, if desired
1 1/2 tablespoons lemon juice   Freshly ground black pepper to taste
4 1/2 tablespoons olive oil   2 tablespoons chicken broth
1/2 teaspoon coriander seeds

1. If the mushrooms are small, leave them whole. Otherwise, cut them into quarters. Put them in a saucepan with lemon juice and stir to coat.

2. Add the remaining ingredients. Cover and cook for 7 to 8 minutes, stirring occasionally. Uncover and cook over high heat for about 5 minutes, shaking the pan occasionally. Remove from the heat and let cool. Remove the garlic clove before serving.

YIELD: ABOUT 2 CUPS.

COTTAGE CHEESE

The back porch of my home in the tiny town in which I was born served as the setting for one of the glories of the past—cottage cheese freshly made from the milk of a herd of family cows. The milk would be put into a churn, stoneware utensil, or urn with a loose-fitting stoneware lid, covered, and let stand overnight. The milk would curdle because of natural bacteria and have a coating of thick yellow cream on top. We would skim off the cream and add the snow-white curds to cheesecloth that would be tied into a bag, then left to hang above a bowl. The whey would drip into the bowl, and when the cheesecloth bag was opened, it would be filled with pure, homemade cottage cheese. My father adored this for lunch or an afternoon snack. He would spoon it into a bowl and add heavy cream and sugar to taste.

You cannot make that cottage cheese with pasteurized milk alone; the natural bacteria will not work properly. You can, however, make a somewhat poorer version using buttermilk as a culture.

My method yields a somewhat firmer, larger-curd cheese than an all-buttermilk recipe.

1 gallon skimmed milk, at room
  temperature
¼ cup cultured buttermilk

1 teaspoon salt, approximately
3 to 4 tablespoons heavy cream,
  optional

1. Mix milk and buttermilk in a large stainless steel, glass, enamel, or ceramic bowl. Cover and set in a warm place (80–90 degrees Fahrenheit, if possible) until the milk has become the consistency of custard, and whey has begun to collect around the edges. This will take 16 to 24 hours.

2. Gently skim or pour off as much whey as possible.

3. Cut down through the curds at 1-inch intervals in two directions, making a crisscross pattern. Then make another row of cuts slanting down through the curds, to roughly cube them.

4. Place the bowl over, not in, a kettle of warm water. Put a dairy thermometer (or a candy or frying thermometer that registers 100 degrees Fahrenheit) into the curds and heat very, very slowly, mixing every 5 minutes or so, until the thermometer registers between 100 and 110 degrees. The water should heat so slowly that this procedure takes about 30 minutes. Remove from the heat, cover, and allow to sit for 20 minutes.

5. Transfer the curds to a sieve or colander lined with cheesecloth. For creamy cottage cheese, allow them to drain for 5 to 10 minutes. The longer the cheese drains, the more compact it will become. The texture will be smoother and less like cottage cheese if it is mixed to break up the curds.

6. Season the cheese with salt to taste and, if desired, stir in the cream. Refrigerate and use within 2 to 3 days.

YIELD: 2 POUNDS.

CORN AND CRAB CHOWDER

5 tablespoons butter
5 tablespoons flour
2 cups Chicken Stock (page 275)
2 1/2 cups milk
1/4 cup finely chopped onion
3/4 cup picked-over fresh or frozen
    crabmeat (about 6 ounces)

1 1/2 cups corn kernels (cut from 3 ears
    cooked corn)
Salt to taste, if desired
Freshly ground pepper to taste
1/8 teaspoon cayenne pepper
1/2 cup heavy cream

1. Melt 4 tablespoons butter in a saucepan. Add the flour, stirring with a wire whisk until blended.

2. Add the stock and milk, stirring rapidly with the whisk. Cook, stirring frequently, about 10 minutes.

3. Meanwhile, melt the remaining 1 tablespoon butter in another saucepan and add the onion. Cook until wilted. Add the crabmeat, corn, salt, pepper, and cayenne. Cook briefly and add to the cream sauce. Add the cream and bring to the boil. Simmer gently about 5 minutes.

YIELD: 4 TO 6 SERVINGS.

OYSTER AND CORN CHOWDER

2 tablespoons unsalted butter
1/2 cup grated onion
1 large garlic clove, peeled and chopped
　fine
4 scallions, white and light green,
　finely chopped
1 1/2 cups milk
1 cup heavy cream
Salt to taste, if desired

1/4 teaspoon freshly ground black
　pepper
About 1 cup oyster liquor
1 dozen fairly large oysters, cut into
　halves (see note)
2 cups fresh corn kernels (cut from 4
　ears of corn)
1 tablespoon freshly chopped chives

1. Melt the butter in a heavy saucepan and add the grated onion, garlic, and scallions. Cook over medium heat for 1 minute.

2. Add the milk and cream and bring to the boil.

3. Add the salt, pepper, oyster liquor, oysters, and corn kernels. Bring to the boil. Remove from the heat and let sit for 5 minutes.

4. Serve sprinkled with chives.

YIELD:　6 SERVINGS.

NOTE:　*Use freshly shucked oysters if possible; canned oysters tend to curdle the milk mixture. If you do use canned oysters, bring the oysters and oyster liquor to a boil separately, then scoop off the scum that may form on top of the oysters and discard. Add the poached oysters and the clear liquid to the soup.*

FRESH CORN AND GROUPER CHOWDER

4 to 8 ears of corn, shucked

2 potatoes (about ³⁄₄ pound)

3 tablespoons cubed salt pork

1 ½ cups finely chopped onions

1 ½ cups water, Fish Stock (page
   274), or Chicken Stock (page 275)

¼ pound nonoily, white-fleshed fish,

such as grouper, striped bass,
   flounder, etc.

Salt to taste, if desired

Freshly ground pepper to taste

Tabasco sauce to taste

3 cups milk

2 tablespoons butter

1. Drop the corn into boiling water and cover. When the water returns to the boil, remove from the heat. Let stand 5 minutes and drain.

2. When the corn is cool enough to handle, cut and scrape the kernels from the cob. There should be about 2 cups.

3. Peel the potatoes and cut them into ½-inch cubes. Drop into cold water and let stand until ready to use.

4. Place the salt pork in a saucepan or small kettle over low heat. When it is rendered of its fat, add the onions and cook until wilted. Drain the potatoes and add them and the 1½ cups water or stock and bring to the boil. Simmer until the potatoes are tender, 5 minutes or longer.

5. Cut the fish into ½-inch cubes and add it to the stock. Add salt, pepper, and Tabasco sauce. Cook about 5 minutes and add the milk. Bring to the boil and add the corn. Add the butter and swirl it in. Serve piping hot.

YIELD: 4 TO 6 SERVINGS.

SHE-CRAB SOUP

She-crab soup, a specialty of Charleston, South Carolina, and of Savannah, Georgia, is one of the simplest of soups to make because its base is merely a white sauce of butter, a little flour, and milk. In theory, the soup should be made with the flesh and eggs of the female crab. Some books state that if you are unable to obtain the female meat and eggs, you may resort to the male flesh and add a few crumbled, hard-boiled egg yolks to the bottom of each soup bowl as a substitute for the real McCoy.

2 tablespoons butter
3 tablespoons flour
3 cups milk
¼ teaspoon freshly grated nutmeg, or more to taste
¼ teaspoon paprika
Salt to taste, if desired

Freshly ground black pepper
⅛ teaspoon cayenne pepper
2 cups picked-over crabmeat, preferably with a certain amount of coral or roe
10 lemon slices
¼ cup sherry

1. Melt the butter in a large saucepan and add the flour, stirring with a wire whisk. Add the milk, stirring rapidly with the whisk. Cook, stirring, until thickened and smooth.

2. Add the nutmeg, paprika, salt, pepper, and cayenne and stir. Add the crabmeat, stirring gently, and bring just to the boil. Add the lemon slices and sherry and pour into a soup tureen or serve in individual bowls.

YIELD: 6 TO 8 SERVINGS.

NAG'S HEAD FISHERMAN'S SOUP

This is a fine fish soup I dined on many years ago in the home of friends who lived on the ocean in Nag's Head, North Carolina.

½ cup olive oil
2 cups finely chopped onions
1½ cups chopped sweet green or red peppers
1 cup cubed carrots
1 small hot green or red pepper, chopped, optional
1½ pounds potatoes, peeled and cut into ¼-inch slices
2 pounds ripe tomatoes, cored and cut into ½-inch cubes, or 4 cups imported canned tomatoes, chopped
Salt to taste, if desired
Freshly ground pepper to taste
7 cups Fish Stock (page 274)

2 teaspoons loosely packed stem saffron
1 tablespoon water
1 teaspoon fennel seeds, crushed
½ teaspoon turmeric
1 thin slice orange peel, white pulp removed
1 teaspoon sugar
1½ pounds fresh scallops, cut in half or quartered if large
1 cleaned 2-pound saltwater fish, such as weakfish
1¼ pounds raw shrimp, the smaller the better, shelled and deveined
24 littleneck clams, well scrubbed

1. Heat the oil in a kettle and add the onions, sweet peppers, carrots, and the hot pepper. Cook, stirring, about 5 minutes. Add the potatoes and cook about 1 minute. Add the tomatoes and salt and pepper. Add the fish stock and bring to the boil.

2. Combine the saffron with the water and add it to the stock. Add the fennel seeds, turmeric, orange peel, and sugar. Simmer about 10 minutes and add the scallops and the fish.

3. Cover and simmer 5 minutes. Add the shrimp and clams and cook about 10 minutes, or until the clams open. If desired, the clams may be steamed separately and added to the soup, layered with the other ingredients. Add salt and pepper to taste. Remove the fish, cut into pieces, and return to the soup. Serve piping hot.

YIELD: 6 SERVINGS.

MUDDLE

This is a recipe prepared for me by Bill Neal, one of the finest young Southern chefs. He is proprietor and chief cook at Crook's Corner in Chapel Hill, North Carolina. The soup is said to be one of the oldest dishes of the Outer Banks of North Carolina. The name originated with the first settlers and means a "mess of fish."

5 slices lean bacon, cut into ¼-inch cubes (about ½ cup loosely packed)

4 onions (about 1½ pounds), peeled and quartered

¾ cup finely diced celery

1 garlic clove, finely minced

½ teaspoon finely grated orange rind

1 can (20 ounces) Italian peeled tomatoes, drained (about 2 cups)

1 pound red, waxy potatoes, peeled

5 cups Fish Stock (page 274) or shrimp broth (see note)

6 sprigs fresh thyme, or ½ teaspoon dried

1 whole dried hot red pepper (about 3 inches long)

Salt to taste, if desired

6 ounces skinless, boneless, white-fleshed nonoily fish, such as grouper or red snapper, cut into ¾-inch cubes

6 ounces shrimp, peeled and deveined

6 ounces bay scallops, left whole, or sea scallops, quartered

4 eggs

½ cup finely chopped scallions, including green part

1½ tablespoons finely chopped fresh basil

1½ tablespoons finely chopped fresh parsley

1. Put the bacon in a kettle and cook, stirring often, until the pieces are crisp and rendered of fat. Remove and reserve the pieces.

2. Cut the quartered onions crosswise into thin slices. There should be about 5 cups.

3. To the fat in the kettle, add the onions, celery, garlic, and orange rind. Cook, stirring, about 2 minutes.

4. Cut the tomatoes into thin slices. Cut the potatoes into ½-inch cubes; there should be about 2 cups. Add the tomatoes to the kettle and cook about 2 minutes. Add the potatoes and fish stock or shrimp broth. Add the thyme, hot red pepper, and salt. Let simmer about 20 minutes, or until the potatoes are tender without being mushy.

5. Add the fish and shrimp and let simmer about 1 minute. Add the scallops and stir.

6. Break 1 egg at a time into a saucer and carefully slide the 4 eggs onto the top of the simmering soup. Cover closely and let the soup simmer slowly, until the whites are firm and the yolks remain runny. As the eggs cook, baste them carefully with some of the hot liquid. Immediately spoon 1 egg into each of 4 hot soup bowls. Spoon the soup with fish and potatoes over all.

7. Blend bacon bits, scallions, basil, and parsley together and garnish each serving with an equal portion of the mixture. Serve immediately.

YIELD: 4 SERVINGS.

NOTE: *To make shrimp broth, put the shells from the 6 ounces of shrimp in this recipe into a saucepan. Add 5 cups water. Bring to the boil and let simmer 1 minute. Strain and reserve the liquid; discard the shells.*

AVOCADO AND TOMATO SOUP

2 to 4 avocados (about 1 pound total
   weight)
Juice of 1 lemon
3 ½ cups Chicken Stock (page 275)
1 tablespoon butter
½ cup finely sliced onion

1 tablespoon flour
2 cups sour cream
1 cup peeled, seeded, chopped tomatoes
Salt to taste, if desired
Freshly ground pepper to taste
Tabasco sauce

1. Peel and cut the avocados in half and remove the pits. Cut the flesh into cubes and put them in the container of a food processor. Add the lemon juice and ½ cup stock. Process until fine in texture; pour mixture into a saucepan.

2. Melt the butter in another saucepan and add the onion. Cook until wilted and sprinkle with flour. Stir to coat the pieces and add the remaining 3 cups stock, stirring rapidly with a wire whisk. When blended and smooth, remove from the heat.

3. Add the sauce to the avocado mixture. Add the sour cream, tomatoes, salt, and pepper. Add Tabasco sauce to taste. Serve hot or chilled.

YIELD: 6 SERVINGS.

TURKEY SOUP

1 turkey carcass	2 whole cloves
1 cup cubed turkey meat for garnish, optional	4 sprigs fresh parsley
	2 sprigs fresh thyme, or ½ teaspoon dried
16 cups water	
Leftover giblet gravy, if any, optional	3 whole carrots, trimmed and scraped
1 cup coarsely chopped onion	3 whole celery ribs, trimmed and scraped
1 bay leaf	
Salt to taste, if desired	½ cup broken vermicelli, cappelini, or spaghettini
Freshly ground pepper to taste	

1. Pick over the carcass and reserve any tender morsels of meat. Use this for the cup of meat indicated, adding more meat as necessary.

2. Place the carcass in a kettle and set the meat aside. Add to the kettle any jellied gravy that may have accumulated on the turkey platter.

3. Add the water to the kettle. Add the leftover giblet gravy, onion, bay leaf, salt, pepper, cloves, parsley, thyme, carrots, and celery. Bring to the boil and simmer 1 hour, skimming the surface as necessary.

4. Strain the soup through a sieve lined with a clean kitchen towel or a double thickness of cheesecloth. Discard all the solids except the carrots and celery.

5. Pour about 2 cups of the soup into a saucepan and add the vermicelli. Cook until just tender.

6. Add this to the soup. Cut the carrots and celery into ½-inch cubes and add them to the soup. Add the cubed turkey meat and bring to the boil. Serve piping hot.

YIELD: ABOUT 14 CUPS.

CREAM OF PUMPKIN SOUP

1 small pumpkin, about 4 pounds   *4 cups Chicken Stock (page 275)*
2 tablespoons butter   *1 teaspoon sugar*
½ cup coarsely chopped onion   *1 cup heavy cream*
4 tablespoons flour

1. Cut off and discard the stem of the pumpkin. Split the pumpkin in half and scoop out and discard the seeds and inner fibers. Cut the pumpkin into eighths. Cut off and discard the tough skin. Cut the pumpkin meat into 1-inch cubes. Set aside.

2. Heat the butter in a saucepan and add the onion. Cook until wilted and sprinkle with flour, stirring with a whisk. When blended, add the stock, stirring rapidly with the whisk. When blended and smooth, add the pumpkin. Simmer about 30 minutes, or until the pumpkin is quite tender.

3. Purée the soup in the container of a food processor or blender or put it through a food mill. Return the purée to the saucepan. Add the sugar and cream and bring just to the boil. Serve piping hot.

YIELD: 10 TO 12 SERVINGS.

OKRA SOUP

3 pounds meaty beef bones, hacked into
  pieces
12 cups water
1¼ pounds fresh okra
3 ripe tomatoes (about 1½ pounds)
2 medium-size onions

1 slice of bacon, or 1 thin slice of
  country ham, cut into small cubes
1 bay leaf
Salt to taste, if desired
Freshly ground pepper to taste

1. Put the bones in a kettle and add cold water to cover. Bring to the boil and simmer 1 minute. Drain and run under cold water until chilled. Put the bones in a clean kettle and add about 12 cups of cold water. Bring to the boil, partly cover, and cook for 2 hours.

2. Meanwhile, cut off and discard the stem ends of the okra. Cut the pods crosswise into ½-inch lengths. There should be about 5 cups. Set aside.

3. Cut away and discard the cores of the tomatoes. Peel the tomatoes and cut them into 1-inch cubes. There should be about 3 cups. Set aside.

4. Peel and finely chop the onions. There should be about 2 cups.

5. When the beef has cooked about 2 hours, strain the liquid and reserve the bones. There should be about 8 cups of liquid. Put the liquid in a kettle and add the okra, tomatoes, onions, and bacon or ham. Add the bay leaf, salt, and pepper. Bring to the boil and cook 2 hours longer.

6. Meanwhile, cut away any meat from the bones and cut the meat into bite-size pieces. Discard the bones. Add the meat to the soup. Heat thoroughly and serve piping hot.

YIELD: 4 TO 6 SERVINGS.

YELLOW BELL PEPPER AND SERRANO CHILI SOUP

All my life I have had a fondness for dishes made with sweet green peppers. I considered it a blessing when, a few short years ago, peppers of various colors came on the market. One of my favorite soups, given to me by a friend in Dallas, is made with sweet yellow pepper (the red version may be substituted) combined with serrano chilies.

1 pound sweet peppers, preferably yellow

1 tablespoon corn, peanut, or vegetable oil

1 cup coarsely chopped onion

1/2 cup coarsely chopped celery

3/4 cup coarsely chopped carrots

3 sprigs fresh thyme, or 1/2 teaspoon dried

1 teaspoon black peppercorns

1 small bay leaf

3 cups Chicken Stock (page 275) or canned chicken broth

1 tablespoon butter, at room temperature

2 tablespoons flour

3 1/3 cups heavy cream

5 serrano chilies (about 1 ounce)

1 cup water

Salt to taste, if desired

12 sprigs fresh coriander

1 1/2 teaspoons lemon juice

1. Place the peppers over a gas flame or under a preheated broiler. Turn often until the peppers are charred all over. Remove and let cool.

2. Heat the oil in a kettle or casserole and add the onion, celery, and carrots. Cook, stirring, over moderately high heat until the onions are wilted and the vegetables start to brown.

3. Add the thyme, peppercorns, and bay leaf and stir. Add the stock or broth and cook about 20 minutes, or until reduced to about 2½ cups.

4. Blend the butter and flour and add to the boiling liquid, stirring rapidly with a wire whisk. Simmer the mixture over low heat, stirring occasionally, for about 5 minutes.

5. Add 3 cups cream and continue cooking over relatively high heat for about 20 minutes. Place a sieve, preferably a chinois, over a bowl. Pour the mixture into the sieve, pressing the solids with a wooden spoon or spatula to extract as much liquid as possible. There should be about 3¼ cups. Pour this mixture into a saucepan and bring to the simmer.

6. Meanwhile, peel the peppers and remove and discard the cores and seeds. Cut the peppers into strips. Put the strips in the container of an electric blender or food processor. Blend thoroughly. There should be about 1 cup. Add the puréed peppers to the soup mixture.

7. Combine the serrano chilies with the water and salt in a saucepan and bring to the boil. Let cook about 6 minutes.

8. Drain the chilies. Run them immediately under cold water and drain. Cut away and discard the stems. Cut the chilies in half and remove the seeds.

9. Put the chilies in the container of an electric blender or food processor and add the fresh coriander. Add ¼ cup of the cream soup and blend as thoroughly as possible.

10. Put the remaining ⅓ cup cream in a bowl and beat until it stands in peaks. Add the chili-and-coriander mixture, folding it into the cream. Add salt to taste and ½ teaspoon lemon juice. Set aside.

11. Add the remaining 1 teaspoon lemon juice and salt to taste to the cream soup. There should be about 4 cups of soup.

12. Pour equal portions of the soup into 4 to 6 soup bowls. Top each serving with a spoonful of the reserved cream-and-coriander mixture.

YIELD: 4 TO 6 SERVINGS.

GOLDEN GAZPACHO WITH CHILIES AND SHRIMP

1½ teaspoons finely chopped fresh
chilies, preferably serrano, although
jalapeños could be used, stems and
seeds removed
¾ cup rich chicken broth
¼ teaspoon saffron threads
2 tablespoons freshly squeezed lime
juice
2 pounds yellow tomatoes (about 6)
3 tablespoons finely chopped sweet
yellow pepper
5 tablespoons finely chopped peeled
cantaloupe

5 tablespoons chopped, peeled, and
seeded papaya
5 tablespoons chopped, peeled, and
seeded mango
½ cup peeled, seeded, and finely diced
cucumber
5 tablespoons peeled, finely diced
jicama, optional (see note)
2 tablespoons finely chopped scallions
Salt to taste, if desired
1 pound cooked, peeled small shrimp
1 tablespoon finely chopped fresh
coriander

1. Combine the chilies, chicken broth, saffron, and lime juice in the
container of a food processor or, preferably, an electric blender. Blend
thoroughly. Pour the mixture into a small mixing bowl and let stand for
a minimum of 10 minutes.

2. Drop the tomatoes into a basin of boiling water and let stand 12
seconds. Drain immediately. Peel the tomatoes, cut them crosswise in half,
and remove the seeds. Cut the tomato flesh into a very small dice. There
should be about 2 cups.

3. Combine the tomatoes, yellow pepper, cantaloupe, papaya, mango,
cucumber, jicama, and scallions in a mixing bowl. Add the chili-and-broth
mixture and stir to blend. There should be about 4 cups. Refrigerate at
least 1 hour. Season with salt, if desired.

4. Cut each shrimp crosswise in half. There should be about 1¼ cups.
Roll the shrimp in chopped coriander.

5. Spoon equal portions of the soup into 4 to 6 chilled soup bowls.
Garnish each bowl with equal portions of the shrimp.

YIELD: 4 TO 6 SERVINGS.

NOTE: *Jicama is a bulbous root that varies widely in size from about the size of a golf ball to a grapefruit. It resembles to a degree a potato with a thin, light-brown skin. The texture has been related to that of a radish or a fresh water chestnut. It is available in many fresh-fruit markets, particularly those that cater to a Latin American clientele.*

POZOLE

One of the great dishes of the Southwest is a stewlike soup made with whole hominy, pork, and chicken. It is served with lime wedges, radishes, chopped lettuce, hot red pepper flakes, and scallions as a garnish. It is called *pozole,* pronunced po-SOH-leh, and the original version is made with half a hog's head and lye hominy, which takes hours of preparation before cooking. This recipe is a modified and excellent version that uses pork shoulder rather than the head, and canned hominy, which merely needs draining before it is added to the kettle.

THE SOUP:

1 ½ pounds lean, boneless pork
  shoulder
1 onion, cut into 1-inch cubes
3 garlic cloves, peeled
6 cups Chicken Stock (page 275)
2 cups water

Salt to taste, if desired
12 peppercorns
8 chicken thighs (about 2 pounds)
1 can (1 pound 14 ounces) whole
  hominy, drained

THE GARNISHES:

12 to 16 lime wedges
¾ cup thinly sliced radishes
3 cups chopped iceberg lettuce
1 avocado, peeled and cut into thin
  slices or small cubes

¼ cup dried oregano
¾ cup finely chopped scallions or red
  onion

1. Cut the pork into 1½-inch cubes. Put them in a kettle and add the onion, garlic, chicken stock, water, salt, and peppercorns. Bring to the boil and cook, skimming the surface to remove scum and foam as necessary, about 15 minutes.

2. Add the chicken thighs and continue cooking, skimming the surface as necessary, about 45 minutes longer.

3. Remove the pork and chicken pieces. Strain the broth into another kettle. Add the drained hominy, bring to the boil, and let simmer 15 minutes.

4. Serve in individual soup bowls with garnishes on the side to be added according to taste.

YIELD: 6 TO 8 SERVINGS.

Fish & Shellfish

FISH CREOLE

1³/4 pounds skinless, boneless fish fillets, such as weakfish, grouper, sea bass, cod, red snapper, or hake
6 tablespoons butter
1 onion, quartered and thinly sliced (about 1 cup)
1 teaspoon chopped garlic
3 cups chopped sweet green and red peppers

Salt to taste, if desired
Freshly ground pepper
2 cups imported peeled tomatoes, preferably with tomato paste and basil
2 tablespoons capers
Tabasco sauce to taste
¹/4 cup finely chopped parsley

1. Preheat the oven to 450 degrees.

2. Cut the fish into 6 individual serving pieces and set aside.

3. Melt 3 tablespoons butter in a saucepan and add the onion. Cook, stirring, until wilted and add the garlic and sweet peppers. Sprinkle with salt and pepper to taste. Toss well and add the tomatoes, capers, Tabasco, and parsley. Cover and cook 15 minutes. Uncover and cook 5 minutes longer.

4. Rub a baking dish with 1 tablespoon butter and sprinkle with salt and pepper. Add the fish pieces and dot with the remaining 2 tablespoons butter. Spoon the sauce over and bake 15 minutes.

YIELD: 6 SERVINGS.

BROILED FISH FILLETS

2 fish fillets (about 1/2 pound each)   1/2 cup fresh bread crumbs
4 tablespoons butter   1/2 teaspoon paprika
Salt, if desired   Lemon wedges for garnish
Freshly ground pepper   Parsley sprigs for garnish

1. Preheat the broiler to high.

2. Select a baking dish just large enough to hold the fish fillets in one layer. Grease the bottom of the dish with 1 tablespoon butter. Sprinkle it with salt and pepper.

3. Arrange the fillets, skin side down, on the dish and sprinkle with salt and pepper to taste.

4. Scatter the bread crumbs on a piece of wax paper. Hold a small sieve over the crumbs. Put the paprika through the sieve and blend paprika and crumbs. Sprinkle the fish fillets with the crumbs. Melt the remaining 3 tablespoons butter and dribble over all. Broil about 6 inches from the source of heat until golden brown. Turn the oven heat to 400 degrees and bake 10 minutes. Garnish with lemon wedges and parsley sprigs.

YIELD: 2 SERVINGS.

FISH FILLETS EN PAPILLOTE

As far as I know, the idea of cooking fish in paper bags originated in Louisiana. Indeed, some sources say that it was created in Antoine's famed New Orleans restaurant in the early 1900s in honor of a well-known Brazilian balloonist named Alberto Santos-Dumont, who was served a dish en papillote because the puffed-up bag resembled a balloon.

In Louisiana, each piece of fish is packaged in a sheet of buttered paper, along with a light cream sauce and crabmeat and shrimp. While pompano is often preferred, many other kinds of fish fillets may be substituted, including weakfish, redfish, and salmon.

4 boneless fillets of fish, such as
   pompano, weakfish, or red snapper,
   with skin left on (about 1 pound)
Salt to taste, if desired
Freshly ground pepper to taste
3 tablespoons butter
1/4 cup finely chopped onion
2 tablespoons flour
1 cup Fish Stock (page 274)
2 tablespoons finely chopped scallions
1/2 pound fresh mushrooms, thinly
   sliced (about 2 cups)

1/2 cup dry white wine
1/4 cup heavy cream
2 tablespoons finely chopped parsley
1 egg yolk
2 tablespoons corn, peanut, or vegetable
   oil
12 small to medium-size shrimp (about
   6 ounces), shelled and deveined
1/4 pound lump crabmeat

1. To make the bags in which the fish will be cooked, it is best to use kitchen parchment. You can use aluminum foil, however. Cut out 4 heart-shaped pieces measuring about 22 inches wide and 15 inches at the center.

2. Preheat the oven to 400 degrees.

3. Sprinkle the fish on both sides with salt and pepper.

4. Heat 1 tablespoon butter in a saucepan and add the onion. Sprinkle with the flour and stir with a wire whisk. Add the stock, stirring rapidly with the whisk. Cook, stirring often, about 5 minutes.

5. Heat the remaining 2 tablespoons butter in a saucepan and add the scallions. Cook briefly, stirring, without browning. Add the mushrooms and cook, stirring, until they give up their liquid. Cook until the liquid is almost gone. Add the wine and cook about 5 minutes.

6. Combine the sauce with the mushroom mixture and add the cream. Bring to the boil and cook about 5 minutes. Season with salt and pepper to taste. Stir in the parsley.

7. Beat the egg yolk and add it to the sauce, stirring vigorously with a wire whisk. Cook about 10 seconds and remove from the heat.

8. Open one of the heart shapes on a flat surface. On one side, brush all over with oil. Fold one half of the heart over the other half and press down to make a crease at the center fold. Open up the heart and place 3 tablespoons of the mushroom sauce in the center of one half.

9. Place 1 piece of fish, skin side down, on the sauce. Arrange 3 shrimp neatly on top of the fish. Arrange one-quarter of the crab over or next to the shrimp. Spoon about 4 tablespoons of the sauce over all. Fold the other half of the heart shape over at the crease. Crimp and fold the edges of the heart over and over to seal. To ensure the bond, you might use paper clips to seal the packages at the top end. Repeat until all 4 packages are filled and sealed.

10. Arrange the packages on 1 or 2 baking sheets and place in the oven. Bake 15 minutes. Serve, if desired, in the paper bags.

YIELD: 4 SERVINGS.

SAUTÉED FRESH ROE

1 pound fresh roe from flounder,
  herring, or weakfish
Salt to taste, if desired
Freshly ground pepper to taste
Flour for dredging

2 tablespoons butter
1 teaspoon finely minced garlic
Juice of ½ lemon
Finely chopped parsley for garnish
Lemon wedges for garnish

1. The size of the roe may vary greatly from about 2 inches in length to 6 or more inches. Prick the roe in several places with a needle or pin.

2. Sprinkle with salt, pepper, and flour. Shake to remove excess flour.

3. Heat the butter in a skillet large enough to hold the roe in one layer. When the butter is quite hot, add the roe. Reduce the heat. Cook until nicely golden on one side. Cooking times will vary depending on size of roe, from 3 to 8 minutes to a side. Turn the roe and cook over gentle heat until golden and cooked through.

4. Remove the roe to a serving dish. Add the garlic to the skillet and cook briefly without browning. Add the lemon juice, stir, and pour the pan sauce over the roe. Serve sprinkled with chopped parsley and lemon wedges.

YIELD: 4 OR MORE SERVINGS.

BLACKENED REDFISH

Within recent memory, a great deal has been made of "American cooking." To my mind, two of the greatest "new" dishes to appear in popular culture are Buffalo chicken wings, distinctly a Yankee creation, and blackened redfish. The latter, of course, is the creation of my good friend Paul Prudhomme, owner of K. Paul's Louisiana Kitchen in New Orleans, who prepared it in my front yard for one special celebration.

"Once a year when I was a child," he explained, "my father would take all thirteen of us kids on a camping trip in Louisiana. Naturally, we did our own cooking, always in a black iron skillet and over an open fire. We'd catch fresh fish and cook it out of doors, and it always had an incredibly good, smoky taste. It never tasted that good at home, so I decided to create my own smoky flavor with the fish I had at hand, mostly redfish or red snapper."

If there is no redfish or red snapper to be had, tilefish cut into thin fillets works admirably well.

3 teaspoons salt, optional
½ teaspoon cayenne pepper
½ teaspoon white pepper
¼ teaspoon black pepper
¼ teaspoon dried thyme
¼ teaspoon dried basil
¼ teaspoon dried oregano

2 teaspoons paprika
8 skinless, boneless fillets of fish,
    preferably redfish, pompano, or
    tilefish (about ¼ pound each) (see
    note)
10 tablespoons butter, melted

1. Combine the salt, cayenne pepper, white pepper, black pepper, thyme, basil, oregano, and paprika in a small bowl.

2. Dip the fish pieces on both sides in butter. Sprinkle on both sides with the seasoned mixture.

3. Heat a black iron skillet over high heat for 5 minutes or longer (the skillet cannot get too hot) until it is beyond the smoking stage and starts to lighten in color on the bottom.

4. Add 2 or more fish pieces and pour about a teaspoon of butter on top of each piece. The butter may flame up. Cook over high heat about 1½ minutes. Turn the fish and pour another teaspoon of butter over each piece. Cook about 1½ minutes. Continue until all the fillets are cooked. Serve immediately.

YIELD: 4 SERVINGS.

NOTE: *Redfish and pompano are ideal for this dish. If tilefish is used, you may have to split the fillets in half. Place the fillet on a flat surface, hold the knife parallel to the surface, and split in half through the center from one end to the other. The fillets must not be more than about 1½ inches thick.*

DEEP-FRIED CATFISH

Like most Southerners, I adore catfish. I'm not certain that my mother ever prepared catfish at home, however. She was too aristocratic for that. Red snapper, yes; but catfish was too common, something to be enjoyed on Sunday outings.

Eating deep-fried catfish was a ritual and the menu was always the same: the cornmeal-coated catfish with its golden-brown crusty exterior and moist white inner flesh; deep-fried hush puppies; deep-fried potatoes; and coleslaw. And ketchup. Deep-fried catfish without ketchup is like a hot dog without mustard.

Now that catfish are being raised in fresh water ponds, they are available frozen all over the country and can be used in any recipe calling for a white nonoily fish. Even after freezing and defrosting, catfish remain snow white and as firm as when taken from the water.

Corn oil for deep-frying
3 catfish fillets (about 1 pound)
½ cup white cornmeal
Salt to taste, if desired

Freshly ground black pepper to taste
Lemon halves
Ketchup
Hush Puppies (page 251)

1. Heat the oil for deep-frying.
2. Cut each fillet in half crosswise.
3. Combine the cornmeal, salt, and pepper.
4. Dredge the fillets in the cornmeal. Pat to make the cornmeal adhere. Drop the fillets in the oil and cook 5 to 10 minutes, or until crisp and brown.
5. Serve with lemon halves, ketchup, and hush puppies.

YIELD: 2 TO 4 SERVINGS.

CATFISH FILLETS IN WHITE WINE SAUCE

I am persuaded that catfish is the most Southern of all fish. I therefore claim that catfish—if it is the basis of whatever preparation—transforms a dish into something "Southern." I never heard of catfish in white wine sauce until we experimented with it in my own kitchen. It is an excellent "Southern" dish with French overtones.

6 catfish fillets (about 2 pounds)
3 tablespoons butter
1/2 cup dry white wine
1/2 pound mushrooms, thinly sliced (about 2 cups)
Salt to taste, if desired
Freshly ground pepper to taste

2 tablespoons flour
1/2 cup milk
Juice of 1/2 lemon
2 tablespoons freshly grated Parmesan cheese
2 tablespoons finely chopped parsley

1. Preheat the oven to 400 degrees.
2. Pat the catfish pieces dry. Rub a baking dish with 1 tablespoon butter. Arrange the fillets in the buttered dish in one layer. Add the wine. Scatter the mushrooms over all and sprinkle with salt and pepper to taste. Place in the oven and bake for 10 minutes.
3. Meanwhile, melt the remaining 2 tablespoons butter in a saucepan and add the flour, stirring with a wire whisk. Add the milk, stirring with the whisk. When blended and smooth, remove from the heat.

4. Pour the liquid from the baked fish into the sauce, stirring. Bring to the boil and cook, stirring often, for about 5 minutes. Stir in the lemon juice. Pour the sauce over the fish and bake for 10 minutes longer. Sprinkle with Parmesan cheese and parsley. Serve hot.

YIELD: 6 SERVINGS.

CATFISH BAKED WITH CHEESE

6 catfish fillets (about 2 pounds)
1/2 cup freshly grated Parmesan cheese
1/4 cup flour
Salt to taste, if desired
Freshly ground black pepper to taste

1 teaspoon paprika
1 egg, lightly beaten
1 tablespoon milk
8 tablespoons butter, melted
1/4 cup sliced almonds

1. Preheat the oven to 350 degrees.
2. Wipe the catfish dry.
3. Blend together the cheese, flour, salt, pepper, and paprika.
4. Combine the egg and milk in a flat dish.
5. Dip the fillets in the egg mixture, and then coat with the cheese mixture. Arrange the fillets in one layer in a baking dish, and pour the butter over all. Sprinkle with the almonds.
6. Place in the oven and bake for 20 minutes.

YIELD: 6 SERVINGS.

NAG'S HEAD CHANNEL BASS
OR RED DRUM STEW

2½ pounds skinned and boned
   channel bass or another fish such as
   blackfish (see note)
6 strips of bacon
2½ cups thinly sliced onions (about 1
   pound)
6 tablespoons flour
2 hot red or green peppers, chopped, or
   ¼ teaspoon or more cayenne pepper
   to taste

3 cups cubed peeled potatoes (about 1
   pound)
5 cups water, approximately
Salt to taste, if desired
Freshly ground pepper to taste
Finely chopped parsley for garnish

1. Cut the fish into 1-inch cubes and set aside.

2. Cut the bacon into fine cubes and put it in a Dutch oven. Cook the bacon, stirring, until crisp.

3. Add the onion to the Dutch oven and cook, stirring, until wilted. Sprinkle with flour and stir. Add the hot peppers and potatoes.

4. Add the water, stirring constantly, until thickened and smooth. Add salt and pepper. Cover and simmer about 15 minutes, or until the potatoes are nearly tender. Watch carefully and stir often from the bottom to prevent sticking. The stew should be thick, but it may be necessary to add a little water.

5. Add the cubed fish and cover. Cook about 6 minutes.

6. Serve in hot soup bowls and sprinkle with parsley.

YIELD: 6 SERVINGS.

NOTE: *Channel bass or red drum, like blackfish, is a firm-fleshed fish whose flesh does not flake easily when it is cooked. These fish are best for this dish, although other fish such as striped bass could be substituted.*

GROUPER WITH LEAF SPINACH

20 thin, skinless, boneless, crosswise
   slices of fresh grouper (about 2
   pounds)
Salt to taste, if desired
Freshly ground pepper to taste
2 pounds fresh spinach, picked over to
   remove any tough stems or blemished
   leaves, or 2 packages (10 ounces
   each) fresh spinach

2 cups water
2 tablespoons butter
1/8 teaspoon freshly grated nutmeg
1/3 cup flour
4 tablespoons corn, peanut, or vegetable
   oil
4 tablespoons olive oil
Juice of 1/2 lemon

1. Preheat the oven to 500 degrees.

2. Each grouper slice should be about 1/4 inch thick. Sprinkle the slices with salt and pepper and set aside.

3. Rinse and drain the spinach. Put the water in a kettle and bring to the boil. Add salt to taste and the spinach. Stir down to wilt.

4. Bring to the boil, stirring occasionally, and cook about 5 minutes. Empty the spinach into a colander and drain. Press with the back of a wooden spoon to extract most of the liquid. Squeeze between the hands to extract additional moisture.

5. Put the spinach on a flat surface and coarsely chop. Heat the butter in a skillet and add the spinach. Add salt, pepper, and nutmeg. Cook, tossing and stirring, just to heat through. Keep warm and set aside briefly.

6. Dredge the fish slices on both sides with flour and pat to make the flour adhere. Shake off the excess.

7. Use a nonstick skillet and add one-half of the corn and olive oils. When they are quite hot and starting to smoke, add half the fish slices. Cook over high heat 1 minute and 15 seconds on one side, and turn the pieces. Cook about 10 seconds, no longer, on the second side.

8. Pour off any fat from the skillet and wipe out the skillet. Add the remaining oils to the skillet and cook the remaining batch of fish as before.

9. Scoop out the spinach onto the center of a preheated ovenproof plate. Smooth it over. Arrange the fish pieces symmetrically over the spinach. Place the fish in the oven and bake 10 seconds, no longer. Sprinkle with lemon juice and serve.

YIELD: 4 SERVINGS.

HALIBUT FILLETS
WITH MANGO AND BASIL SAUCE

This is another example of what has been called "nouvelle" Southern cooking. It is a splendid dish, the creation of an inspired chef who presides over a fine restaurant kitchen in Dallas.

4 tablespoons plus 1½ teaspoons corn, peanut, or vegetable oil
1 cup thinly sliced fresh mushrooms
¼ cup finely chopped shallots
¼ cup dry white wine
2 sprigs fresh thyme, or ½ teaspoon dried
1¼ cups Fish Stock (page 274), approximately
1½ cups heavy cream

2 to 3 ripe, unblemished mangoes (about 1 pound)
5 fresh basil leaves
Salt to taste, if desired
Freshly ground pepper to taste
1½ cups Powdered Bread Crumbs (see following instructions)
½ cup macadamia nuts
4 skinless, boneless halibut fillets (about 1 pound total weight)

1. Heat 1½ teaspoons oil in a saucepan and add the mushrooms. Cook, stirring, until the mushrooms give up their liquid. Continue cooking until the liquid evaporates. Add the shallots and cook, stirring, about 1 minute.

2. Add the wine and thyme and continue cooking until the wine evaporates. Add 1 cup of the fish stock and continue cooking until the broth is reduced by half.

3. Add the cream and bring to the boil. Let boil over relatively high heat about 8 minutes, or until the sauce is reduced to about 1½ cups.

4. Line a saucepan with a fine sieve, preferably a chinois. Pour the sauce through, pressing the solids in the sauce with a wooden spoon or spatula to extract as much liquid as possible.

5. Peel and cut away the pulp from the seeds of the mangoes. There should be about 1½ cups pulp. Blend thoroughly in a food processor or electric blender.

6. Add this pulp to the cream sauce. Add the remaining ¼ cup fish stock, the basil leaves, salt, and pepper. Bring to the simmer and let cook about 10 minutes. Set aside.

7. Preheat the oven to 400 degrees.

8. Combine the powdered bread crumbs and macadamia nuts in a food processor or electric blender and blend for about 1 minute, no longer. If you overblend, the nuts will lose too much oil.

9. Sprinkle the fillets with salt and pepper. Dip each halibut fillet in the macadamia nut mixture and coat well on both sides. Pat to make the coating adhere.

10. Use 1 or 2 ovenproof skillets in which to cook the fish. Heat enough of the remaining oil in the skillet or skillets to barely cover the bottom. Add the fish fillets and cook 1 to 1½ minutes on a side, or until nicely browned. Turn carefully in the skillet. Place the skillet in the oven. Bake 5 to 7 minutes, depending on the thickness of the fillets.

11. Remove the basil leaves from the sauce and reheat it. If necessary, add a little fish stock to thin the sauce to the desired consistency.

12. Place a fillet in the center of each of 4 warm plates. Spoon the sauce around the fish, and serve.

YIELD: 4 SERVINGS.

POWDERED BREAD CRUMBS

Preheat the oven to 250 degrees. Split 1 or 2 loaves of French bread in half lengthwise. Quarter each half by cutting crosswise. Place on a rack in the oven and bake 20 to 30 minutes, or until the bread is dried throughout without browning. Break or cut the bread into small pieces and put the pieces in the container of a food processor or electric blender. Blend to a fine powder. The yield will depend on the size of the loaves.

BARBECUED MACKEREL

2 fresh, cleaned mackerel (about 1
    pound each)
Salt to taste, if desired
Freshly ground pepper to taste

2 tablespoons peanut, vegetable, or corn
    oil
Southern Barbecue Sauce (page 273)

1. Prepare a charcoal grill and have it ready. The coals must be white-hot but not overly plentiful, or the food will cook too fast. Arrange the grill 6 to 8 inches over the coals.

2. Sprinkle the fish with salt and pepper and brush lightly with oil.

3. Arrange the fish on the grill and cook until lightly browned on one side. Turn and baste the top side with sauce. Cook, turning the fish and basting as necessary, until the fish flakes easily with a fork, 20 to 25 minutes.

4. Give the fish a final brushing with the sauce and remove to a serving dish.

YIELD: 2 TO 4 SERVINGS.

BREADED FILLETS OF POMPANO

2 pounds skinless, boneless pompano
    fillets or striped bass, sole, or
    flounder
3/4 cup flour
Salt to taste, if desired
Freshly ground pepper to taste
1 egg, lightly beaten

3 tablespoons plus 1 teaspoon peanut,
    vegetable, or corn oil
2 tablespoons water
3/4 cup fine fresh bread crumbs
1 tablespoon butter
Lemon wedges
Mustard Sauce (page 267)

1. Cut the fish into serving pieces.

2. Combine the flour, salt, and pepper and set aside.

3. Beat the egg with 1 teaspoon oil, the water, salt, and pepper.

4. Coat the fish pieces all over in the seasoned flour. Dip them well in the egg, then coat them all over with crumbs.

5. Heat the remaining 3 tablespoons oil and the butter in a heavy skillet. Cook the fish pieces until golden brown on one side. Turn and cook on the other side, basting frequently with the oil and butter in the skillet. Cooking time may range from 10 to 15 minutes, depending on the thickness of the fish.

6. Serve with lemon wedges and mustard sauce.

YIELD: 4 TO 6 SERVINGS.

STEAMED RED SNAPPER

1 whole red snapper (2 1/2 pounds)

1. The best utensil for steaming a fish is a fish cooker. You can improvise, however, by using a Chinese steamer, a small roasting pan, and so on. The important thing is to have a rack that can be slightly elevated above a basin of boiling water. As the fish cooks, the steaming utensil should be covered to allow as little steam to escape as possible.

2. If a fish cooker is to be used, place 2 small plates, such as after-dinner coffee-cup saucers, upside down at each end of the cooker. Add the steaming rack and enough water to come up almost but not quite to the bottom of the rack.

3. Remove the rack and place the fish on it. If you bend the handles of the rack slightly toward the center, the lid of the steamer will fit snugly on top. If you do not bend the handles, you will have to cover the fish closely with heavy-duty aluminum foil.

4. Bring the water to the boil in the steamer. Add the rack with the fish on it.

5. Cover closely. Steam the fish for 10 to 12 minutes. Do not overcook. The fish is properly cooked when the bones along the backbone can be pulled out easily with the fingers.

YIELD: 4 SERVINGS.

POACHED RED SNAPPER

1 red snapper (3 1/2 pounds cleaned
   weight), with head and tail left on
5 quarts water
1 onion, peeled and thinly sliced
4 carrots, scraped and cut into cubes
   (about 1 1/2 cups)
1 1/2 cups coarsely chopped celery with
   leaves

4 garlic cloves, peeled and crushed
6 sprigs fresh parsley
1 teaspoon dried thyme
24 whole cloves
4 bay leaves
1/4 cup black peppercorns
1 bottle dry white wine

1. The bass must be scrupulously cleaned of scales. Using scissors, cut off and discard the back and side fins. Leave the head and tail intact.

2. If available, use a fish cooker. In the cooker combine the water, onion, carrots, celery, garlic, parsley, thyme, cloves, bay leaves, peppercorns, and wine. Do not add salt. Do not add the fish.

3. Cover and place on the stove. Bring the liquid to the boil and cook 20 minutes.

4. Uncover, add the fish, and let it simmer about 13 minutes. Remove from the heat and let rest about 5 minutes before draining and serving.

5. Remove the skin from the fish and serve.

YIELD: 4 SERVINGS.

RED SNAPPER WITH BASIL AND ROSEMARY

*1 red snapper (7 pounds), with head
    and tail attached but gills removed*
Juice of 1 lemon
Salt to taste, if desired
Freshly ground pepper to taste
20 fresh basil leaves
6 fresh rosemary sprigs

3 whole garlic cloves, peeled
2 tablespoons olive oil
2 teaspoons paprika
¼ cup dry sherry
*8 hot, freshly cooked peeled shrimp for
    garnish*
Parsley sprigs for garnish

1. Preheat the oven to 400 degrees.

2. Using a small boning or paring knife, make incisions lengthwise down the back of the fish, running the knife about 1 inch deep on each side of the backbone, holding the knife close to the bone.

3. Sprinkle the fish inside the incisions, inside the cavity, and on the outside with lemon juice, salt, and pepper. Distribute the basil leaves and rosemary sprigs evenly within the incisions and cavity of the fish. Insert garlic cloves inside the fish.

4. Lay out a large rectangle of heavy-duty aluminum foil on a baking sheet and rub the center with 1 tablespoon olive oil. Place the fish on the center of the foil and brush the top with remaining 1 tablespoon oil. Hold a small sieve over the fish and dust evenly with paprika. Pour sherry over all. Bring up the edges of foil tent style, folding and crimping the edges. Leave a small air pocket between the top of the fish and the foil. Seal ends of foil as neatly and tightly as possible. Place foil-wrapped fish in the oven and bake 40 minutes.

5. Open the foil and carefully transfer the fish to a hot serving dish. Serve garnished with shrimp and parsley sprigs.

YIELD: 4 TO 6 SERVINGS.

BAKED RED SNAPPER
WITH SHRIMP AND OYSTER DRESSING

2 red snappers (2 1/2 to 3 pounds each)
5 slices of bread
1 can (2 pounds, 3 ounces) Italian
  plum tomatoes, not packed with
  tomato paste
2 medium onions, finely chopped
2 large stalks of celery, finely chopped
1 small sweet green pepper, seeded and
  finely chopped
2 garlic cloves, finely minced
4 tablespoons softened butter
1 large egg

Salt to taste, if desired
1/8 to 1/4 teaspoon cayenne pepper, to
  taste
1/2 pound shrimp, peeled, deveined, and
  coarsely chopped
18 oysters, coarsely chopped
1 to 2 cups water, as needed
3 bay leaves
Juice of 1 lemon
Freshly ground black pepper to taste
Extra 1/2 pound shrimp, peeled and
  deveined, optional garnish

1. Preheat the oven to 350 degrees.

2. The snappers should be split and eviscerated, but not cut completely through. Heads may be cut off, but the final result looks better, and the juices stay in the fish more satisfactorily, when heads are intact. The fish may be boned, making them easier to serve, but this results in some wasted meat, and the fish will be a little less firm and flavorful. It is possible for the fish man to split the fish, leaving the bones in. Rinse and dry thoroughly.

3. Toast the bread, and when it has cooled slightly, crumble it to coarse crumbs, preferably in a blender or a food processor.

4. Drain the tomatoes, reserving the juice. There should be about 3 cups juice. Chop or coarsely break up the tomatoes and add to the bread crumbs. Stir in the onions, celery, green pepper, and garlic. Blend in the softened butter and egg. Season to taste with salt and cayenne. Stir in the chopped shrimp and oysters.

5. Spoon the filling into the fish cavities, using about two-thirds in all between the 2 fish. Sew the fish closed with heavy kitchen thread. If you have a pan large enough to allow both fish to lay flat with a little space between them, use it to bake the fish together. Otherwise use 2 open baking pans. (Oval, enameled cast-iron baking pans are especially nice for this because the fish can be brought to the table in them.) Arrange the fish in the pan and spoon the remaining stuffing around it. Pour in the reserved tomato liquid, dividing it in half if you use 2 baking dishes. Add 1 cup of water to each pan, or 1½ cups if baking both fish in the same pan. Add bay leaves, lemon juice, and a little salt and pepper. Baste the fish with liquid. If you like, extra whole shrimp can be added to the pan.

6. Place in the preheated oven and bake for 45 minutes to 1 hour, or until fish flakes when tested with a fork. Baste several times during baking and add a little more water to the pan if sauce thickens too much.

7. Remove the thread and cut the fish into serving portions; spoon sauce over each. Serve with steamed rice.

YIELD: 4 TO 6 SERVINGS.

SHRIMP-STUFFED SHAD

One of the finest Southern dishes I can recall was served to me in the home of friends in Nag's Head, North Carolina. It was shad fillets served with deveined shrimp. Here is one version of that dish.

8 tablespoons butter
½ cup finely chopped celery
½ cup finely chopped onion
10 to 12 medium-size shrimp, peeled,
    deveined, and coarsely chopped
Salt to taste, if desired
Freshly ground pepper to taste

⅛ teaspoon cayenne pepper
1½ cups heavy cream
2 shad fillets (about 1 pound each)
½ cup dry white wine
2 teaspoons chopped chives or parsley
Juice of ½ lemon

1. Preheat the oven to 425 degrees.

2. In a small saucepan, heat 2 tablespoons butter and add the celery and onion. Cook, stirring, until the onion is translucent.

3. Put the shrimp into the container of an electric blender and add salt, pepper, cayenne, and ½ cup heavy cream. Blend, stirring down as necessary, to make a fine paste.

4. Spoon the shrimp paste into a mixing bowl and add half the vegetable mixture. Reserve the rest.

5. Lay 1 of the shad fillets, skin side down, on a flat surface. Note that there are two flaps on either side of the fillet where the bones were removed. Open these. Spoon the shrimp mixture down the center of the fillet and bring the flaps back up to make a three-sided "box."

6. Open the flaps of the other fillet and center the fillet, skin side up, over the shrimp mixture to close the box. Tie the box crosswise in about four places with string.

7. Butter a flameproof dish and sprinkle with salt and pepper. Arrange the fish in the dish and dot it with 4 tablespoons butter. Scatter the remaining vegetables around the fish. Sprinkle with salt and pepper and add the white wine. Cover the dish closely with foil. Bring to the boil on top of the stove, then put the dish in the oven. Bake 30 minutes.

8. Pour the liquid that has accumulated in the dish into a saucepan. Keep the fish warm. Bring the liquid to the boil over high heat and reduce it by one-third. Add the remaining 1 cup cream and simmer 5 minutes.

9. Swirl in the remaining 2 tablespoons butter and add the chives and lemon juice.

10. Remove the string from the stuffed fish. Cut it crosswise into serving pieces, and serve with the hot sauce spooned over.

YIELD: 6 TO 8 SERVINGS.

SHAD STUFFED WITH SHAD ROE

6 rectangular portions of boneless shad
  fillets with skin left on (about 2¼
  pounds total weight)
Salt to taste, if desired
Freshly ground pepper to taste
¼ cup dry white wine
2 tablespoons olive oil
2 tablespoons plus ¼ cup finely
  chopped fresh chervil (or use a blend
  of parsley and tarragon)

2 pairs of shad roe (about ¾ pound
  total weight)
6 tablespoons unsalted butter
½ cup finely chopped onion
1 cup finely diced whole wheat bread
2 hard-cooked eggs put through a sieve
  (about ½ cup)
6 thin, seedless lemon slices with rind

1. Preheat the oven to 475 degrees. Cut out 6 rectangles of parchment or aluminum foil measuring 12 × 16 inches.

2. Arrange the shad fillets, skin side down, on a baking dish in which the portions will fit snugly in one layer. Sprinkle with salt and pepper.

3. Blend the wine, oil, and 2 tablespoons chervil. Sprinkle this over the fish.

4. Pull off and discard the connecting membranes of the roe. Cut the roe crosswise into ½-inch-thick slices.

5. Heat the butter in a small skillet and add the onion. Cook, stirring, until wilted. Add the pieces of roe and cook, stirring briefly, just until the roe starts to lose its raw look and is partly cooked.

6. Put the bread in a mixing bowl and add the ¼ cup chopped chervil. Add the roe mixture and the sieved eggs. Blend well. Divide the mixture into 6 equal portions.

7. Lay out the 6 rectangles of parchment paper or foil and place 1 piece of fillet, skin side down, on each piece of paper. Spoon equal portions of the marinade over each. Open up the flaps (from which the bones were removed) and stuff each opening with equal portions of the roe mixture. Pack it loosely. Top each serving with a lemon slice. Fold the paper neatly and compactly, envelope fashion. Arrange each filled paper envelope, sealed side down, on a baking sheet.

8. Place in the oven and bake 13 minutes. Remove the fish from the envelopes and serve.

YIELD: 6 SERVINGS.

CREAMED SHAD ROE

Oddly enough, we rarely had access to shad roe—and certainly not to boned shad—in my home. For special occasions, my mother would use canned shad roe to serve in a cream sauce. Here is a version of creamed roe prepared from the fresh fish eggs.

2 pairs of shad roe
Salt to taste, if desired
Juice of 1/2 lemon
2 tablespoons butter
1 tablespoon flour
1/2 cup milk
1/2 cup heavy cream

Freshly ground pepper to taste
1 tablespoon finely chopped shallots
1 tablespoon finely chopped parsley
1/3 cup dry white wine
4 teaspoons freshly grated Parmesan
   cheese

1. Place the shad roe in a skillet and add boiling water to cover. Add salt to taste and the lemon juice. Simmer about 5 minutes if small, 10 minutes if medium, and 15 minutes if large. Drain, cool, and cut each half into bite-size morsels.

2. Heat 1 tablespoon butter in a saucepan and add the flour. Add the milk and cream, stirring vigorously with a whisk. Season to taste with salt and pepper and simmer about 10 minutes, stirring frequently.

3. Meanwhile, combine the shallots, parsley, and wine in a small saucepan and cook to reduce until there are only 2 tablespoons liquid left. Add this to the cream sauce.

4. Heat the remaining 1 tablespoon butter in a skillet and add the cubed shad roe, salt, and pepper. Toss briefly to heat through, about 2 minutes. Add all but ⅓ cup of the sauce and blend. Spoon the shad roe into 4 ramekins and cover with equal amounts of the remaining sauce. Sprinkle each serving with a teaspoon of Parmesan cheese and run under the broiler until bubbling and golden brown.

YIELD: 4 SERVINGS.

SHAD ROE POACHED IN BUTTER

1 pair of shad roe
Salt to taste, if desired
Freshly ground pepper to taste

¼ pound butter
1 tablespoon finely chopped parsley
Lemon wedges

1. Trim off excess membranes. Do not split the pair of roe in half although it may separate as it cooks. Puncture the roe in several places with a pin. Sprinkle with salt and pepper to taste.

2. Melt the butter in small skillet or casserole with a tight-fitting lid. Add the roe, cover, and let cook over gentle heat about 3 minutes. Using a spatula, carefully turn the roe. Cover and let simmer 8 or 10 minutes on the second side.

3. If roe has not split, divide it carefully. Transfer the pieces to 2 hot serving plates. Spoon a little butter over each. Sprinkle with parsley and serve with lemon wedges.

YIELD: 2 SERVINGS.

SMELTS MEUNIÈRE

8 smelts
Salt to taste, if desired
Freshly ground pepper to taste
¼ cup lemon juice

Flour
4 tablespoons butter
Chopped parsley

1. Split and clean the smelts or have the fish dealer do this for you. Cut 5 diagonal gashes on each side of the fish. Sprinkle with salt, pepper, and lemon juice. Cover and let stand 5 minutes.

2. Roll the fish in flour. Melt the butter in a skillet and sauté the fish until golden brown, about 4 minutes.

3. Arrange the fish on serving dishes, pour the juice from the skillet over them, and sprinkle with chopped parsley.

YIELD: 4 TO 6 SERVINGS.

TROUT MEUNIÈRE

When the chefs of New Orleans first created their dishes, supposedly based on the classic cooking of the French, they may have been in the traditional mold. But I have found that their preparations are at variance with the teachings of Escoffier and in certain dishes have re-created recipes that hark back to the classics. It is true of most of the recipes for trout printed here, including this Trout Meunière.

8 small trout (about 5 ounces each), or
   4 large trout (8 to 10 ounces each)
1/2 cup milk
1/4 cup flour
Salt to taste, if desired
Freshly ground pepper to taste

1/2 to 1 cup peanut, vegetable, or corn
   oil
Juice of 1 lemon
8 tablespoons butter
8 lemon slices, seeded
1/4 cup finely chopped parsley

1. Put the trout in a shallow dish and add the milk. Turn the fish in the milk.

2. Drain the trout, one at a time, but do not pat dry.

3. Blend the flour with salt and pepper. Dip each trout in the mixture and shake off the excess.

4. Heat 1/2 cup oil in a skillet (or use 2 skillets, using 1/2 cup oil in each). Fry 4 trout at a time in 1 skillet, or cook all 8 in 2 skillets. The oil must be quite hot when the trout are added.

5. When the trout are browned on one side, about 3 minutes, turn them. Spoon the oil over the trout as they cook. A 5-ounce trout should be cooked in about 5 minutes total cooking time; about 1 minute per ounce.

6. When all the trout are cooked, transfer them to a serving platter and pour the lemon juice over.

7. Heat the butter in a clean skillet, swirling it around until it foams. Continue cooking, swirling it around, until the butter is a hazelnut color. Pour this over the trout. Garnish each trout with 1 lemon slice and top with finely chopped parsley.

YIELD: 4 TO 8 SERVINGS.

TROUT MARGUERY

1 trout (about ³/₄ pound), preferably
   boned but not filleted
2 tablespoons butter
2 teaspoons finely chopped shallots
Salt to taste, if desired
Freshly ground pepper to taste
4 raw shrimp, shelled and deveined
2 mushrooms, thinly sliced

¹/₄ cup dry white wine
¹/₄ cup Fish Stock (page 274) or fresh
   or bottled clam juice
¹/₂ cup heavy cream
1 egg yolk
Juice of ¹/₂ lemon
2 tablespoons whipped cream, optional

1. Preheat the oven to 400 degrees.

2. Rinse the trout and pat dry inside and out.

3. Select a baking dish large enough to hold the trout and butter it with 1 tablespoon butter. Sprinkle with the shallots and add the trout (do not open it up). Sprinkle lightly with salt and pepper to taste.

4. Scatter the shrimp and mushrooms around the trout. Add the wine and fish stock and cover loosely with a piece of lightly buttered wax paper. Bake 20 minutes.

5. Remove the fish and shrimp and keep warm. Pour and scrape the cooking liquid and mushroom slices into a saucepan. Bring to the boil and let cook until quite thick. Do not let the sauce stick or burn.

6. Carefully pull away and discard the skin on both sides of the trout. This is easily done with the fingers. Leave the skin on the head and tail. Using the fingers, remove the thin backbone from the back of the fish. Arrange the trout on a heatproof serving dish.

7. Using a fork, carefully remove the mushrooms from the sauce and arrange them over the fish. Arrange the shrimp on either side.

8. Stir the heavy cream into the sauce. Bring to the boil. Spoon out about ¼ cup of the sauce and to this add the egg yolk and lemon juice, beating well with a fork. Spoon and scrape this mixture into the sauce and cook, stirring constantly, just until the sauce thickens. Swirl in the remaining 1 tablespoon butter. Add salt and pepper to taste. Strain the sauce over the fish and, if desired, run the trout under a very hot broiler until lightly glazed. The sauce will glaze better if whipped cream is folded into the sauce before running the trout under the broiler, but the whipped cream is not essential.

YIELD: 2 SERVINGS.

CRAB-STUFFED TROUT

2 trout (¾ pound each), preferably boned but not filleted
8 tablespoons butter
¼ cup finely chopped celery
¼ cup finely chopped onion
¼ cup finely chopped sweet green pepper
1 cup fresh crabmeat, preferably lump or backfin
½ cup fresh bread crumbs
1 egg, lightly beaten

1 tablespoon finely chopped parsley
Salt to taste, if desired
Freshly ground pepper to taste
⅓ cup Fish Stock (page 274) or bottled clam juice
4 tablespoons dry sherry
1½ teaspoons paprika
¾ cup heavy cream
1 egg yolk
1 teaspoon imported mustard, such as Dijon or Düsseldorf

1. Preheat the oven to 400 degrees.
2. Rinse the trout and pat dry inside and out. Set aside.
3. Heat 2 tablespoons butter in a saucepan and add the celery, onion, and green pepper. Cook until the onion is wilted. Add the crabmeat and bread crumbs. Add the egg, parsley, and salt and pepper to taste. Mix well.

4. Sprinkle the trout inside and out with salt and pepper to taste. Stuff the trout with the crabmeat mixture. Arrange the trout in a buttered baking dish. Dot each trout with 3 tablespoons butter. Pour the fish stock and 3 tablespoons sherry around the fish. Bake, uncovered, 20 minutes, basting often.

5. Pour the cooking liquid into a saucepan and bring to the boil. Using the fingers, pull off and discard the skin from both sides of the fish but not from the heads and tails. Using the fingers, remove the thin backbones from the backs of the fish. Arrange the trout on a hot serving dish. Keep warm.

6. Add the paprika and cream to the sauce and bring to the boil. Beat the yolk, and add a little of the hot sauce to it. Return this mixture to the saucepan, stirring rapidly. Do not boil. Stir in the mustard and remaining sherry and strain the sauce over the fish.

YIELD: 4 SERVINGS.

TROUT VÉRONIQUE

8 small trout (about 5 ounces each), or
   4 large trout (8 to 10 ounces each)
2 tablespoons butter
2 tablespoons finely chopped shallots
Salt to taste, if desired

Freshly ground pepper to taste
1 cup dry white wine
1 cup white seedless grapes
1 cup heavy cream

1. Preheat the oven to 400 degrees.

2. Select a baking dish large enough to hold the trout in one layer. Rub the bottom with butter and sprinkle the shallots over it. Sprinkle with salt and pepper to taste.

3. Arrange the trout neatly in the baking dish. Pour the wine over the trout. Sprinkle the grapes over all. Place in the oven and bake small trout about 10 minutes, large trout about 16 minutes.

4. Remove the trout from the oven. Scrape and peel the skin from both sides of each trout, leaving the heads and tails intact. Arrange the trout in one layer in a serving dish and cover closely with wax paper.

5. Pour and scrape the cooking liquid and grapes into a shallow casserole. Bring to the boil and cook over moderately high heat until the sauce is quite syrupy and almost reduced. Add the cream and bring to the boil. Cook until the sauce is reduced by half. Pour the sauce over the trout and serve.

YIELD: 4 TO 8 SERVINGS.

DEVILED CRAB

Deviled dishes, meaning those with special spices and generally containing dry mustard, were commonplace in my childhood. Although deviled foods are a part of a national pattern in American kitchens (you will also find foods "à la diable" or devil's style in French cookery), I have always considered deviled—or well-spiced—dishes, such as the following recipe for crabmeat, to be particularly Southern. The dish is seasoned with those two most basic Southern staples, Tabasco and Worcestershire sauces, seasonings my mother could not have cooked without. It can be made with any kind of crab—blue crab, Dungeness, Alaskan king, or whatever.

1 pound lump crabmeat
2 hard-cooked eggs
1/4 cup chopped parsley
4 tablespoons plus 8 teaspoons butter
1/2 cup finely chopped onion
3/4 cup finely chopped celery
1/3 cup finely chopped sweet green
  pepper
3 tablespoons chopped pimiento
2 cups bread crumbs
1/4 cup fresh or bottled clam juice

2 tablespoons dry sherry
1 1/2 teaspoons chopped scallions or
  chives
1/4 teaspoon Tabasco sauce, or to taste
1/4 teaspoon Worcestershire sauce, or to
  taste
Salt to taste, if desired
Freshly ground pepper to taste
1 egg
1/4 cup Hot Mustard (page 267)
Lemon wedges

1. Pick over the crabmeat to remove any trace of shell or cartilage. Place the crabmeat in a mixing bowl.

2. Chop the eggs and add them to the crab. Add the parsley.

3. Heat 4 tablespoons butter in a skillet and add the onion, celery, and green pepper. Cook, stirring, until the onion is translucent. Add to the crabmeat mixture along with the chopped pimiento.

4. Fold in 1½ cups bread crumbs and moisten with the clam juice and sherry. Add the scallions, Tabasco, Worcestershire, salt, and pepper.

5. Beat the egg lightly and add it to the crab mixture. Fold all the ingredients together until well blended.

6. Pile equal parts of the mixture into 8 or 10 crab shells, scallop shells, or ceramic ramekins. Smooth over the tops and brush each with mustard. Sprinkle with the remaining bread crumbs. Dot with the remaining butter.

7. When ready to cook, preheat the oven to 400 degrees.

8. Place the shells on a baking sheet and bake 20 to 30 minutes, until piping hot throughout and golden brown on top. Serve with lemon wedges.

YIELD: 4 TO 6 SERVINGS.

CRAB NORFOLK

Crab Norfolk is a specialty of Norfolk, Virginia, where it was first created by W. O. Snowden of the once popular, now defunct, Snowden and Mason Restaurant, which opened in that city in 1924. The dish was originally cooked in specially designed, small oval aluminum pans. In some establishments in Norfolk it is still cooked and served in those pans.

1 pound lump crabmeat	Salt to taste, if desired
¼ cup white or cider vinegar	Freshly ground pepper to taste
¼ pound butter, preferably unsalted	4 drops Tabasco sauce, or more to taste

1. Pick over the crabmeat to remove any trace of shell or cartilage, handling the meat gently.

2. Put the crabmeat in a bowl and sprinkle it with vinegar.

3. Heat the butter in a skillet and add the crab, salt, pepper, and Tabasco. Stir the crab, turning it as gently as possible, leaving the lumps as large as possible. Cook only until heated through.

4. Serve hot with buttered rice on the side.

YIELD: 4 SERVINGS.

CRAB CAKES

1 pound lump crabmeat (about 2½ cups)
2 cups fine fresh bread crumbs
2 eggs, well beaten
1 tablespoon Dijon or Creole mustard
½ teaspoon Worcestershire sauce
2 tablespoons finely chopped parsley

¼ cup finely chopped scallions
1 teaspoon Old Bay Seasoning, optional
½ cup Mayonnaise (page 263)
Corn, peanut, or vegetable oil
Lemon wedges
Tartar Sauce (page 264)

1. Put the crabmeat in a mixing bowl and add 1½ cups bread crumbs, the eggs, mustard, Worcestershire sauce, parsley, scallions, Old Bay Seasoning, and mayonnaise. Blend well but gently, leaving the crab lumps as large as possible.

2. Shape the mixture into 10 portions of equal size. Shape each into a flat patty about 1 inch thick or slightly less.

3. Coat each patty with the remaining bread crumbs. Chill until ready to cook.

4. When ready, the crab cakes may be cooked in deep fat heated to 365 degrees for 2 to 3 minutes, or until golden brown all over. Or they may be cooked, one batch at a time, in 2 tablespoons oil heated in a heavy skillet, adding more oil as necessary as each batch is cooked. Cook each batch about 2½ minutes on each side, or until golden brown on both sides.

5. Drain on paper towels. Serve hot with lemon wedges and tartar sauce.

YIELD: 10 CAKES.

DEEP-FRIED SOFT-SHELL CRABS

8 soft-shell crabs, cleaned

2 eggs, well beaten

1/4 cup cold water

Salt to taste, if desired

Freshly ground pepper to taste

1 1/2 cups fine fresh bread crumbs

1/2 cup flour

6 cups peanut, vegetable, or corn oil

Dill Mayonnaise (page 263)

1. Pat the crabs dry and set aside.

2. Beat the eggs with water, salt, and pepper. Put the mixture into a dish for dipping.

3. Put the bread crumbs in another dish for coating. Season the flour with salt and pepper and put in a third dish.

4. Dip the crabs in flour to coat well. Shake off the excess. Dip in egg to coat and then in bread crumbs.

5. Heat the oil to 350 degrees. Add the crabs, a few at a time, and cook until crisp and well browned, about 3 minutes. Remove and drain well on paper towels.

6. Continue cooking until all are well done. Serve with dill mayonnaise on the side.

YIELD: 4 SERVINGS.

CRAWFISH ÉTOUFFÉE

Curiously enough, the word étouffée is not unrelated to smothered, as in smothered chicken. The verb étouffer in French means to suffocate, choke, or smother. The cooking term étouffée in French kitchens refers to foods, principally meats, that have been cooked in a tightly covered utensil. No doubt the Creole étouffée and the original French term are related, but in this recipe the dish is not tightly covered.

1/3 cup corn, peanut, or vegetable oil
1/3 cup flour
1/4 cup finely chopped sweet green pepper
1/4 cup finely chopped celery
1/2 cup finely chopped onion
1 teaspoon finely minced garlic
1 1/2 cups Fish Stock (page 274)
2 tablespoons butter
1/2 cup finely chopped scallions

3 pounds crawfish tails (see following instructions)
1/4 cup crawfish fat
Salt to taste, if desired
Freshly ground pepper to taste
1 tablespoon finely chopped fresh basil, or 1 1/2 teaspoons dried
1/8 teaspoon cayenne pepper
2 tablespoons fresh lemon juice

1. Heat the oil in a heavy kettle and add the flour. Cook, stirring almost constantly, for about 20 minutes, or until the flour becomes reddish brown. Take care that the flour does not burn or it will develop a bitter taste.

2. Add the green pepper, celery, and onion. Cook, stirring, about 5 minutes. Add the garlic and stir. Add the stock, stirring with a wire whisk.

3. Heat the butter in a wide saucepan and add the scallions and crawfish tails. Cook, stirring, about 1 minute. Add the thickened sauce, crawfish fat, salt, and pepper and stir. Cook, stirring often, about 8 minutes. Add the basil, cayenne, and lemon juice. Serve with rice.

YIELD: 4 SERVINGS.

TO REMOVE CRAWFISH TAIL AND FAT

Turn the crawfish upside down. Break or twist the tails from the main body. Inside the shell there will be a creamy white mass that you should scoop out with the tip of a knife or a small spoon. This is crawfish fat. Break open the tail portions and pull away the tail meat.

OYSTERS FRIED IN CORNMEAL

24 large oysters, shucked, with their
   liquor
1/2 cup cornmeal, preferably yellow,
   although white may be used
1/2 teaspoon freshly ground black
   pepper

1/8 teaspoon cayenne pepper
1/8 teaspoon paprika
Salt to taste, if desired
Corn, peanut, or vegetable oil for
   deep-frying

1. Drain the oysters briefly and discard the liquor.

2. Combine the cornmeal, black pepper, cayenne pepper, paprika, and salt. Blend well.

3. Heat the oil to 375 degrees.

4. Dredge the oysters in the cornmeal mixture. Drop them, a few at a time, in the hot fat and cook, stirring often, until they are golden brown all over, less than 2 minutes. Do not overcook. Remove and drain.

5. Let the fat return to the proper temperature before adding successive batches. Serve, if desired, with tartar sauce, mayonnaise, or Southern-style —with ketchup flavored with Worcestershire sauce, a dash of Tabasco, and lemon juice.

YIELD: 2 SERVINGS.

CREAMED OYSTERS

2 cups shucked oysters with their
   liquor
Water or bottled clam juice
2 tablespoons butter
2 tablespoons flour
1/4 cup heavy cream
Salt to taste, if desired

Freshly ground pepper to taste
1/2 teaspoon Worcestershire sauce
1/8 teaspoon freshly grated nutmeg
1/8 teaspoon cayenne pepper
Toast triangles
3 teaspoons freshly chopped parsley

1. Line a mixing bowl with a sieve and pour in the oysters. Reserve the oyster liquor and add enough water or bottled clam juice to make 1 cup. Pat the oysters with paper towels to remove excess moisture.

2. Heat the butter in a saucepan and add the flour, stirring with a wire whisk. When blended and smooth, add the oyster liquor mixture, stirring rapidly with the whisk. When blended and smooth, add the cream and stir.

3. Add salt, pepper, Worcestershire, nutmeg, and cayenne. Add the oysters and cook briefly over gentle heat until the edges curl.

4. Serve over hot buttered toast triangles. Sprinkle each serving with an equal amount of chopped parsley.

YIELD: 4 TO 6 SERVINGS.

BOILED SHRIMP

In the days of my youth, we feasted on shrimp, fresh from the Gulf Coast, whenever they were available. The shrimp were simply boiled with seasonings and eaten at table, hot out of the shell. No one bothered with the refinement of "cleaning" or deveining the shrimp. They were simply shelled, dipped into melted butter to which a small amount of lemon juice,

Worcestershire sauce, and Tabasco sauce had been added, and popped into the mouth.

1 pound fresh shrimp	*Salt to taste, if desired*
Water to cover	*1 bay leaf*
8 whole allspice	*10 peppercorns*
1 hot red pepper	*Tail ends of 12 dill sprigs, optional*
1 garlic clove, crushed	

Combine all the ingredients in a saucepan and bring to the boil. Simmer about 30 seconds. Remove the saucepan from the heat and let the shrimp cool in the cooking liquid. Drain well.

YIELD: 4 SERVINGS.

SHRIMP CREOLE

It is conceivable that the first Creole dish I ever sampled (how many decades ago!) and the one I have eaten most often because of my affection for it is shrimp Creole. The following is one of the most basic and best recipes for the dish. It is made with what Paul Prudhomme has referred to as the "holy trinity" of Creole foods: chopped celery, green pepper, and onion. It is a recipe that served me well, long before I became professionally involved in the food field, when I set up a bachelor kitchen in Chicago after my years in military service.

1 pound fresh shrimp	*2 sprigs fresh thyme, or ¹/₂ teaspoon*
3 tablespoons butter	* dried*
³/₄ cup coarsely chopped onion	*1 bay leaf*
3 small celery ribs, coarsely chopped	*Tabasco sauce to taste*
1 sweet green pepper, cored, seeded, and	*¹/₂ teaspoon grated lemon rind*
* coarsely chopped*	*Salt to taste, if desired*
3 garlic cloves, finely minced	*Freshly ground pepper to taste*
2 cups canned tomatoes, preferably	*2 tablespoons finely chopped parsley*
* Italian peeled tomatoes*	*Juice of ¹/₂ lemon*

1. Shell and devein the shrimp. Rinse and pat dry. Set aside.

2. Melt the butter in a saucepan and add the onion. Cook, stirring, until the onion is wilted, and add the celery, green pepper, and garlic. Cook briefly, stirring. The vegetables must remain crisp.

3. Add the tomatoes, thyme, bay leaf, Tabasco, lemon rind, salt, and pepper. Simmer 10 minutes uncovered.

4. Add the shrimp and cover. Cook 3 to 5 minutes, no longer. Add the chopped parsley, lemon juice, and, if desired, more Tabasco sauce to taste. Serve with rice.

YIELD: 2 TO 4 SERVINGS.

SHRIMP AND EGGPLANT CREOLE

1 1/2 pounds eggplant
Flour for dredging
Salt to taste, if desired
Freshly ground pepper to taste
1/2 cup olive oil, approximately

24 raw shrimp, shelled and deveined
2 cups Tomato Sauce with Mushrooms
  (page 272)
1 teaspoon dried oregano
Juice of 1 lemon

1. Preheat the oven to 400 degrees.

2. Cut the eggplant into 12 slices, each about 3/4 inch thick. Pare each slice into a round about 3 inches in diameter.

3. Dredge the slices on all sides in flour seasoned with salt and pepper.

4. Heat about 1/4 cup olive oil in a heavy skillet, and when it is hot and almost smoking, add the eggplant slices. Cook quickly until golden on one side, and turn to brown the other side. It may be necessary to add a little more oil to prevent burning or sticking. Drain the slices and continue cooking the remaining slices.

5. Arrange the slices in one layer in a baking dish. Arrange 2 shrimp on each slice and spoon equal amounts of tomato sauce over the shrimp. Sprinkle with the oregano, lemon juice, and 1/4 cup additional olive oil.

6. Bake 30 minutes and serve piping hot.

YIELD: 6 SERVINGS.

SHRIMP WITH CHEESE GRITS

3 1/2 cups water
3/4 cup regular grits (do not use
   quick-cooking grits)
Salt to taste, if desired
1 pound fresh shrimp in the shell
12 drops Tabasco sauce
6 ounces sharp Cheddar cheese, finely
   grated
3 tablespoons butter
2 1/2 ounces bacon, finely diced (about
   1/2 cup)

1/4 cup corn, peanut, or vegetable oil
1 cup finely chopped scallions,
   including green part
6 ounces mushrooms, thinly sliced
   (about 3 cups)
1 garlic clove, finely minced
Juice of 1 lemon
1/4 cup finely chopped parsley

1. Bring the water to the boil and gradually add the grits, stirring. Add salt. Cook uncovered, stirring often, about 15 minutes. Cover closely and continue cooking over low heat for 25 minutes, or until done.

2. Meanwhile, shell and devein the shrimp and put in a bowl. Set aside.

3. When the grits are cooked, remove from heat. Stir in 6 drops Tabasco sauce, the cheese, and butter.

4. Place 2 heavy skillets on the stove. Add the diced bacon to 1 skillet; pour the oil in the other. Cook the bacon, stirring, until it starts to brown. Add the shrimp and cook, tossing and stirring so that they cook evenly, about 3 minutes. Add the scallions and cook briefly.

5. As the shrimp cook, put the mushrooms in the hot oil in the other skillet and cook, tossing and stirring, until the mushrooms give up their liquid. Add the garlic and cook briefly, stirring. Add the lemon juice and stir.

6. Combine the shrimp and mushroom mixtures in one skillet and sprinkle with parsley and the remaining 6 drops Tabasco. Stir to blend.

7. Spoon equal portions of the cheese grits onto 6 hot plates. Spoon equal portions of the shrimp-and-mushroom mixture over each serving. Serve immediately.

YIELD: 4 SERVINGS.

SHRIMP PILAU

The word *pilau* is widely used in Southern kitchens, primarily those of the Carolinas. It is related to the words *pilaf, pilaff, pilaw,* and rarely, *plaw.* It is derived from the Turkish word *pilaw* and it invariably refers to almost any rice dish, plain or cooked with other foods, such as shrimp.

2 pounds shrimp	1 cup Carolina long-grain rice
6 strips of bacon	3 tablespoons butter
1/2 cup finely chopped onion	Salt to taste, if desired
1/4 cup finely chopped sweet green pepper	Freshly ground pepper to taste
1 3/4 cups canned tomatoes, partly drained and crushed	6 drops Tabasco Sauce
	1/8 teaspoon ground mace

1. Peel and devein the shrimp and set aside.

2. Bring 6 cups water to the boil in a saucepan. Add the shrimp. Cover and cook about 2 minutes, no longer. Turn off the heat.

3. Drain the shrimp, but reserve 1½ cups of the cooking liquid. Use this liquid to cook the rice for the pilau.

4. Cook the bacon in a skillet until crisp. Drain. When the bacon is cool, crumble it and set aside.

5. Pour off all but 1 tablespoon bacon fat from the skillet. Add the chopped onion and green pepper to the skillet and cook until wilted.

6. Add the tomatoes and cook, stirring occasionally, about 5 minutes.

7. Add the rice and reserved 1½ cups cooking liquid. Stir to blend. Cover and simmer 18 minutes.

8. Add the butter and stir until the butter is melted and blended. Add salt, pepper, Tabasco, and mace. Stir. Add the shrimp and bacon. Stir from the bottom to blend. Reheat gently.

YIELD: 8 OR MORE SERVINGS.

JAMBALAYA

There is some dispute as to the exact origin of the name *jambalaya,* the excellent blend of rice and other ingredients including—depending on your recipe—sausage, shrimp, crawfish, and ham, among other things. In the most definitive book on Creole and Cajun cooking, *Chef Paul Prud-homme's Louisiana Kitchen,* the author quotes the *Acadian Dictionary,* written by Rita and Gabrielle Claudet and published in Houma, Louisiana, in 1981. Jambalaya, the dictionary declares, "comes from the French 'jambon' meaning ham, the African 'ya' meaning rice, and the Acadian [language] where everything is 'à la.' " If you really want to be authentic, the ham used in a basic jambalaya is a Cajun specialty called tasso. It is a highly seasoned ham and rarely found outside Louisiana.

¼ pound salt pork, cut into small cubes

¾ pound hot link sausages, such as chorizos or hot Italian sausages

4 cups finely chopped onions

3 cups finely chopped celery

3 tablespoons finely minced garlic

4 cups chopped sweet green peppers

1 cup chopped sweet red peppers, or an additional cup of chopped sweet green peppers

3 pounds porkette (smoked boneless pork butt), available in supermarkets, or a cooked ham in 1 thick slice

3 bay leaves

3 sprigs fresh thyme, or 1 teaspoon dried

1 can (35 ounces) tomatoes, preferably imported Italian tomatoes

1 cup finely chopped parsley

Salt to taste, if desired

Freshly ground pepper to taste

Tabasco sauce to taste

1 quart shucked oysters with their liquor

4 cups Fish Stock (page 274) or bottled clam juice, approximately

4 cups water, approximately

5 cups rice

5 pounds raw shrimp, shelled and deveined

1½ pounds fresh bay scallops

1. Using a large kettle or Dutch oven, cook the salt pork cubes, stirring often, until rendered of fat.

2. Cut the sausages into ½-inch-thick slices and add them to the kettle. Cook about 8 minutes, stirring occasionally, and add the onions. Cook, stirring often, until wilted, and add the celery, garlic, green peppers, and red peppers.

3. Cut the porkette or ham into 1-inch cubes and add it to the kettle. Add the bay leaves, thyme, tomatoes, parsley, salt, pepper, and Tabasco sauce. Continue cooking. Drain the oysters and add the liquor, ½ to 1 cup, to the pot.

4. Add 2 cups fish stock and 2 cups water. Cook, stirring once or twice from the bottom, about 10 minutes.

5. Add the rice and stir gently. Cover and cook about 15 minutes. If necessary, add a little more stock and water to prevent sticking and to keep the jambalaya from becoming too dry.

6. Add the remaining stock and water, the shrimp, scallops, and oysters. Cook, stirring often from the bottom, 15 to 20 minutes. If necessary, add more liquid to prevent scorching and drying out.

7. Serve with a bottle of Tabasco sauce on the side.

YIELD: 24 OR MORE SERVINGS.

BAKED EGGPLANT AND SHRIMP

1 ¼ pounds eggplant
3 tablespoons flour
Salt, if desired
Freshly ground pepper
¾ cup olive oil, approximately
1 ½ pounds ripe tomatoes, or 3 cups
   drained imported canned tomatoes

1 ½ pounds fresh raw shrimp, shelled
   and deveined
¾ cup fresh bread crumbs
1 tablespoon finely chopped parsley
2 tablespoons finely chopped garlic
½ teaspoon dried thyme

1. Preheat the oven to 375 degrees.

2. Trim off and discard the ends of the eggplant and peel the eggplant. Cut it into 1-inch cubes. There should be 4 or 5 cups.

3. Dredge the cubes in flour seasoned with salt and pepper to taste.

4. Heat about one-third of the oil in a skillet, and when it is piping hot add half the eggplant. Cook, tossing and stirring, until the eggplant is browned. Drain the eggplant, and add more oil and the remaining eggplant cubes. Cook, tossing and stirring, until the eggplant is browned. Drain the eggplant very well to rid it of excess oil. Reserve the oil.

5. If fresh tomatoes are used, peel and seed them. Cut the tomatoes into 1-inch cubes. There should be about 3 cups. If canned tomatoes are used, chop them. Put in a saucepan and simmer about 10 minutes. Add salt and pepper to taste.

6. Put the reserved oil in a skillet and add the shrimp. Sprinkle with salt and pepper and cook just until the shrimp turn pink.

7. Spoon equal amounts of eggplant into 6 baking dishes. Add equal portions of shrimp to each dish. Spoon equal amounts of tomato over the shrimp.

8. Combine the bread crumbs, parsley, garlic, and thyme. Blend well and sprinkle this over each dish. Drizzle about 1 teaspoon olive oil over each serving and bake 10 minutes. Run briefly under the broiler to glaze.

YIELD: 6 SERVINGS.

ROUX

Of all the techniques used in the preparation of foods, nationally or internationally, I think that one of the most difficult to describe is the making of a roux in the Cajun or Creole style. I specify Cajun or Creole because in the French kitchen a roux—pronounced rue—is nothing more than the blending of a fat, generally butter, with flour. And to your roux you add a liquid of almost any sort, chicken broth, beef broth, fish stock, and so on. The roux in this case is made without browning.

In the Cajun or Creole kitchen, the roux is almost invariably browned or cooked until it achieves one degree of color or another—it might be a light to medium brown color; it might be light or dark red; or it might be the color of dark caramel or even black. My friend Paul Prudhomme has noted that the light or medium brown roux are to be used in the preparation of sauces that cover or are served with dark meats such as game, or with dark-fleshed birds such as duck or goose, or with game birds such as pheasant. Dark-colored roux are the bases for sauces to be served with lighter or white meats, such as pork and veal, or with saltwater or fresh water fish and seafood such as crawfish or red snapper. The latter are also preferable for gumbos because, in his opinion, dark roux produce the thinnest of gumbos.

Roux are best cooked in a heavy kettle or casserole, preferably one with curved sides. This enables the cook to stir all over the bottom with greater facility. The best kettles or casseroles are those made of cast iron or those that are enamel-coated. You cook your roux according to the color indicated in any given recipe and proceed from there. You must stir constantly and it may require a good deal of patience and time. The ratio of flour to fat in the preparation of a roux is about 1:1. You should prepare all the ingredients that go into your dish before you begin preparation of the roux. I strongly feel that one of the most important ingredients in the preparation of a roux is self-confidence. Remember that the chances are your roux will not burn if it is properly stirred and if it is removed from the heat once you have achieved the desired color.

SEAFOOD GUMBO

This gumbo was prepared in my kitchen by that greatest of Cajun and Creole chefs, Paul Prudhomme, whose name appears frequently in this book. To be absolutely authentic, he told me, you would have to use smoked *andouille*, a staple in New Orleans meat markets, but, like tasso, not widely available outside Louisiana. The Polish sausage, kielbasa, is used as a substitute and is widely available.

¾ cup peanut, vegetable, or corn oil
1 cup flour
2 tablespoons butter
3 ½ cups finely chopped onions
3 cups finely chopped sweet green
   peppers
2 cups finely chopped celery
1 tablespoon finely minced garlic
1 ½ pounds Polish sausage (kielbasa),
   cut into ½-inch cubes
¼ teaspoon dried oregano
½ teaspoon dried thyme
2 bay leaves

½ teaspoon cayenne pepper
¼ teaspoon white pepper
½ teaspoon freshly ground black
   pepper
Salt to taste, if desired
2 cups chopped fresh or drained canned
   imported tomatoes
2 quarts Seafood Stock (see following
   recipe)
4 live blue crabs, optional
2 pounds shrimp, shelled and deveined;
   reserve the shells for Seafood Stock
1 pound lump crabmeat

1. Put the oil and flour in a heavy kettle. Cook, stirring with a wire whisk or flat wooden spoon, until the flour goes through several changes of color: beige, light brown, dark brown, light red, and a slightly darker red. You must keep stirring constantly. The cooking will take 5 minutes or slightly longer. This is a roux. Set aside.

2. Heat the butter in a saucepan and add the onions, green peppers, celery, and garlic. Cook, stirring, until wilted. Add the sausage and stir.

3. Add the oregano, thyme, bay leaves, cayenne, white and black peppers, salt, tomatoes, and stock. Bring to the boil and let simmer 15 minutes.

4. Add the tomato-and-sausage mixture to the roux. Bring to the boil, stirring, and let cook 1 hour.

5. If the blue crabs are used, pull off and discard the apron at the base on the underside of each crab. Cut the crabs in half and pull off and discard the spongy "dead man's fingers." Cut each crab half in 2 pieces and add to the kettle. Let simmer 1 minute.

6. Add the shrimp and crabmeat. Stir. Cover and set aside 15 minutes. Serve with rice.

YIELD: 8 OR MORE SERVINGS.

SEAFOOD STOCK

4 pounds fish bones, preferably with
head on but gills removed
3 quarts water
1 1/2 cups coarsely chopped onions

1 1/2 cups coarsely chopped celery
2 cups cored, coarsely chopped tomatoes
Shells from 2 pounds of shrimp

1. Combine all the ingredients in a kettle. Bring to the boil. Cook the stock down until about 2 quarts of liquid are left.
2. Cook 5 to 7 hours longer, but always keep the liquid replenished so that it remains at approximately 2 quarts. Strain, discarding the solids.

YIELD: 2 QUARTS.

SEAFOOD GUMBO WITH OKRA

1/3 cup plus 3 tablespoons vegetable oil,
bacon fat, or lard
1/3 cup flour
1 pound raw shrimp in the shell
4 cups Fish Stock (page 274)
2 cups finely chopped onions
1 cup chopped sweet green peppers
1/4 cup chopped long hot or mild green
chilies, optional
1 cup chopped celery
1/2 cup chopped scallions
1 tablespoon finely chopped garlic
1 cup oysters with their liquor
1 cup canned Italian peeled tomatoes
1 bay leaf
1 or 2 dried hot red peppers, or 1/2
teaspoon dried hot red pepper flakes

16 whole allspice
6 whole cloves
4 sprigs fresh thyme, or 1/2 teaspoon
dried
1/8 teaspoon grated nutmeg
Salt to taste, if desired
Freshly ground pepper to taste
3/4 pound fresh okra, trimmed and cut
into 1/2-inch pieces, or 1 package
(10 ounces) frozen cut okra
1/3 cup dry white wine or dry
vermouth
Juice of 1/2 lemon
1/2 to 1 teaspoon Worcestershire sauce
1/2 pound cooked crabmeat, or 1
package (6 ounces) frozen and
defrosted crabmeat, optional

1. Put ⅓ cup oil and the flour in a heavy 4- or 5-quart casserole or Dutch oven. Cook over low heat, stirring with a wooden spoon, 20 to 40 minutes or longer, until the flour is nicely browned.

2. Peel and devein the shrimp and reserve the shells. Refrigerate the shrimp until ready for use. Combine the shells and fish stock and simmer about 5 minutes. Strain and set aside.

3. When the roux is ready, add the onions, stirring with the spoon. Cook, stirring, until the onions wilt. Add the green peppers, chilies, celery, scallions, and garlic and continue stirring—it will be a thick mass—about 5 minutes to brown lightly. Add the oysters, tomatoes, and strained fish stock, stirring constantly with a wire whisk. When the mixture is thickened and boiling, add the bay leaf and hot red peppers. Tie the allspice, cloves, and thyme in a small cheesecloth bag and add it. Add the nutmeg, salt, and pepper. Let simmer. The shrimp may be added now or reserved until later if you wish them to remain firm.

4. Heat the remaining 3 tablespoons oil in a skillet and add the okra. Add salt and pepper to taste. Toss and stir until the okra starts to brown. Add it to the gumbo.

5. Add the wine, lemon juice, and Worcestershire. Add the crabmeat if it is to be used.

6. Add more salt and pepper, if desired, according to taste. Cook the mixture 45 minutes to 1 hour. If the shrimp have not been added, add them at least 5 minutes before serving. While the gumbo cooks it must be stirred frequently from the bottom to make sure it does not stick and burn, and it is best to cook it on a flame-guarding device such as a Flame Tamer. When the gumbo is ready, remove the bay leaf and spice bag. Add more Worcestershire sauce and lemon juice to taste. Serve with fluffy rice.

YIELD: 6 TO 8 SERVINGS.

ဘၚ
CAJUN-STYLE GUMBO

This Cajun-Style Gumbo was prepared in my home some time ago by Paul Prudhomme. The preferred ham for this dish is the specially cured New Orleans version known as tasso, but it is seldom available outside Louisiana. In substituting a store-bought ham, choose one that is not heavily smoked.

1 cup melted pork lard, or peanut, corn, or vegetable oil

3/4 cup flour

2 cups finely chopped onions

1 1/2 cups finely chopped sweet green peppers

1 cup finely chopped celery

10 small or 5 large bay leaves

1 3/4 teaspoons cayenne pepper

2 teaspoons freshly ground white pepper

2 teaspoons freshly ground black pepper

1 tablespoon plus 1 teaspoon finely minced garlic

1 1/2 pounds fresh, tender young okra, cut crosswise into 1/4-inch-thick

rounds, or 3 packages (10 ounces each) frozen cut okra, thawed

3 cups smoked ham pieces (each about 1 inch long and 1/2 inch wide)

3/4 teaspoon garlic powder

Salt to taste, if desired

4 cups peeled, seeded, and coarsely chopped fresh tomatoes (about 2 pounds), or chopped imported canned tomatoes

6 cups Fish Stock (page 274)

1 pound peeled, Blanched Crawfish Tails (see following instructions)

Filé powder to be added as desired, optional

1. A heavy, black iron skillet is almost essential for the preparation of this dish. It is also strongly recommended that all the ingredients be chopped and assembled before starting to cook. Combine and assemble them in the order in which they will be used so that they may be added without hesitation.

2. Heat 1/2 cup melted lard or oil in the skillet until it is barely smoking. Add the flour and stir vigorously and constantly with a wire whisk, about 3 minutes, or until the mixture is the color of dark chocolate. Take care that it does not burn.

3. Quickly add 1 cup onion, 1/2 cup green peppers, and 1/2 cup celery. Reduce the heat and cook, stirring, about 3 minutes. Add 4 small bay leaves or 2 large ones, 1 teaspoon cayenne pepper, 1 teaspoon white pepper, and 1/2 teaspoon black pepper. Cook, stirring, about 1 minute. Add 1 teaspoon minced garlic and cook briefly, stirring. Remove from the heat. Scrape the mixture into a large casserole and set aside. There should be about 1 1/2 cups.

4. Heat the remaining ½ cup melted lard or oil in a black iron skillet over very high heat. When it is hot and almost smoking, add the okra. Cook, stirring often, about 15 minutes. Frozen okra will require a shorter cooking time. Add the remaining onion, green peppers, celery, and minced garlic, 1 cup ham pieces, and the remaining bay leaves. Continue cooking over high heat, stirring occasionally, for 5 minutes, and add the remaining cayenne pepper, white pepper, and black pepper, and the garlic powder. Add salt, if desired.

5. Cook until the mixture is quite dry, about 5 minutes. Stir in the tomatoes. Cook over high heat, stirring often, about 10 minutes. Stir carefully and often all over the bottom to prevent sticking and burning.

6. Pour and scrape this mixture into the large casserole containing the browned flour. Add the fish stock and the remaining ham. Cook over moderately high heat for about 1 hour. Stir often all over the bottom. (The base of this gumbo may be made to this point several days in advance and refrigerated. It also may be frozen.)

7. Add the crawfish tails and bring to the boil. Let simmer about 5 minutes.

8. When ready to serve, remove the bay leaves. Serve the filé powder separately to be added by each guest according to taste. Serve with plain boiled or steamed rice.

YIELD: 10 OR MORE SERVINGS.

BLANCHED CRAWFISH TAILS

1 pound crawfish

1. Place the crawfish in a large kettle and add cold water to cover and ¼ cup salt for each gallon of water. Let stand, stirring often, for about 10 minutes.

2. Drain the crawfish, and pour boiling water over them until covered. Cover and let stand 10 minutes. Drain.

3. Tear off the tail of each crawfish and break the tail covering from the underside to expose the tail. Remove the meat.

4. The crawfish fat is the yellowish or golden-white matter in the upper body of the crawfish. Scrape or push this out with the fingers or a spoon.

FROGS' LEGS CREOLE

12 large pairs frogs' legs, or 24 small
* pairs*
1 cup milk
1 cup flour, approximately
Salt to taste, if desired
Freshly ground pepper to taste

1 can (28 ounces) peeled tomatoes,
* drained*
½ cup vegetable or salad oil
10 tablespoons butter
1 tablespoon finely chopped garlic
¼ cup finely chopped parsley

1. Prepare one pair of frogs' legs at a time. Slip one leg in between the two muscles of the lower part of the other leg to keep the frogs' legs flat.

2. Soak the legs briefly, about 5 minutes, in the milk.

3. Drain the legs but do not dry, then dredge each pair in flour seasoned with salt and pepper.

4. Meanwhile, pour the tomatoes into a saucepan and simmer until thickened, 20 to 30 minutes. Season to taste with salt and pepper.

5. In a large skillet, heat the oil and 4 tablespoons butter. Cook the legs until golden on one side, then turn and cook the other side until golden.

6. Lightly butter a heatproof serving dish and arrange the frogs' legs on it in a symmetrical fashion. Spoon the tomato sauce neatly over the centers of the frogs' legs.

7. Discard the fat from the skillet and wipe out the skillet with paper towels. Melt the remaining butter in the skillet and add the garlic. When the butter is hot and foaming, pour it over the frogs' legs. Sprinkle with parsley and serve.

YIELD: 4 TO 6 SERVINGS.

Poultry

CHICKEN POT PIE

Chicken is to my way of thinking the most Southern of main-course ingredients. That may be because chicken is, by far, the least expensive of all "meats" and it often appeared on my mother's table at least once, and frequently twice, a day. Our servant named Joe was an exceptionally fine cook, and the chicken dish that I coveted most—next to fried chicken, of course—was Joe's chicken pot pie. This is my revised version of his dish.

THE PASTRY:

2 cups flour
8 tablespoons butter
4 tablespoons lard

Salt, if desired
2 to 3 tablespoons cold water

THE FILLING:

5 tablespoons butter

*2 chickens (2 1/2 pounds each), cut into
serving pieces*

Salt to taste, if desired

Freshly ground pepper to taste

1/2 cup coarsely chopped carrots

1/2 cup coarsely chopped celery

1 cup small white onions, peeled

1/2 pound mushrooms, thinly sliced

3 sprigs fresh parsley

2 whole cloves

*3 sprigs fresh thyme, or 1/2 teaspoon
dried*

4 tablespoons flour

1 cup dry white wine

4 cups Chicken Stock (page 275)

A few drops of Tabasco sauce

5 strips of bacon

3 hard-cooked eggs, peeled

1 cup heavy cream

1 teaspoon Worcestershire sauce

1 egg, beaten

1. For the pastry, put the flour in a mixing bowl and add the butter, lard, and salt to taste. Using a pastry blender, work the mixture until it looks like coarse cornmeal. Add the water, a little at a time, working the dough lightly with the fingers. Add just enough water to have it hold together. Shape the dough into a ball and wrap it in wax paper. Refrigerate dough at least 30 minutes.

2. To make the filling, melt 3 tablespoons butter in a skillet and add the chicken, skin side down. Sprinkle with salt and pepper to taste. Cook over low heat without browning, about 5 minutes, turning once. Scatter the carrots, celery, and white onions over.

3. Heat the remaining 2 tablespoons butter in another skillet and add the mushrooms. Cook, stirring, until they give up their liquid. Continue cooking until most of the liquid evaporates. Add the mushrooms to the chicken.

4. Tie together the parsley, cloves, and thyme in a cheesecloth square. Add it to the chicken mixture. Cook, stirring frequently, about 10 minutes. Do not let the mixture burn.

5. Sprinkle with the flour, stirring to distribute it evenly. Add the wine and stock. Add the Tabasco sauce and cover. Simmer 30 minutes.

6. Preheat the oven to 400 degrees.

7. Meanwhile, cut the bacon into 2-inch lengths. Cook the pieces until crisp and brown. Drain.

8. Strain the chicken and pour the cooking liquid into a saucepan. Discard the cheesecloth bag. Arrange the chicken and vegetables in a baking dish (a 16 × 10½ × 2-inch oval dish works well). Cut the eggs into sixths and arrange them over the chicken and vegetables. Scatter the bacon bits over the chicken and vegetables.

9. Skim off and discard the fat from the cooking liquid. Bring the liquid to the boil and add the heavy cream. Bring the sauce to the boil. Simmer about 20 minutes. Add the Worcestershire sauce and salt and pepper to taste.

10. Pour the sauce over the chicken mixture.

11. Roll out the pastry. Cut an oval just large enough to fit the baking dish. Arrange it over the chicken mixture and cut a small hole in the center to allow steam to escape. Brush with the beaten egg. Bake 30 minutes.

YIELD: 6 TO 8 SERVINGS.

ROAST CHICKEN WITH PECAN STUFFING

1 roasting chicken (about 3½ pounds), with giblets	1 cup fine, fresh bread crumbs
2 tablespoons butter, or the fat rendered from the inner chicken fat	1 egg, lightly beaten
	Salt to taste, if desired
½ pound bulk sausage	Freshly ground pepper to taste
1 cup finely chopped onion	1 cup toasted pecans
1 tablespoon loosely packed leaf sage	1 onion, peeled and quartered
¼ cup finely chopped parsley	¼ cup water

1. Preheat the oven to 400 degrees.

2. Remove the gizzard, heart, and liver from the chicken. Cut away and discard the tough outer membrane of the gizzard. Chop the soft, fleshy part of the gizzard, heart, and liver.

3. Heat the butter in a saucepan and add the sausage, breaking it up with the flat side of a metal kitchen spoon. Add the liver mixture and chopped onion. Cook, stirring, about 3 minutes, and add the sage.

4. Cook about 3 minutes more, stirring, or until the sausage is cooked. Add the parsley, bread crumbs, egg, salt and pepper to taste, and the pecans. Blend well and let cool.

5. Sprinkle the chicken inside and out with salt and pepper to taste. Stuff the chicken with the pecan mixture and truss. Place the chicken on its side in a shallow baking dish and scatter the quartered onion around it.

6. Roast the chicken 20 minutes. Turn the chicken to the other side and continue roasting, basting often, about 20 minutes.

7. Turn the chicken on its back and continue roasting, basting often, about 20 minutes.

8. Ten minutes before the chicken is done, add the water and continue baking.

9. Remove from the oven and let stand 10 minutes before carving. Serve with the pan juices.

YIELD: 4 OR MORE SERVINGS.

BARBECUED CHICKEN

Barbecues were a focal point of my early nourishment. When I was young, hundreds of guests would arrive on special occasions for barbecues that consisted of long trenches specially dug on my father's property. Wire was laid over these trenches to hold hundreds of pounds of chicken and ribs of pork, which were then basted for hours until the meat shredded at a touch.

1 chicken (about 2½ pounds)
Salt to taste, if desired
Freshly ground pepper to taste
1 tablespoon oil or, preferably, softened
  lard

Southern Barbecue Sauce (see page 273)

1. Prepare a charcoal grill and have it ready. The coals must be white-hot but not overly plentiful, or the food will cook too fast. Arrange the grill 6 to 8 inches above the coals.

2. Split the chicken in half for grilling. Place it skin side up on a flat surface and flatten it lightly with a flat mallet. This will help it lie flat on the grill. Sprinkle the chicken with salt and pepper. Sprinkle with oil or rub with lard.

3. Place the chicken, skin side down, on the grill and cook until browned, about 10 minutes. Brush the top with barbecue sauce and turn. Brush the skin side with sauce. Continue grilling and turning, brushing often with sauce, until chicken is thoroughly cooked, 30 minutes or less.

4. Give the chicken a final brushing with the sauce and remove to a serving dish.

YIELD: 2 TO 4 SERVINGS.

SOUTHERN FRIED CHICKEN

1 chicken (2 1/2 to 3 pounds), cut into
  serving pieces
Milk to cover
1/4 teaspoon Tabasco sauce
1 cup flour

1 1/2 to 2 teaspoons salt, if desired
2 teaspoons freshly ground black pepper
1 pound lard, or 2 cups corn oil
1/4 pound butter

1. Put the chicken pieces in a bowl and add milk to cover. Add the Tabasco sauce and stir. Refrigerate 1 hour or longer.

2. Combine the flour, salt, and pepper (the flavor of pepper in this recipe is important) in a flat baking dish. Blend well.

3. Remove the chicken pieces, 2 or 3 at a time, and dip them into the flour mixture, turning them in the flour to coat well.

4. Heat the lard and butter in a skillet, preferably a black iron skillet large enough to hold the chicken pieces in one layer without touching, over high heat. Add the chicken pieces, skin side down, and cook until golden brown on one side. Turn the pieces and reduce the heat to medium-low. Continue cooking until pieces are golden brown and cooked through. The total cooking time should be 20 to 30 minutes. As the pieces are cooked, transfer them to paper towels to drain.

YIELD: 4 SERVINGS.

HONEY-FRIED CHICKEN
WITH THYME AND MINT SAUCE

1 chicken (about 4 pounds), cut into
serving pieces
1/2 cup honey
2 1/2 tablespoons vinegar, preferably
raspberry or other fruit-flavored
vinegar
Salt to taste, if desired
Freshly ground pepper to taste
1/2 cup lard
1/2 cup corn, peanut, or vegetable oil

1/2 cup all-purpose flour
2 tablespoons whole wheat flour
1/2 cup dry white wine
1/2 cup rich chicken broth
1 1/2 cups heavy cream
1 tablespoon finely chopped fresh thyme
leaves, or 1 teaspoon dried
1 teaspoon freshly grated lemon rind
1 1/2 tablespoons finely chopped fresh
mint leaves

1. Put the chicken pieces in a mixing bowl. Blend the honey and vinegar and pour it over the chicken. Stir to coat the pieces evenly. Let stand at least 2 hours, stirring occasionally. Drain the chicken pieces on paper towels, but reserve and set aside 2 tablespoons of the marinade. Sprinkle the chicken pieces with salt and pepper.

2. Heat the lard and oil in a 12-inch frying pan to a temperature of 360 degrees, if a thermometer is available.

3. Meanwhile, combine the all-purpose flour with the whole wheat flour. Add the chicken pieces and stir to coat all over. Shake off the excess.

4. Place the pieces, skin side down, in the hot fat and cook, turning the pieces often, until they are golden brown all over and cooked through, about 20 minutes or longer. The dark-meat pieces generally require a longer cooking time than the white-meat pieces. Drain the chicken on paper towels as it is cooked.

5. Pour off most of the fat from the pan, leaving the brown particles that may cling to the bottom and sides of the pan. Do not wipe out the skillet.

6. Combine the wine and chicken broth. Heat the skillet and add the wine mixture, stirring to dissolve the brown particles that cling to the bottom and sides. Cook until reduced by half.

7. Add the cream, thyme, lemon rind, mint, and the 2 tablespoons reserved marinade. Cook until reduced to about 2 cups. Put the sauce through a fine sieve, pressing to extract all the juices from the solids. Reheat and season with salt and pepper to taste. Spoon the sauce over the chicken and serve.

YIELD: 4 SERVINGS.

CHICKEN GUMBO

Gumbo is as essential to the lexicon of Southern cookery as clam chowder is to that of New England or scrapple is to that of the Pennsylvania Dutch country. The word derives from the Bantu word *gombo,* meaning okra, and first appeared in American print in the year 1803. The name was brought over, of course, by the slaves.

2 1/2 cups peanut, vegetable, or corn oil
2 1/2 cups flour
2 cups finely chopped sweet green peppers
2 cups finely chopped onions
2 cups finely chopped celery
1 chicken (5 to 6 pounds), cut into serving pieces

10 cups Chicken Stock (page 275) or canned chicken broth
1/2 teaspoon cumin
3/4 teaspoon cayenne pepper
1 teaspoon white pepper
Salt to taste, if desired
2 bay leaves

1. Heat a large heavy skillet and add 1 cup oil. When it starts to smoke, add 1½ cups flour and cook, stirring, until the roux becomes quite dark, a rusty caramel color. Do not let it burn or it will become bitter. Add the green peppers, onions, and celery. Cook, stirring, over low heat about 10 minutes.

2. Meanwhile, dredge the chicken pieces in the remaining 1 cup flour. Heat the remaining 1½ cups oil in a skillet and brown the chicken pieces on both sides.

3. Add the stock to the celery-and-pepper mixture, stirring constantly. This sauce will be quite thin. As the chicken is browned on both sides, transfer it to the sauce.

4. Continue cooking about 30 minutes. Add the cumin, cayenne, white pepper, salt, and bay leaves. Cook 10 minutes longer.

5. Serve with rice.

YIELD: 10 SERVINGS.

CHICKEN AND SAUSAGE GUMBO

1 chicken (2 1/2 pounds), cut into
  serving pieces
Salt to taste, if desired
1 teaspoon finely ground black pepper
1 1/4 teaspoons finely ground white
  pepper
1 teaspoon dry mustard
1 1/2 teaspoons cayenne pepper
1 1/2 teaspoons paprika
2 teaspoons finely minced garlic
1 teaspoon filé powder, optional
1 1/2 cups flour

2 1/2 cups corn, peanut, or vegetable oil
3/4 cup finely chopped onion
3/4 cup finely chopped celery
3/4 cup finely chopped sweet green
  peppers
9 cups Chicken Stock (page 275)
1 3/4 cups chopped or thinly sliced
  smoked sausage such as kielbasa (see
  note)
1 bay leaf
2 cups cooked rice

1. Put the chicken pieces in a bowl. Blend the salt, black and white peppers, mustard, cayenne pepper, paprika, 1 teaspoon garlic, and filé powder. Rub 4 teaspoons of the mixture over the chicken. Reserve 2 teaspoons of the spice mixture and discard the rest.

2. Put the flour and the reserved spice mixture in a bowl. Blend well.

3. Heat a 10-inch black iron skillet and add the oil. Dredge the chicken pieces in the flour mixture to coat well, shaking off the excess. Reserve the leftover flour.

4. When the oil is hot and almost smoking, add the chicken pieces, skin side down. Cook about 2 minutes on one side until golden brown. Turn and cook about 3 minutes on the second side until nicely browned. Drain thoroughly on paper towels.

5. Pour off all but 1 cup of fat from the skillet. Heat this oil over high heat until it is almost smoking and add the reserved seasoned flour. Stir rapidly and constantly with a wire whisk until the mixture starts to look like dark chocolate. Do not burn. This is a roux.

6. Add the chopped onion, celery, and green peppers to the roux and stir to blend well. Remove from the heat without allowing it to burn.

7. Meanwhile, bring the stock to a boil in a large saucepan.

8. Add about ½ cup of the roux mixture to the stock, stirring rapidly with the whisk. Continue adding the roux mixture to the stock, ½ cup at a time, always stirring rapidly and constantly.

9. Add the smoked sausage and stir. Cook over high heat, stirring often from the bottom, about 15 minutes.

10. Add the chicken pieces, bay leaf, and remaining teaspoon garlic. Continue cooking about 40 minutes.

11. Remove the chicken pieces. Cut the meat from the bones and discard the bones. Cut the chicken meat into cubes and add it to the gumbo. Serve with rice spooned into the gumbo.

YIELD: 6 OR MORE SERVINGS.

NOTE: *The smoked pork sausage traditionally used to prepare this dish is known as andouille.*

BRUNSWICK STEW

The name of the following dish is derived from the place of its origin, Brunswick County, Virginia. The dish was originally made with squirrel, but chicken makes a practical and palatable substitute. The dish was created in the early 1800s, and one source states specifically in the year 1828 at a political rally. Some authorities state that only onions were used in the original recipe and that corn and lima beans (which to my taste are essential to the goodness of the dish) were added with the passage of time.

1 chicken (about 5 pounds), cut into
   serving pieces
Salt to taste, if desired
Freshly ground pepper to taste
8 tablespoons butter
2 cups thinly sliced onions
2 cups coarsely chopped celery
1 cup diced sweet green peppers
1 ham bone (about 2 pounds),
   preferably from a Smithfield or
   country ham

2 cups crushed canned tomatoes
1/4 cup finely chopped parsley
1 dried hot red pepper
1 tablespoon Worcestershire sauce
1 pound potatoes, peeled and quartered
3 cups lima beans, preferably freshly
   shelled, although frozen lima beans
   may be used
3 cups fresh corn kernels or defrosted
   frozen whole-kernel corn

1. Sprinkle the chicken pieces with salt and pepper.

2. Heat 4 tablespoons butter in a large heavy kettle and brown the chicken on all sides. Add the onions, celery, and green peppers and cook, stirring, until the vegetables are wilted.

3. Add the ham bone, tomatoes, water to cover by about 1 inch above the level of the solids, parsley, hot red pepper, and Worcestershire sauce. Bring to the boil and cover closely. Cook about 45 minutes, or until the chicken is tender.

4. Transfer the chicken to a warm dish. Replace the cover and continue cooking the stew for 1 hour.

5. Meanwhile, peel the potatoes and put them in a saucepan or kettle. Add cold water to cover and salt to taste. Bring to the boil and cook until the potatoes are tender. Put them through a food mill or ricer.

6. When the stew has cooked for the indicated time, add the lima beans and cook 20 minutes more.

7. Cut off any tender meat from the chicken pieces and the ham bone if there is any. Cut the meat into 1-inch cubes and return it to the stew. Add the remaining 4 tablespoons butter and the corn and cook uncovered 10 minutes. Add the mashed potatoes and stir to blend evenly. Cook 10 minutes longer.

8. Serve hot with plain rice.

YIELD: 6 TO 8 SERVINGS.

KENTUCKY BURGOO

Some people believe that the word *burgoo* is related to a mispronunciation of the word *barbecue,* and the dish is, of course, frequently cooked out of doors for one or another festival or political rally. But John Mariani, in *The Dictionary of American Food and Drink,* states that the word was known to British sailors in the mid-1700s as an oatmeal porridge, and that the name then was associated with the Turkish cracked-wheat product known as burghul or bulgur. He adds that around the turn of the century a so-called Kentucky burgoo king named James T. Looney was used to serving crowds of people numbering up to ten thousand.

This is the recipe of a friend of mine who told me that in making a burgoo, which is first cousin to a Louisiana gumbo, "It is customary to begin with chicken, then add to the kettle something that happens to run by—a squirrel, possum, or rabbit." He added that nothing ran by when he made this version, so he added ham for depth of flavor.

1 fowl (4 1/2 to 5 pounds)
1 quart beef stock
6 large ripe tomatoes, cut up
2 medium-size onions, whole and
*   unpeeled*
2 teaspoons curry powder
1 tablespoon black pepper
1 tablespoon coarse salt, if desired
1 1/2 cups 100-proof bourbon
2 chicken breasts, skinned, boned, and

*   cut into large pieces*
1 cup diced country ham trimmings,
*   optional*
2 cups corn kernels, fresh or frozen
*   and thawed*
1 cup diced raw potatoes
2 cups shelled fresh lima beans
2 1/2 cups okra, trimmed of stems and
*   cut in half*
1 tablespoon filé powder, optional

1. Place the whole, cleaned fowl in a large stockpot with 3 quarts water and the beef stock. Bring to the boil, reduce to a simmer, and skim off foam as it rises to the surface. When the broth is clear, add the tomatoes, onions, curry powder, pepper, and salt. Simmer gently but steadily, partly covered, for 2 hours.

2. Add 1 cup bourbon and simmer gently but steadily, partly covered, for 4 more hours.

3. Remove all the chicken. Trim off and discard skin and bones. Reserve the meat in large pieces.

4. Strain the soup, removing the onion skin and rubbing any remaining tomato and onion solids through a sieve into the broth. Cool completely, then skim fat from the surface.

5. Return the soup to a rinsed pot. Add the remaining ½ cup bourbon, the reserved cooked chicken, raw breast meat, ham, and all the vegetables. Simmer gently but steadily, partly covered, for 30 minutes. Adjust the seasonings. If you are using filé powder, add it to the hot soup as soon as it is removed from the heat. If filé has been added, the soup should not be reheated because it will become gummy, so do not add filé to any more burgoo than you expect to serve at one time.

6. Traditionally, burgoo is ladled into the mugs from which mint juleps are drunk, but any mugs or bowls can, of course, be substituted. Eat with spoons.

YIELD: SIXTEEN 1-CUP SERVINGS.

BASIC SMOTHERED CHICKEN

One dish that was very much a part of my Mississippi childhood was dubbed smothered chicken. I suppose it could be regarded as soul food, basic, easy to prepare; in my books, it belongs in the "comfort" category, a food that gives solace to the spirit when you dine on it.

In its most basic form, it consists of cooking a chicken that has been split down the back and opened up, as for broiling. You cook it skin side down in a black iron skillet with a plate on top. The plate is weighted down and it is this method that contributes the name *smothered*. The chicken is turned over and continues to cook in a flour-thickened gravy until it is exceptionally tender, the meat almost falling from the bones.

*1 chicken (3½ pounds), butterflied
(split down the backbone, breast left
intact and unsplit)*
Salt to taste, if desired
Freshly ground pepper to taste

2 tablespoons butter
2 tablespoons flour
*1½ cups Chicken Stock (page 275) or
canned chicken broth*

1. A black iron skillet is essential for the authentic preparation of this dish. Sprinkle the chicken on both sides with salt and pepper. Select a skillet large enough to hold the chicken comfortably when it is opened up, as for broiling. Fold the chicken wings under to hold them secure.

2. Melt the butter in the skillet and add the chicken, skin side down. Cover the chicken firmly with a plate that will fit comfortably inside the skillet. Add several weights, approximately 5 pounds, to the top of the plate. Cook over low heat until the skin of the chicken is nicely browned, about 25 minutes. Turn the chicken, skin side up, replace the plate and weights, and continue cooking 15 minutes.

3. Remove the chicken and pour off all but 2 tablespoons fat from the skillet. Add the flour, stirring with a wire whisk. Gradually add the chicken stock, and, when thickened, return the chicken to the skillet, skin side up. Add salt and pepper. Cover with the plate and weights and continue cooking over low heat about 30 minutes longer, or until the chicken is exceptionally tender. Spoon the sauce over.

4. Cut the chicken into serving pieces, and serve with the sauce and fluffy rice.

YIELD: 4 SERVINGS.

SMOTHERED CHICKEN CREOLE STYLE

*1 chicken (3 1/2 pounds), butterflied
(split down the backbone, breast left
intact and unsplit)*
Salt to taste, if desired
Freshly ground pepper to taste
2 tablespoons butter
1 cup finely chopped onion
1 cup finely chopped celery

*1 cup finely chopped sweet green
peppers*
1 1/2 teaspoons finely minced garlic
2 tablespoons flour
*1 3/4 cups crushed or chopped imported
canned tomatoes*
1 bay leaf
2 tablespoons finely chopped parsley

1. A black iron skillet is essential for the authentic preparation of this dish. Sprinkle the chicken on both sides with salt and pepper. Select a skillet large enough to hold the chicken comfortably when it is opened up, as for broiling. Fold the chicken wings under to hold them secure.

2. Melt the butter in the skillet and add the chicken, skin side down. Cover the chicken firmly with a plate that will fit comfortably inside the skillet. Add several weights, approximately 5 pounds, to the top of the plate. Cook over low heat until the skin side of the chicken is nicely browned, about 25 minutes.

3. Remove the chicken to a warm platter. Add the onion, celery, green peppers, and garlic to the skillet and cook, stirring, until onion is wilted.

4. Sprinkle with flour and stir to blend. Add the tomatoes, bay leaf, salt, and pepper, stirring rapidly with a whisk. Bring to the boil.

5. Return the chicken, skin side up, to the sauce. Cover with the plate and weights and continue cooking over low heat 45 minutes longer. Remove the chicken to a warm platter and cook down the sauce briefly, stirring. Pour the sauce over the chicken and sprinkle with parsley.

YIELD: 4 SERVINGS.

SMOTHERED CHICKEN WITH MUSHROOMS

1 chicken (3 1/2 pounds), butterflied
  (split down the backbone, breast left
  intact and unsplit)
Salt to taste, if desired
Freshly ground pepper to taste
4 tablespoons butter
1/2 pound mushrooms, sliced, cut in
  half, or quartered, depending on size

16 very small white onions (about 1
  pound), peeled and left whole
1 bay leaf
1/4 teaspoon dried thyme
1/2 cup dry white wine
1/2 cup Chicken Stock (page 275) or
  canned chicken broth
2 tablespoons finely chopped parsley

1. A black iron skillet is essential for the authentic preparation of this dish. Sprinkle the chicken on both sides with salt and pepper. Select a skillet large enough to hold the chicken comfortably when it is opened up, as for broiling. Fold the chicken wings under to hold them secure.

2. Melt 2 tablespoons butter in the skillet and add the chicken, skin side down. Cover the chicken firmly with a plate that will fit comfortably inside the skillet. Add several weights, approximately 5 pounds, to the top of the plate. Cook over low heat until the skin side of the chicken is nicely browned, about 25 minutes.

3. Pour off most of the fat from the skillet and add the remaining 2 tablespoons butter. Turn the chicken skin side up. Scatter the mushrooms over the chicken. Scatter the onions around it. Add the bay leaf, thyme, wine, and chicken stock. Replace the plate and the weights and continue cooking over low heat about 45 minutes longer.

4. Remove the chicken to a warm platter. Spoon the mushrooms and onions around the chicken. Cook down the skillet liquid until reduced by half. Pour this over the chicken and sprinkle with parsley.

YIELD: 4 SERVINGS.

COUNTRY CAPTAIN

No one knows precisely the origin of the dish known throughout Georgia and much of the South as country captain. The theory is that it was introduced to the port of Savannah by the captain of a vessel that plied the spice route from India in the early 1800s.

1/4 cup dried currants
1 frying chicken (about 2 1/2 pounds),
cut into serving pieces
1/2 cup flour
Salt to taste, if desired
Freshly ground pepper to taste
2 tablespoons butter
2 tablespoons corn, peanut, or vegetable oil

1/2 cup finely chopped onion
3/4 cup finely chopped sweet green peppers
1 teaspoon finely minced garlic
1 tablespoon curry powder
2 cups chopped canned tomatoes
Cooked rice
1/4 cup toasted, slivered almonds
Chutney

1. Put the currants in a mixing bowl and pour very hot water over them. Let stand at least 20 minutes.

2. Dredge the chicken pieces on all sides in the flour seasoned with salt and pepper. Shake off the excess.

3. Heat the butter and oil in a heavy skillet large enough to hold the chicken pieces in one layer without crowding. Brown the chicken pieces on all sides, turning the parts so that they cook evenly. Remove the chicken.

4. To the skillet add the onion, green peppers, garlic, and curry powder and cook, stirring, until the vegetables are wilted. Add the tomatoes and salt and pepper to taste. Bring to the boil, stirring, and add the chicken pieces, skin side up. Cover and cook until the chicken is cooked throughout, about 20 minutes. Drain the currants and add them. Stir to blend.

5. Serve with cooked rice, toasted almonds, and chutney on the side.

YIELD: 4 SERVINGS.

CHICKEN SAUTÉ WITH PECANS

2 chickens (2 1/2 to 3 pounds each), cut
  into serving pieces
Salt to taste, if desired
Freshly ground pepper to taste
4 tablespoons butter
1/2 cup finely chopped onion
1/2 cup finely chopped celery
1 bay leaf

1/2 teaspoon dried thyme, or 2 sprigs
  fresh
1/4 teaspoon grated nutmeg
2 whole cloves
1 bottle (3 cups) dry red wine
1/2 cup heavy cream
1/2 cup chopped pecans

1. Sprinkle the chicken pieces with salt and pepper to taste.

2. Heat the butter in a heavy skillet and brown the chicken pieces all over. Scatter the onion, celery, bay leaf, and thyme around the chicken. Sprinkle with nutmeg. Add the cloves, wine, and salt and pepper to taste.

3. Cover and simmer 30 minutes, or until the chicken is tender.

4. Remove the chicken pieces and keep warm. Skim off the fat from the surface of the sauce. Reduce the sauce to about 2 cups. Add the cream. Return the chicken pieces to the skillet and bring the sauce to the boil. Add the pecans and serve hot.

YIELD: 6 TO 8 SERVINGS.

CHICKEN À LA KING

To my mind, it would be inconceivable to print a Southern cookbook without a recipe for chicken à la king. When I was a child, it was standard party fare, and in my earliest youth, conceivably the most delectable of all main courses. It was served in my home for special occasions, when my mother entertained, for Sunday dinners, for birthday parties, and so on. The French version of this dish is called *poulet à la reine,* and it underwent a sort of sea change between here and France. I do not know why it seems so typically Southern.

1 chicken (about 3 pounds)
5 cups water or chicken broth
1 bay leaf
1 small onion stuck with 2 cloves
2 allspice
1 carrot, trimmed, scraped, and cut
  into large cubes
3 ribs celery, cut into large cubes
Salt to taste, if desired
8 peppercorns
3 tablespoons butter

2 tablespoons flour
1 cup heavy cream
Freshly ground pepper to taste
1 teaspoon freshly squeezed lemon juice
2 egg yolks, beaten
3/4 cup thinly sliced mushrooms
1/2 cup thinly sliced canned pimientos
1/8 teaspoon Tabasco sauce
1 tablespoon dry sherry, optional
6 toast triangles

1. Put the chicken in a kettle and add the water or broth, bay leaf, onion, allspice, carrot, celery, salt, and peppercorns. Bring to the boil, partly cover, and simmer about 30 minutes, or until the chicken is tender. Let cool in the broth.

2. Remove the chicken and strain the broth. Reserve both. Discard the solids from the broth.

3. Remove the flesh from the chicken. Discard the skin and bones. Cut the chicken into 1/2-inch cubes. Set aside.

4. Melt 2 tablespoons of butter in a saucepan and add the flour, stirring with a wire whisk. When blended, add 1 cup of the reserved broth. The remaining broth may be put to other uses such as for soups and sauces. Stir rapidly with the whisk until the sauce is blended and smooth. Cook about 5 minutes, stirring. Add the cream and simmer about 10 minutes. Add salt and pepper to taste. Add the lemon juice.

5. Spoon 1/2 cup of the hot sauce over the egg yolks, stirring rapidly. Scrape this mixture back into the sauce and bring barely to the simmer, stirring. Remove from the heat.

6. Heat the remaining tablespoon of butter in a skillet and add the mushrooms. Cook, stirring, until the slices are wilted and they have given up their liquid. Cook until this liquid evaporates. Add the pimientos and Tabasco and stir. Cook just to heat through.

7. Add the cubed chicken and the mushroom-and-pimiento mixture to the sauce. Stir in the sherry, if desired.

8. Serve piping hot over toast triangles.

YIELD: 6 SERVINGS.

HOMINY AND CHICKEN CASSEROLE

2 tablespoons olive oil
3 cups finely chopped onions
2 tablespoons finely minced garlic
1 1/2 pounds ground beef
5 1/2 cups imported canned tomatoes
1/2 cup tomato paste
2 cups Chicken Stock (page 275)
1/2 cup, more or less to taste, finely chopped, seeded fresh or canned jalapeño peppers
2 teaspoons crumbled dried oregano

Salt to taste, if desired
Freshly ground pepper to taste
5 cups Basic Cream Sauce (page 268)
6 cans (1 pound 13 ounces each) hominy, drained (about 18 cups)
6 cups shredded chicken made from Poached Chicken Thighs (see following recipe)
6 cups grated sharp Cheddar cheese (about 1 1/2 pounds)

1. Heat the oil in a saucepan with a capacity of approximately 6 quarts and add the onions and garlic. Cook, stirring, until wilted. Add the beef, breaking up lumps with the side of a heavy metal spoon. Cook, stirring, until meat loses its raw look.

2. Add the tomatoes, tomato paste, chicken stock, jalapeño peppers, oregano, salt, and ground pepper. Cook, stirring often, 30 or 40 minutes, until thickened. Add the cream sauce and stir.

3. Meanwhile, preheat the oven to 350 degrees.

4. Butter two 8-quart casseroles. Add a layer of hominy, a layer of chicken, a layer of sauce, and a layer of cheese in each. Continue making layers, ending with a layer of cheese.

5. Place the casseroles in the oven and bake 45 minutes, or until piping hot and bubbling throughout.

YIELD: 20 TO 24 SERVINGS.

POACHED CHICKEN THIGHS

20 chicken thighs (about 6 pounds)
2 cups water
2 bay leaves
1 teaspoon dried thyme
2 medium-size onions, each stuck with
   2 cloves

1 1/4 cups coarsely chopped celery
6 parsley sprigs
Salt to taste, if desired
14 peppercorns

1. Combine the thighs, water, bay leaves, thyme, onions, celery, parsley, salt, and peppercorns in a kettle. Bring to the boil, partly covered, and let simmer 20 minutes.

2. Remove from the heat and let stand until ready to use. Remove the thighs, strain the broth, and skim off the fat.

YIELD: 20 COOKED THIGHS, PLUS 2 CUPS BROTH.

MY MOTHER'S CHICKEN TURNOVERS

THE FILLING:

2 tablespoons butter
2 tablespoons all-purpose flour
1 cup milk
1/2 cup heavy cream
2 lightly beaten egg yolks

Salt to taste, if desired
Freshly ground pepper to taste
1/2 teaspoon Worcestershire sauce
1/8 teaspoon freshly grated nutmeg
1 1/2 cups cubed cooked chicken

THE PASTRY:

2 cups sifted cake flour
2 teaspoons baking powder
1 teaspoon salt

3 tablespoons butter or chicken fat
1/2 cup milk, approximately

THE COOKING:

Corn oil for deep-frying
Golden Sauce (see following recipe)

1. To prepare the filling, melt the butter in a saucepan and add the all-purpose flour, stirring with a wire whisk. Add the milk and cream, stirring rapidly with the whisk.

2. Pour a little of the hot sauce over the yolks, stirring rapidly with a fork. Scrape this mixture into the remaining sauce, stirring rapidly with the whisk. Add salt and pepper to taste, Worcestershire, and nutmeg. Stir in the chicken. Set aside.

3. Prepare the pastry. Put the sifted cake flour in a sifter and add the baking powder and salt. Sift this into a mixing bowl and make a well in the center. Put the butter or chicken fat into the well and blend well with a pastry blender until the mixture has the texture of coarse cornmeal. Add the milk gradually while stirring and blending with the fingers. Add only enough to make a soft, workable dough.

4. Turn the dough out onto a lightly floured board and roll it out to a thickness of about ⅛ inch. Cut the dough into circles, each 5 to 6 inches in diameter (if desired, use a saucer placed over the dough and trace around it with a small sharp pointed knife). Spoon equal portions of the filling into the center of each pastry round and fold the dough over to enclose the filling. Press around the edges of the crescent shapes with the tines of a fork to seal them.

5. Heat the oil for deep-frying (360 degrees, or hot enough to brown a cube of bread in 1 minute). Cook the turnovers for 5 minutes, until golden brown.

6. Serve with golden sauce on the side.

YIELD: 8 SERVINGS.

GOLDEN SAUCE

4 tablespoons butter or chicken fat
1 cup thinly sliced mushrooms
1 cup diced sweet green peppers
¼ cup flour
2 cups Chicken Stock (page 275) or
 canned chicken broth

¼ cup heavy cream
Salt to taste, if desired
Freshly ground pepper to taste

1. Heat the butter in a saucepan and cook the mushrooms and peppers, stirring constantly, until the mushrooms start to take on a little color.

2. Sprinkle with flour and blend. Add the stock and cream, stirring constantly with a wire whisk until thickened. Season to taste with salt and pepper.

YIELD: ABOUT 2½ CUPS.

MY MOTHER'S CHICKEN SPAGHETTI

This recipe has been printed on many occasions, for it, more than any other dish, was my favorite as a child and I still prepare it. I have no idea of the origin of the dish, but find it notably akin to certain authentic Italian sauces, notably a *ragù bolognese* made with ground meat in a tomato and cream sauce. I believe it was strictly my mother's own creation, and she was famous for it up and down the Mississippi Delta. One of the stipulations in the original recipe is that the spaghetti, including all the ingredients, be combined at least 4 hours before baking.

1 chicken (about 3½ pounds), with
    giblets
Chicken broth to cover
Salt to taste, if desired
3 cups canned tomatoes, preferably
    Italian peeled tomatoes
7 tablespoons butter
3 tablespoons flour
½ cup heavy cream
⅛ teaspoon grated nutmeg
Freshly ground pepper to taste
½ pound fresh mushrooms (see note)
2 cups finely chopped onions

1½ cups finely chopped celery
1½ cups chopped sweet green peppers
1 tablespoon or more finely minced
    garlic
¼ pound ground beef
¼ pound ground pork
1 bay leaf
½ teaspoon hot red pepper flakes,
    optional
1 pound spaghetti or spaghettini
½ pound Cheddar cheese, grated (2 to
    2½ cups)
Grated Parmesan cheese

1. Place the chicken with neck, gizzard, heart, and liver in a kettle and add chicken broth to cover and salt to taste. Bring to the boil and simmer until the chicken is tender without being dry, 35 to 45 minutes. Let cool.

2. Remove the chicken and take the meat from the bones. Shred the meat, cover, and set aside. Return the skin and bones to the kettle and cook the broth down 30 minutes or longer. There should be 4 to 6 cups of broth. Strain and reserve the broth. Discard the skin and bones.

3. Meanwhile, put the tomatoes in a saucepan and cook down to half the original volume, stirring. There should be 1½ cups.

4. Melt 3 tablespoons butter in a saucepan and add the flour, stirring to blend with a wire whisk. When blended and smooth, add 1 cup of the reserved hot broth and the cream, stirring rapidly with the whisk. When thickened and smooth, add the nutmeg, and salt and pepper to taste. Continue cooking, stirring occasionally, about 10 minutes. Set aside.

5. If the mushrooms are very small or button mushrooms, leave them whole. Otherwise, cut them in half or quarter them. Heat 1 tablespoon butter in a small skillet and add the mushrooms. Cook, shaking the skillet occasionally and stirring the mushrooms, until they are golden brown. Set aside.

6. Heat the remaining 3 tablespoons butter in a deep skillet and add the onions. Cook, stirring, until wilted. Add the celery and green peppers and cook, stirring, about 5 minutes. Do not overcook. The vegetables should remain crisp-tender.

7. Add the garlic, beef, and pork and cook, stirring and chopping down with the edge of a large metal spoon to break up the meat. Cook just until the meat loses its red color. Add the bay leaf and red pepper flakes. Add the tomatoes and the white sauce made with the chicken broth. Add the mushrooms.

8. Cook the spaghetti in boiling salted water until it is just tender. Do not overcook. Remember that it will cook again when blended with the chicken and meat sauce. Drain the spaghetti and run under cold running water.

9. Spoon enough of the meat sauce over the bottom of a 5- or 6-quart casserole to cover it lightly. Add about one-third of the spaghetti. Add about one-third of the shredded chicken, a layer of meat sauce, a layer of grated Cheddar cheese, and another layer of spaghetti. Continue making layers, ending with a layer of spaghetti topped with a thin layer of meat sauce and grated Cheddar cheese.

10. Pour in up to 2 cups of the reserved chicken broth, or enough to almost but not quite cover the top layer of spaghetti. Cover and let the spaghetti stand for 4 hours or longer. If the liquid is absorbed as the dish stands, add a little more chicken broth. Remember that when this dish is baked and served, the sauce will be just a bit soupy rather than thick and clinging.

11. When ready to bake, preheat the oven to 350 degrees.

12. Place the spaghetti casserole on top of the stove and bring it just to the boil. Cover and place it in the oven. Bake 15 minutes and uncover. Bake 15 minutes longer, or until the casserole is hot and bubbling throughout and starting to brown on top. Serve immediately with grated Parmesan cheese on the side.

YIELD: 12 OR MORE SERVINGS.

NOTE: *If fresh mushrooms are not available, as they frequently weren't when this recipe was prepared some fifty years ago, use drained canned button mushrooms.*

CHICKEN OR TURKEY CROQUETTES

There were very few leftovers in my home during my early youth. The servants all had "toting" privileges, which they took advantage of to feed themselves, their children, and animals. If there were leftovers, however, from chicken or turkey, the meat was almost invariably turned into croquettes. The recommendation to serve mushroom sauce with these croquettes is my own idea. We did not have access to fresh mushrooms during my childhood.

2 tablespoons butter
3 tablespoons finely minced onion
3 tablespoons flour
1 1/2 cups Chicken Stock (page 275)
3 1/2 cups coarsely chopped cooked
   chicken or turkey meat, including
   skin
Salt to taste, if desired
Freshly ground pepper to taste
1/4 teaspoon freshly grated nutmeg

3 drops Tabasco sauce
3 egg yolks
Flour for dredging
1 egg, lightly beaten
3 tablespoons water
1 1/2 cups fine fresh bread crumbs
Peanut, vegetable, or corn oil for
   deep-frying
Mushroom Sauce (page 269)

1. Melt the butter in a saucepan and add the onion, stirring to wilt. Sprinkle with flour and stir with a wire whisk until blended. Add the stock, stirring rapidly with the whisk. Stir in the chicken. Add salt and pepper to taste, nutmeg, and Tabasco. Remove the sauce from the heat and add the yolks, stirring vigorously with the whisk. Cook briefly, stirring, and remove from the heat.

2. Spoon the mixture into a dish (one measuring 8 × 8 × 2 inches is convenient) and smooth it over. Cover with a piece of buttered wax paper and refrigerate, preferably overnight.

3. Remove the paper and, using the fingers, divide the mixture into 12 to 14 portions. Shape into balls and roll lightly in flour. The portions may be shaped finally into balls or cylinders. Combine the egg and water. When the balls or cylinders are smooth on the surface and neatly coated with flour, dredge in the egg-water mixture, then in the bread crumbs. Arrange on a rack and chill until ready to cook.

4. Heat the oil. When it is hot, add the balls or cylinders, a few at a time. Cook 2 or 3 minutes, until golden and cooked through.

5. Serve hot with mushroom sauce.

YIELD: 6 TO 8 SERVINGS.

OVEN-BARBECUED CHICKEN WINGS

24 chicken wings (about 5 pounds)
Salt to taste, if desired
2 teaspoons freshly ground black pepper
3 teaspoons paprika
½ cup corn, peanut, or vegetable oil
1 cup ketchup
¼ cup honey

6 tablespoons white vinegar
2 tablespoons Worcestershire sauce
1 teaspoon Tabasco sauce
1 tablespoon Dijon mustard
1 tablespoon finely minced garlic
4 tablespoons butter
1 bay leaf

1. Preheat the oven to 400 degrees.

2. Fold the small tips of the chicken wings under the main wing bones. Arrange the wings in one layer in a baking dish so that they bake comfortably close together without crowding.

3. Sprinkle with salt, pepper, and 2 teaspoons paprika. Pour ¼ cup oil over all, and turn the wings in the mixture so that they are evenly coated. Rearrange them in one layer with the small wing side down.

4. Place in the oven and bake 15 minutes.

5. Meanwhile, combine the ketchup, remaining ¼ cup oil, honey, vinegar, Worcestershire, Tabasco, mustard, garlic, butter, bay leaf, and remaining 1 teaspoon paprika. Bring to the boil.

6. Brush the wings lightly with sauce and turn them on the other side. Brush this side with sauce and continue cooking 15 minutes.

7. Brush the wings with the sauce again. Turn the pieces and brush the other side again. Continue baking 15 minutes.

8. Continue turning, brushing, and baking the chicken for 15 minutes longer, for a total cooking time of about 1 hour.

YIELD: 6 OR MORE SERVINGS.

DEEP-FRIED CHICKEN LIVERS

1 pound chicken livers   *Freshly ground pepper to taste*
⅓ cup flour   *Fat for deep-frying*
Salt to taste, if desired

1. Cut the livers in half crosswise. Trim the livers of any connecting membranes and put the pieces in a mixing bowl. Add cold water to cover and stir. Let stand 15 minutes.

2. Drain the livers but do not pat them dry.

3. Combine the flour, salt, and pepper in a brown paper bag. Add the livers and toss to coat well. Remove the livers and shake off the excess flour.

4. Heat the oil to a temperature of about 365 degrees. Add the livers, a few at a time, and cook until crisp and golden brown on the outside. Drain on paper towels, and continue cooking the livers until all are crisp and browned.

YIELD: 4 SERVINGS.

TRUSSING

Poultry was rarely trussed in my home and I suppose it was rarely done outside commercial restaurants. I doubt that my mother ever saw or heard of a trussing needle. If you wish to truss your turkey, however, here is how to go about it.

HOW TO TRUSS A TURKEY

Stuff the body and the neck cavity of a turkey that is ready to cook.

Make a gash 2 inches from the tail tip of the turkey and push the tail tip into the cavity. Truss the cavity opening with string. Push the legs forward and shove the needle through one leg at the point where the cavity and thigh meet. Push needle through cavity and bring it out the other side, going through the opposite leg where cavity and thigh join.

Twist the wings securely under the back of the turkey. Push the needle through the center of the second wing joint, then weave it through the neck skin, sewing this to the surface skin at the tip of the backbone. Run the needle through the center of the second wing joint on the other side. Cut off the cord and tie the ends together securely.

Run the needle through the base of the thigh, just above the thigh bone. Run it all the way through the same position of the opposite thigh. Bring the needle up and around a leg, running the needle through the tender, cartilage-like, V-shaped base of the breastbone.

Bring the cord around the other leg and cut off the cord. Tie the ends to secure the legs close to the body.

ROAST FRESH TURKEY

1 fresh turkey (17 to 20 pounds), neck and giblets reserved

8 to 9 cups stuffing (see following recipes)

4 tablespoons peanut, vegetable, or corn oil

1 large onion (about ¾ pound)

Salt to taste, if desired

Freshly ground pepper

2 cups water

1 cup turkey or chicken broth

1. Preheat the oven to 375 degrees.

2. Fill the turkey cavity with stuffing, pushing the tail inside the cavity to secure the stuffing. Stuff the neck cavity, fold skin over, and truss the turkey according to the instructions opposite.

3. Coat the bottom of a shallow roasting pan with 1 tablespoon oil. Set the turkey, breast side up, in the pan. Add the turkey neck and onion to the pan. Rub the entire surface of the turkey with the remaining 3 tablespoons oil. Sprinkle with salt and pepper. Roast, basting frequently with pan juices, until the turkey is golden brown, 45 minutes to 1 hour.

4. Reduce the oven temperature to 350 degrees. Cover the turkey loosely with foil and continue roasting 1 hour, basting often.

5. Reduce the oven temperature to 325 degrees. Add 1 cup water to the pan. Continue roasting for 1 hour, basting frequently. Add the broth and continue roasting until the turkey tests done (a thermometer inserted in the dressing should register about 160 degrees).

6. Transfer the turkey to a carving platter and keep warm. Add the remaining 1 cup water to the roasting pan and place on top of the stove over direct heat. Bring to the boil, stirring constantly and scraping up any browned bits clinging to the pan. Strain and degrease. Serve hot with the carved turkey.

YIELD: 16 TO 20 SERVINGS.

JALAPEÑO CORN BREAD STUFFING

7 cups crumbled Jalapeño Corn Bread (page 245)

4 cups toast cubes

3 hard-cooked eggs, chopped

4 tablespoons unsalted butter

2 cups finely chopped onions

1 teaspoon finely minced garlic

1 1/2 cups finely chopped sweet green peppers

1 cup finely chopped celery

Turkey gizzard, trimmed and finely chopped

Turkey liver, chopped

Turkey heart, chopped

Salt to taste, if desired

Freshly ground pepper to taste

3 eggs, lightly beaten

1/2 cup turkey or chicken broth, approximately

1. Combine the corn bread, toast cubes, and chopped eggs in a large bowl and toss lightly to mix well. Set aside.

2. Melt the butter in a large skillet over medium heat. Add the onions and garlic and sauté until softened. Add the green peppers and celery and cook until crisp-tender, about 3 minutes. Add the gizzard, liver, and heart and sauté just until they lose their raw color. Season with salt and a generous grinding of pepper. Let cool slightly.

3. Add the onion mixture to the corn bread mixture and blend well. Stir in the beaten eggs. Blend in enough broth to moisten lightly.

YIELD: 8 TO 9 CUPS.

RICE AND LIVER STUFFING

1 pound chicken livers
1 turkey liver, chopped
Salt to taste, if desired
Freshly ground pepper to taste
1 pound fresh mushrooms
2 tablespoons butter

1/2 cup finely chopped onion
1/3 cup corn oil
1/4 cup dry sherry
4 1/2 cups cooked rice
1 egg, lightly beaten

1. Preheat the oven to 350 degrees.

2. Pick over the livers. Cut away and discard the tough connecting membranes. Cut the chicken and turkey livers into small cubes. Sprinkle with salt and pepper and set aside.

3. Cut the mushrooms into quarters and slice them. There should be about 4 cups.

4. Heat the butter in a heavy skillet and add the onion. Cook, stirring, until wilted. Sprinkle with salt and pepper. Add the mushrooms and cook, stirring, until the mushrooms give up their liquid. Continue cooking until the liquid evaporates.

5. Heat the oil in another heavy skillet and add the livers. Cook over very high heat, stirring frequently, about 1 1/2 minutes.

6. Add the livers to the mushrooms. Stir and cook briefly. Add the sherry and cook briefly over high heat until the sherry evaporates. Add the rice and stir. Add the egg, stirring. Let cool.

YIELD: ABOUT 8 CUPS.

SAUSAGE-PECAN STUFFING

1 pound prepared sausage meat in bulk
1/4 pound butter
3 cups finely chopped onions
1 1/2 cups chopped celery
4 cups dried bread crumbs, or use
   prepared stuffing mix

1 teaspoon dried thyme
1/2 teaspoon dried sage
Salt to taste, if desired
Freshly ground pepper to taste
2/3 cup hot water
1/2 pound pecans, coarsely chopped

1. Put the sausage in a skillet and cook, breaking up the lumps with the side of a kitchen spoon. Cook until it has lost its raw color. If desired, drain off part or all of the fat.

2. Melt 2 tablespoons butter in a skillet and cook the onions and celery until the onions are wilted.

3. Add the sausage. Melt the remaining 6 tablespoons butter and add it. Add all the remaining ingredients and blend well. Let cool.

YIELD: SUFFICIENT STUFFING FOR AN 8- TO 10-POUND TURKEY.

NOTE: *For a 19- to 20-pound turkey, the quantities should be doubled exactly except for the sausage meat, which should be increased to 2 1/2 pounds.*

BREAD AND APPLE DRESSING

In the South, the terms *stuffing* and *dressing* are synonymous. If the ingredients are baked alone to be served as a side dish, with roast poultry, for example, it is most often referred to as a dressing.

8 cups coarsely blended or crumbled
   fresh bread crumbs
2 cups dark raisins
4 cups peeled, cored, seeded, and cubed
   apples
1/3 cup finely chopped parsley
1/2 teaspoon finely minced garlic

1 teaspoon ground mace
1 teaspoon dried ground or rubbed sage
1/2 teaspoon freshly grated nutmeg
1/2 teaspoon ground cloves
1/4 pound butter, melted
Salt to taste, if desired
Freshly ground pepper to taste

1. Preheat the oven to 350 degrees.

2. In a mixing bowl combine the bread crumbs, raisins, apples, parsley, garlic, mace, sage, nutmeg, cloves, butter, salt, and pepper. Blend well.

3. Butter the inside of a baking dish measuring about 13 × 9 × 2 inches. Pour the dressing into the dish and smooth over the top. Place in the oven and bake 1 hour.

YIELD: 12 OR MORE SERVINGS.

ROAST WILD TURKEY

1 wild turkey (about 13 pounds, cleaned weight)
Salt to taste, if desired
Freshly ground pepper to taste
1 onion, peeled and cut into quarters
2 celery ribs, cut crosswise in half
½ pound salt pork, cut lengthwise into thin slices
2 celery ribs, left whole
1 cup thinly sliced carrot rounds
1½ cups thinly sliced onions
¼ cup coarsely chopped parsley
2 bay leaves
3 sage leaves, or ½ teaspoon dried
4 sprigs fresh thyme, or ½ teaspoon dried
6½ cups Chicken Stock (page 275), or canned chicken broth or beef broth

1. Preheat the oven to 475 degrees.

2. Sprinkle the turkey inside and out with salt and pepper. Put the quartered onion and halved celery ribs inside the cavity of the turkey.

3. Place the turkey, breast side up, in a roasting pan. Cover the top of the turkey with slices of salt pork.

4. Place the turkey in the oven and bake about 30 minutes. Rotate the pan occasionally as the turkey bakes.

5. Scatter the whole celery ribs, carrot rounds, sliced onions, parsley, bay leaves, sage, and thyme around the turkey. Pour the stock around the turkey. Cover the roasting pan and continue cooking 1 hour.

6. Reduce the oven heat to 350 degrees. Continue cooking, basting often, about 1 hour more.

YIELD: 12 TO 16 SERVINGS.

TURKEY GUMBO

1 turkey carcass with meat
2 to 2½ quarts water
1 large carrot
1 large onion
2 celery ribs with leaves
6 tablespoons butter
2 tablespoons minced raw bacon or
   lean ham
1 garlic clove, minced
1 large onion, chopped

1 sweet green pepper, seeded and
   chopped
1 pound okra, sliced
3 cups chopped canned tomatoes
1 teaspoon dried thyme
1 large bay leaf
Pinch of cayenne
3 tablespoons flour
Salt to taste, if desired
Steamed white rice

1. Discard the turkey skin. Scrape the herbs and all the stuffing from the turkey carcass carefully, especially if sage was used. Break up the carcass. Put it in a tall straight-sided 4-quart soup pot and add the water to cover. If that amount doesn't cover, the pot is too wide. Bring to the boil and skim off the foam. When the broth is clear, add the carrot, whole onion, and celery. Cover and simmer for 1 hour.

2. Remove the carcass. Pick off meat and dice it. Discard the vegetables. Strain and skim stock and return the turkey meat to it.

3. Heat 2 tablespoons butter with the bacon or ham. In the combined fat slowly sauté the garlic, chopped onion, green pepper, and okra until golden brown and okra is no longer stringy, about 25 minutes. Add to the soup along with tomatoes, thyme, bay leaf, and cayenne.

4. Simmer the soup gently for 30 minutes, adjusting seasoning as you do so.

5. Heat the remaining 4 tablespoons butter in a small heavy-bottomed saucepan. When bubbling, add the flour and stir until smooth. Cook very, very slowly, stirring almost constantly, for about 10 minutes, or until the roux is a dark coffee color. The flour will seem to take a long time before it begins to color, but once it does it burns quickly, so give it your undivided attention. When the roux is a good dark espresso color (but not burned), cool slightly, then stir it into the simmering soup. Cook 30 minutes more.

6. Adjust the seasoning and serve in a bowl with a mound of white rice heaped in the center of each serving.

YIELD: 8 OR MORE SERVINGS.

ROAST PHEASANT

1 pheasant (1 1/2 to 2 pounds)
Salt to taste, if desired
Freshly ground pepper to taste
1/4 teaspoon dried thyme

10 tablespoons butter
3 tablespoons water
Watercress for garnish

1. Preheat the oven to 450 degrees.

2. It is best if the pheasant has been hung. In any event, wipe the outside of the pheasant with a damp cloth. If it has been freshly cleaned, do not wipe the cavity. That would remove some of the special flavor.

3. Combine the salt, pepper, and thyme and sprinkle the cavity with the mixture. Add 4 tablespoons butter to the cavity. Rub the outside of the bird with 2 tablespoons butter.

4. Use a casserole with a tight-fitting cover. Place the pheasant, breast side up, in the pan and cover. Place in the oven and roast for 15 minutes.

5. As the pheasant cooks, melt the remaining 4 tablespoons butter in a small saucepan. Use this to baste the bird every 15 minutes of cooking time, which should be about 1½ hours.

6. When the pheasant is done, place the casserole on top of the stove. Remove the pheasant. Add the water to the casserole, stirring to dissolve the brown particles that cling to the bottom and sides of the casserole. Strain the sauce and reheat before serving.

7. The pheasant may be served hot with the sauce or cold. Garnish with watercress. If you are to serve the pheasant cold, pour the sauce over and chill in a covered bowl overnight.

YIELD: 2 TO 4 SERVINGS.

BARBECUED DUCK

1 duck (about 4 ½ pounds), quartered
Salt to taste, if desired
Freshly ground pepper to taste

¾ cup Maryland-Style Barbecue
Sauce (page 274)

1. Prepare a charcoal grill and have it ready. The coals must be white-hot but not overly plentiful, or the duck will cook too fast. Arrange the grill 6 to 8 inches above the coals.

2. Place the duck pieces on a flat surface and use a sharp knife to cut away the excess, peripheral skin fat that surrounds the pieces. Discard the fat. Place the pieces skin side up and pound them with a flat mallet. This will help the pieces to lie flat on the grill. Sprinkle the pieces with salt and pepper to taste.

3. Marinate for about an hour in the barbecue sauce. Remove and place the duck, skin side down, on the grill. Cook, basting often and turning the duck pieces as often as necessary, until the skin is crisp and the flesh is cooked. Cooking time should be about 40 minutes, more or less. Do not overcook or the flesh will be tough and dry.

YIELD: 2 TO 4 SERVINGS.

ROAST QUAIL

Wild bird and game hunting seems to be to a great degree regional. It is a popular sport in the West and Southwest, in certain parts of the North, and particularly throughout the South. Quail figured often on the tables of my childhood, and it was an integral part of Christmas-morning breakfast. It is a thought that is essentially romantic but I invariably think of quail as a Southern staple.

8 cleaned quail (¼ pound each)
Salt to taste, if desired
Freshly ground pepper to taste
1 tablespoon butter

8 thin slices lean fatback, each slice
*   sufficiently large to amply cover a*
*   quail breast*
3 tablespoons water

1. Preheat the oven to 475 degrees.
2. Sprinkle the quail with salt and pepper. Grease a metal baking pan with the butter and arrange the quail on their backs in the dish. Cover each quail with fatback.
3. Bake 10 minutes. Remove but reserve each piece of fatback. Brush the quail with pan drippings, then cover once more with fatback. Do not turn the quail. Bake 5 minutes longer and remove the fatback. Bake 3 minutes longer.
4. Transfer the quail to serving dishes.
5. Place the baking pan on top of the stove and add the water. Simmer, scraping the bottom and sides of the pan to dissolve the brown particles that cling to the bottom and sides. Spoon the pan drippings over the birds and serve.

YIELD: 4 TO 8 SERVINGS.

CHARCOAL-GRILLED STUFFED QUAIL

The following is a recipe demonstrated for me by a young master chef from Chapel Hill, North Carolina—Bill Neal, owner and chief cook of the Crook's Corner Restaurant. I would label it nouveau Southern. It is excellent.

8 cleaned quail (¼ pound each)

⅛ pound streaky bacon or salt pork,
  cut into small cubes (about ½ cup)

1 tablespoon finely chopped garlic

2½ tablespoons fine dry bread crumbs

2½ tablespoons finely diced carrot

2½ tablespoons finely diced celery

1 tablespoon finely chopped fresh basil

1 tablespoon finely chopped parsley

½ teaspoon finely chopped fresh thyme,
  or ¼ teaspoon dried

Salt to taste, if desired

Freshly ground pepper to taste

2 tablespoons bacon fat or corn oil

1. Preheat a charcoal grill until white ash forms on top of the coals.

2. Split each quail neatly along the backbone. Set aside.

3. Put the bacon or salt pork and garlic on a flat surface and chop until almost a paste. Put the mixture in a mixing bowl and add the bread crumbs, carrot, celery, basil, parsley, thyme, salt, and pepper. Blend thoroughly with the fingers.

4. By hand, carefully separate a portion of the breast meat from the bone to form a small pocket. Push equal portions of the stuffing into the cavities. Push any additional stuffing under the skin of the birds, without breaking the skin. Brush the birds all over with bacon fat or oil.

5. Place the quail, skin side down, on the grill and cook until nicely browned on one side, 4 to 5 minutes. Turn and press the outer portions together to give the bodies more of their original shape. Let cook 4 to 5 minutes on the second side, or until the desired doneness.

YIELD: 4 TO 8 SERVINGS.

LOW-COUNTRY GRILLED QUAIL WITH OYSTER SAUCE

THE QUAIL:

12 quail, main body bones and wings
  removed but with leg and thigh
  bones intact (about 3 pounds
  ready-to-cook weight)

Freshly ground pepper to taste

6 slices bacon, each cut crosswise
  in half

¼ cup olive oil

1 tablespoon balsamic vinegar

1 tablespoon finely minced fresh thyme

THE OYSTER SAUCE:

1 tablespoon butter
1/4 cup finely chopped country ham or
  prosciutto
1/4 cup finely minced leeks

2 cups heavy cream
2 tablespoons finely chopped pimiento
1 cup (1 half-pint) small oysters,
  drained

1. Preheat the oven to 475 degrees.

2. Sprinkle the quail inside and out with freshly ground pepper and arrange them breast side up on a baking sheet. Wrap each quail around the breast portion with half a slice of bacon.

3. Blend the oil, vinegar, and thyme and spoon equal amounts of the sauce over each quail. Place in the oven and bake 13 to 15 minutes. Place under the broiler briefly to crisp the bacon.

4. To prepare the oyster sauce, heat the butter in a heavy skillet or casserole and add the prosciutto and leeks. Cook about 1 minute, stirring, and add the cream and pimiento. Cook over relatively high heat about 10 minutes, or until reduced to about 1 cup.

5. Put the oysters in a small skillet and cook over moderately high heat, shaking the skillet briefly until the oysters just start to bubble. Take care not to overcook the oysters or they will toughen. Drain the oysters and add them to the sauce. Spoon the sauce over the quail and serve immediately.

YIELD: 6 SERVINGS.

SMOTHERED QUAIL

6 cleaned quail (about 1/4 pound each)
Salt to taste, if desired
Freshly ground pepper to taste
5 tablespoons butter

3 tablespoons flour
2 1/2 cups Chicken Stock (page 275)
1 teaspoon Worcestershire sauce
6 toast triangles

1. Preheat the oven to 325 degrees.
2. Sprinkle each quail inside and out with salt and pepper.

3. Heat the butter in a skillet, preferably of black iron, and when it is quite hot add the quail. Brown the birds on all sides, turning occasionally to brown evenly, about 5 minutes.

4. Transfer the quail to a platter. Sprinkle the fat remaining in the skillet with flour. Cook, stirring rapidly, until the flour starts to take on color. Add the stock, stirring rapidly with a wire whisk. Add the Worcestershire sauce. Return the quail to the skillet and turn them in the sauce. Cover with a tight-fitting lid. Place in the oven and bake 45 minutes or longer, until the quail are thoroughly tender.

5. Serve each quail on a toast triangle with sauce spooned over.

YIELD: 3 TO 6 SERVINGS.

QUAIL WITH APPLE, HONEY, AND THYME SAUCE

6 cleaned quail (about ⅓ pound each)
Salt to taste, if desired
Freshly ground pepper to taste
3 tablespoons corn, peanut, or vegetable
  oil
⅓ cup cubed smoked ham, preferably
  Virginia ham

1 apple, cored and thinly sliced
Fresh thyme sprigs
Apple, Honey, and Thyme Sauce (see
  following recipe)

1. Preheat the oven to 400 degrees.
2. Cut off the quail wings, which may be used for stock.
3. Split the quail down the back, cutting through the backbone.
4. Sprinkle the quail inside and out with salt and pepper.
5. Heat the oil in an ovenproof skillet large enough to hold all the quail in one layer once they are added. Arrange the quail on one side and cook over relatively high heat until nicely browned, about 1½ minutes.
6. Turn the quail and place in the oven. Bake about 12 minutes. Remove the skillet from the oven and sprinkle the ham around the quail. Cook about 1 minute on top of the stove. Let the quail rest for 5 minutes before serving.

7. You may serve the quail whole, or cut off the legs and carefully cut the breast meat from each side of each quail. Count on 2 breast halves and 2 legs for each serving. Garnish each serving with thin slices of quartered apples, a few sprigs of fresh thyme, and the ham cubes. Spoon the hot sauce around the quail, and serve.

YIELD: 6 SERVINGS.

APPLE, HONEY, AND THYME SAUCE

1 or 2 apples, preferably Granny
  Smith (about ³/₄ pound)
1 tablespoon honey

6 sprigs fresh thyme
2 cups Chicken Stock (page 275)
1 tablespoon butter

1. Cut the apple or apples into quarters but do not peel. Cut away the cores. Cut each quarter into thin crosswise slices. There should be about 3 cups.

2. Heat the honey in a heavy saucepan and cook, shaking the skillet in a flat, circular motion, until the honey takes on the color of dark caramel. Do not burn. Add the thyme and apple slices and cook, shaking the skillet and stirring the apple slices, about 2 minutes, until the apple slices are well coated.

3. Add the stock and cook about 15 minutes. Strain through a sieve, pressing with a wooden spoon or rubber spatula to extract as much of the apple as possible. Reheat the sauce. Just before serving, swirl in the butter.

YIELD: ABOUT 2 CUPS.

ROAST DOVES

36 whole doves or quail (about 6 1/2
   pounds, cleaned weight)
1/2 cup olive oil
1 tablespoon dry mustard
1 tablespoon curry powder
1 tablespoon chopped garlic

Salt to taste, if desired
Freshly ground pepper to taste
1 cup water
1/3 cup freshly squeezed lemon juice
3/4 cup freshly squeezed orange juice
1/4 cup Worcestershire sauce

1. Preheat the oven to 225 degrees.

2. Put the doves in a heavy casserole and add the olive oil, mustard, curry powder, garlic, salt, pepper, and water. Cover and place in the oven. Bake about 1 hour and 15 minutes.

3. Increase the oven temperature to 325 degrees and continue baking about 45 minutes. Add the lemon juice, orange juice, and Worcestershire sauce and stir to blend. Continue baking 30 minutes longer.

YIELD: 12 TO 16 SERVINGS.

Meat

SMITHFIELD, VIRGINIA, OR COUNTRY HAM

1 cured Smithfield, Virginia, or
country ham (14 to 16 pounds)

40 to 60 whole cloves
½ cup brown sugar

1. Place the ham in a large kettle or roasting pan and add cold water to cover. Soak overnight. The water should be changed often to get rid of excess salt.

2. Preheat the oven to 300 degrees.

3. Drain the ham and trim or scrape off all mold on the "face" side (this is opposite the skin side).

4. It is not essential, but you will facilitate carving the ham after cooking if you run a boning or other knife around the contours of the hipbone on the underside of the ham. Run the knife down deep around the bone, but do not remove the bone at this time. It will be removed after cooking.

5. Place the ham in a roaster with 10 cups water and cover closely with a lid or heavy-duty aluminum foil. Place in the oven and bake 20 to 23 minutes to the pound. Remove the ham from the oven, leaving the heat on.

6. Using the fingers, pull against the hipbone that was carved around earlier. Run the carving knife around the bone and pull with the fingers to remove it.

7. Increase the oven heat to 425 degrees.

8. Slice away the skin from the ham, leaving a thick layer of fat. Using a sharp knife, score the ham at 1-inch intervals, making a diamond-shaped pattern. Stud the fat with cloves. Sprinkle the surface with the brown sugar and bake 15 minutes.

YIELD: 12 TO 20 SERVINGS.

RED-EYE GRAVY

Red-eye gravy, to those unaccustomed to the nobler things in life, requires first a good, well-cured country ham. Smithfield and genuine Virginia hams are ideal for this.

Take a slice of uncooked ham with most or much of the fat left on. Fry the ham in its own fat until nicely browned on both sides. When it is cooked, transfer the ham to a warm platter and add boiling black coffee to the skillet, scraping to dissolve the brown particles that cling to the bottom and sides.

That is red-eye gravy, which you pour over the ham and serve.

The name *red-eye gravy* (sometimes referred to as red-ham gravy) derives from the fact that a circle or oval of liquid fat with a slightly reddish cast will form on the surface of the gravy when it is slightly reduced. This is the "eye" of the name.

HAM CROQUETTES

3 tablespoons butter
3 tablespoons finely chopped onion
1/4 cup flour
1 1/2 cups milk
4 cups coarsely chopped cooked ham
3 egg yolks
1/4 teaspoon freshly grated nutmeg
Salt to taste, if desired

Freshly ground pepper
Flour for dredging
1 egg, lightly beaten
3 tablespoons water
1 1/2 cups fine fresh bread crumbs
Peanut, vegetable, or corn oil for
   deep-frying
Tomato Sauce (see page 271)

1. Melt the butter in a saucepan and add the onion, stirring with a wire whisk. Add the flour, stirring to blend. When blended, add the milk, stirring rapidly with the whisk. When blended and smooth, add the meat. Bring to the boil and remove from the heat.

2. Add the yolks, stirring rapidly with the whisk. Return to the heat and cook briefly. Add the nutmeg, salt (if the ham is salty, do not add salt), and pepper to taste. Spoon the mixture into a dish and cover closely with buttered wax paper. Refrigerate, preferably overnight.

3. Remove the paper and, using the fingers, divide the mixture into 12 to 14 portions. Shape into balls and roll lightly in flour. The portions may be shaped finally into balls, cylinders, or pyramid shapes. Combine the egg and water. When the shapes are smooth on the surface and neatly coated with flour, dredge in the egg-water mixture, and then in the bread crumbs. Arrange on a rack and chill until ready to cook.

4. Heat the oil; when it is hot, add the croquettes, a few at a time. Cook 2 or 3 minutes, or until golden and cooked through.

5. Serve hot with tomato sauce.

YIELD: 6 TO 8 SERVINGS.

NOTE: *Leftover beef, lamb, or pork may be used in place of the ham.*

BAKED FRESH HAM

1 fresh ham with bone in (about 14
    pounds), or 1 boneless fresh ham
    (about 9 pounds)
Salt to taste, if desired
Freshly ground pepper to taste
1 tablespoon dried rosemary

2 garlic cloves, finely minced
2 tablespoons corn, peanut, or vegetable
    oil
2 onions, peeled and left whole
2 cups Chicken Stock (page 275)

1. Preheat the oven to 400 degrees.

2. Using a sharp knife held parallel to the bone, score the fat from one side to the other. Continue scoring at 1-inch intervals from bottom to top of the fat layer. Sprinkle the ham on all sides with salt and pepper.

3. Chop the rosemary as fine as possible and blend with the garlic. If you have a spice mill, grind the two together. In any event, rub the ham all over with the mixture.

4. Brush the ham on all sides with oil. Arrange the ham, fat side up, in a large roasting pan. Place in the oven and bake 1 hour, or 45 minutes for a boneless ham. Reduce the oven heat to 350 degrees and place the onions in the pan. Bake 1½ hours longer, basting often with the pan drippings. As the ham bakes, rotate the pan in the oven so that it bakes evenly.

5. After 2½ hours total baking time (2¼ hours for boneless ham), pour off the fat from the pan and return the ham to the oven. Continue baking, basting and rotating the pan occasionally, about 30 minutes.

6. Pour off all the fat from the pan. If the ham has a bone in, you will facilitate carving if you pull out the very thin bone from the short end of the ham. If the ham is done, it should come out easily. Add the chicken stock to the pan and return the ham to the oven. Continue baking about 15 minutes. If you use a meat thermometer, the temperature at the thickest part of the ham should register 165 degrees. Transfer the ham to a warm platter.

7. Line a saucepan with a sieve and pour the pan juices into it. Skim off the fat. Bring the pan juices to the boil and serve with the ham.

YIELD: 10 TO 18 SERVINGS.

OVEN-BARBECUED SPARERIBS

This recipe was given to me by a first-rate chef, Gene Hovis, a native North Carolinian who now lives and works in New York City. It was given to him by his Aunt Rosie.

*2 slabs of lean spareribs (about 4
    pounds each)*

*Salt to taste, if desired
Freshly ground pepper to taste*

THE BARBECUE SAUCE:

¹/₄ pound butter
2 teaspoons finely minced garlic
2 cups finely chopped onions
2 cups ketchup
¹/₄ cup soy sauce
1 ¹/₂ tablespoons chili powder

¹/₄ teaspoon Tabasco sauce, or more,
*   according to taste*
¹/₄ cup sherry wine vinegar or red
*   wine vinegar*
3 tablespoons dark brown sugar

1. Preheat the oven to 400 degrees.

2. Sprinkle the spareribs with salt and pepper. Arrange slabs in each of 2 large baking dishes and bake 1 hour. Turn the ribs and bake 10 minutes longer. Pour off the fat.

3. Meanwhile, heat the butter in a large saucepan and add the garlic and onions. Cook, stirring, until onions are wilted. Add the ketchup, soy sauce, chili powder, Tabasco sauce, vinegar, and sugar. There should be about 3 cups of sauce. Bring to a boil and let simmer about 5 minutes.

4. Brush each slab of ribs on the underside with sauce and return to the oven, brushed side up. Bake 30 minutes, brushing every 10 minutes on the same side with the sauce.

5. Turn the ribs. Brush generously with all the remaining sauce. Return to the oven and bake 30 minutes.

6. Cut apart the spareribs into individual ribs. Serve hot or at room temperature.

YIELD: 6 TO 8 SERVINGS.

BOILED PIGS' FEET

I have a distinctly childish recollection of an old saying that in the South they eat every part of the pig except for the squeal, and they always put that in a Model-T Ford. I loved pigs' feet as a child and prize them highly as an adult.

6 to 8 pigs' feet (4 to 4 1/2 pounds)
Salt to taste, if desired
Freshly ground black pepper to taste

4 celery ribs, broken in half
2 medium-size onions, cut in half

1. Put the pigs' feet in a kettle and add cold water to barely cover. Bring to the boil, cover, and cook about 45 minutes.

2. Add salt and a generous grinding of black pepper. Add the celery and onions. The cooking liquid should be kept at a depth of 1 inch at all times. As it evaporates, add a little more boiling water.

3. Continue cooking, covered, about 2 hours, or until pigs' feet are very tender and almost but not quite falling off the bone.

YIELD: 6 TO 8 SERVINGS.

CHITTERLINGS (CHITLINS)

Although I have eaten chitlins (the authentic Southern pronounciation for the small intestines of pigs) all my life, this is the recipe given to me by a fine cook and neighbor, Laura Sandifer. Please note that they should always be served with vinegar, hot red pepper sauce, and finely chopped onion on the side. Chitterlings (as they are spelled by all Yankees) are not necessarily peculiar to the South. They are much prized in French kitchens, where they are known as *andouilles* or *andouillettes,* large or small chitterling sausages, generally grilled and eaten with mustard on the side.

10 pounds chitterlings (see note)
1 large celery rib, cut in quarters
*1 medium-size onion, peeled and
  quartered*

1 tablespoon finely minced garlic
Salt to taste, if desired
Freshly ground pepper to taste

1. If using frozen chitterlings, let them stand at room temperature or in the refrigerator until thoroughly defrosted.

2. Hold the chitterlings under cold running water and, as carefully as possible, pick over the inside of each to remove fat and foreign matter. Total cleaning time will be about 45 minutes.

3. When the chitterlings have been thoroughly cleaned, put them in a kettle or casserole. Do not add water; they will create their own liquid. Add the celery, onion, garlic, salt, and a generous grinding of black pepper. Bring to the boil and cover. Cook about 3 hours. The liquid should remain at a depth of about 1 inch. If it reduces below that, add water. Test the chitterlings for tenderness. If not tender, it may be necessary to add about 1 cup water. Cover and continue cooking until tender, 30 minutes to 1 hour longer.

4. Serve the chitterlings with cider vinegar, hot pepper sauce, and finely chopped onion on the side.

YIELD: 6 SERVINGS.

NOTE: *Chitterlings are available fresh or frozen in many pork stores in metropolitan areas.*

GRILLADES AND GRITS

One of the most traditional main courses in Louisiana is a combination called grillades and grits. It is made with braised slices of veal or round steak. The meat is well browned and cooked with tomatoes. It is served, of course, with freshly cooked grits.

³⁄₄ pound veal, preferably from the leg, or round of beef, cut into 3 slices of equal width
1 teaspoon finely chopped garlic
2 tablespoons flour
Salt to taste, if desired
Freshly ground pepper to taste
¹⁄₄ teaspoon cayenne pepper

1 tablespoon solid white shortening or lard
1 cup finely chopped onion
1 cup cored and diced tomatoes
1 cup beef broth
1 cup raw grits, cooked according to package directions

1. Cut the veal or beef slices crosswise in half to produce 6 pieces. Put on a flat surface and pound lightly without breaking the fibers. Rub on all sides with garlic. Sprinkle with flour seasoned with salt, pepper, and cayenne. Pound the meat lightly all over with a heavy dinner plate.

2. Heat the shortening in a heavy skillet and add the meat. Cook 2 or 3 minutes over high heat, until nicely browned. Turn and cook about 3 minutes on the other side. It must be well browned to give a proper slightly dark color to the sauce.

3. Remove the meat briefly. Add the onion to the skillet and cook, stirring, until wilted. Add the tomatoes, beef broth, salt, and pepper and return the meat to the sauce. Turn the meat in the sauce. Cover and cook 20 to 30 minutes, turning the meat occasionally as it cooks.

4. Serve with hot grits on the side.

YIELD: 6 BREAKFAST OR LUNCHEON SERVINGS.

SMOKED COUNTRY SAUSAGE

One of my earliest recollections of life in the tiny village of Sunflower, Mississippi, where I was born was of the smokehouse used in late fall and early winter by my father for smoking hams and homemade sausage. I remember the structure and I remember the smells. The following is my version—my recollection of the taste—of the sausages that he cured in that smokehouse. We moved to a larger town when I was very young and he never cured or smoked meats thereafter.

3 1/2 pounds lean pork, cut into 2-inch cubes
2 pounds solid pork fat, cut into 2-inch cubes
2 1/2 tablespoons rubbed sage, or more to taste
4 tablespoons sweet paprika
Salt to taste, if desired

2 teaspoons finely ground or cracked black pepper
12 dried hot red pepper pods, or about 1 tablespoon dried hot red pepper flakes
10 to 12 feet of sausage casings (see page 164)

1. Put the pork and pork fat into a large mixing bowl and add the sage, paprika, and salt.

2. If preground black pepper is used, add it. Otherwise, grind the pepper, using a peppermill. Or grind it in a small, clean coffee grinder. Add it to the mixture.

3. If hot red pepper flakes are used, add them. Otherwise, grind the pepper pods in a small, clean coffee grinder. Add it to the mixture.

4. Mix well with the hands, cover, and let stand in the refrigerator overnight.

5. Put the mixture through a meat grinder fitted with the largest blade. Remove all the meat left in the grinder and clean the grinder blade.

6. Return the blade to the grinder and fit it, along with the special sausage attachment, to the mouth of the grinder. Slide 1 prepared sausage casing onto the attachment and tie the end. Grind the meat, holding the casing to permit free entry of the filling into the casing. When about 16 inches of casing have been filled, pinch the casing at the end of the sausage attachment. Pull it out to leave about 4 inches of empty casing at that end. Tie that end. Tie both ends of the sausage together. Set aside. Continue making sausages in this manner until all the stuffing has been used.

7. Hang the sausages in a smoker and smoke according to the manufacturer's instructions.

YIELD: 6 TO 8 SAUSAGE RINGS, WEIGHING ¾ TO 1 POUND EACH.

CHAURICE SAUSAGES

1½ pounds lean pork, trimmed of all
  fat
⅔ pound fatback or hardest pork fat
  available
1 cup finely chopped onion
½ cup finely chopped parsley
1½ tablespoons finely minced garlic
2 tablespoons finely chopped fresh hot
  red chilies, or 1 teaspoon or more
  dried hot red pepper flakes

2½ teaspoons cayenne pepper
2 teaspoons freshly ground black pepper
1 teaspoon dried thyme
½ teaspoon ground allspice
1 tablespoon salt, if desired
⅛ teaspoon saltpeter, optional
5 or 6 prepared sausage casings (see
  following instructions for
  preparation)

1. Grind the pork and pork fat, using a meat grinder.

2. Add the onion, parsley, garlic, chilies, cayenne pepper, black pepper, thyme, allspice, salt, and saltpeter. Blend well.

3. Test the mixture by making a small patty and cooking it on both sides until done. Adjust the seasonings according to taste.

4. Put the mixture through the meat grinder a second time.

5. Stuff the sausage casings, following the instructions outlined in the recipe for Smoked Country Sausage, page 163.

6. When ready to cook, prick the sausages all over with a fork to prevent bursting. Fry in a little oil.

YIELD: ABOUT 2½ POUNDS.

HOW TO PREPARE SAUSAGE CASINGS

Sausage casings, available in pork stores in metropolitan areas, are normally preserved in salt. When ready to use, put them in a basin of cold water and let stand about 30 minutes.

Drain and return to a basin of cold water.

To determine if the casings have holes in them, fill with water and examine for leaks. Discard sections with holes and use the partial casing.

ROSEMARY AND SAGE SAUSAGE

2 pounds pork chops, with fat
Salt to taste, if desired
1 tablespoon leaf sage or to taste
1 teaspoon chopped fresh rosemary, or
  ½ teaspoon dried

½ teaspoon coarsely ground black
  pepper, or to taste
½ teaspoon dried hot red pepper flakes,
  or to taste, optional

1. Remove the meat and fat from the bones. Reserve the bones for another use, such as tomato sauce, if desired.

2. Put the meat and fat through a meat grinder, and put it through again. Add the remaining ingredients to the ground meat and mix well. Shape the mixture into 4 or 6 patties.

3. To cook, put the patties in a cold skillet. Cook on both sides until well browned and thoroughly cooked.

YIELD: 4 TO 6 SERVINGS.

PORK SAUSAGE CAKES

Breakfasts in my mother's boardinghouse were copious affairs, and her paying guests could order any of a variety of meats—country sausage, sausage cakes, fried ham slices, crisp bacon, and so on—plus grits and eggs, any style. There were always breakfast biscuits hot from the oven and an assortment of jams and jellies, most of them homemade, plus molasses, which was produced locally.

2/3 pound lean pork
1/3 pound pork fat (see note)
Salt to taste, if desired
Freshly ground pepper to taste

1 tablespoon chopped dried sage, or
* 1 1/2 teaspoons ground (see note)*
1 teaspoon dried red pepper flakes,
* optional*

1. Cut the lean pork and pork fat into 1-inch cubes. Put into the container of a food processor equipped with the steel blade and blend. Or grind the pork and fat, using a meat grinder.

2. Add the remaining ingredients and blend 15 to 30 seconds, or until the meat is coarse-fine. Do not overblend or the consistency will be too fine.

3. Store the sausage in a container in the refrigerator for future use, or shape it into 4 or 6 patties and fry in a skillet, turning as necessary, until the sausage cakes are thoroughly browned and cooked through.

YIELD: 4 TO 6 SAUSAGE CAKES.

NOTE: *If you wish leaner sausage cakes, simply decrease the amount of pork fat and increase the lean pork. You may omit the sage and add about 1 teaspoon or more crushed fennel seeds.*

SPICED SAUSAGE

1 pound ground pork
1/4 teaspoon freshly ground black
    pepper
1/4 teaspoon crushed dried hot red
    pepper flakes

1/8 teaspoon ground allspice
Pinch of ground cloves
Pinch of ground cinnamon
2 tablespoons cold water
Salt to taste, if desired

1. Combine the pork, black pepper, red pepper flakes, allspice, cloves, cinnamon, water, and salt to taste in a mixing bowl. Blend thoroughly. If desired, you may substitute 1 1/2 teaspoons crumbled sage for the allspice, cloves, and cinnamon.

2. To test the mixture for seasoning, shape a small patty with the fingers. Heat a small skillet and cook the patty on both sides until thoroughly cooked. Taste, and add more seasoning as desired.

3. Shape into patties and fry on both sides in an ungreased skillet until thoroughly cooked.

YIELD: 4 TO 6 PATTIES.

NATCHITOCHES MEAT PIES

One of the most popular pies in America comes from the city of Natchitoches, Louisiana. It is a turnover and it is celebrated farther afield than the state limits. It is made with ground meat, is quite spicy, and is deep-fried. The name of that town, incidentally, is pronounced NACK-i-tosh.

Pastry for Deep-Fried Turnovers (see
following recipe)
3 tablespoons bacon fat or corn oil
¾ cup finely chopped onion
1½ teaspoons finely minced garlic
½ pound ground lean beef
¾ pound ground lean pork
1 cup finely chopped scallions

½ cup finely chopped parsley
Salt to taste, if desired
Freshly ground black pepper to taste
2 teaspoons finely chopped hot red or
green pepper
Corn, peanut, or vegetable oil for
deep-frying

1. Prepare the pastry and let stand, covered, while preparing the filling.

2. Heat the bacon fat or oil in a skillet or saucepan and add the onion and garlic. Cook, stirring, until wilted. Add the beef and pork and cook, stirring and chopping down with the side of a metal spoon to break up any lumps. Cook until the meat loses its raw look. Add the scallions, parsley, salt, black pepper, and hot pepper. Let cool.

3. On a lightly floured board, roll out one quarter of the dough at a time to the thickness of about ⅛ inch or less.

4. With a cutter 6 inches in diameter, cut out circles. Use a lid of a saucepan or a saucer as a guide.

5. Gather the scraps of dough and quickly form a ball. Roll out this dough to the same thickness, and cut it into 6-inch circles. Continue rolling and cutting circles until all the dough has been used.

6. Fill one-half of each circle of dough with about 3 tablespoons filling, leaving a margin for sealing when the dough is folded. Moisten all around the edges of the circle of dough. Fold the unfilled half of dough over to enclose the filling. Press around the edges with the tines of a fork to seal well.

7. Heat the oil to 375 degrees in a skillet or deep-fryer. Add the meat pies, 4 to 6 at a time, without crowding. Cook, turning the pies in the hot fat until nicely browned and cooked through, about 8 minutes. Drain well on absorbent paper towels. Serve hot.

YIELD: ABOUT 20 MEAT PIES.

NOTE: *If you wish to freeze the meat pies, it is best if you deep-fry them as indicated in the recipe. Drain, and let stand at room temperature until cool. Wrap each individually in foil and freeze. To reheat, preheat the oven to 350 degrees. Bake them without defrosting on a baking sheet for about 25 minutes.*

PASTRY FOR DEEP-FRIED TURNOVERS

¼ cup lard	*4½ cups flour*
¼ cup olive oil	*Salt to taste, if desired*
1⅓ cups water	

1. Heat the lard, oil, and water in a saucepan just until the lard is melted.
2. Put the flour and salt into the container of a food processor. Start processing while gradually adding the lard mixture.
3. Remove the dough and shape it into a ball. Set it on a lightly floured board and cover with a cloth. Let stand about 15 minutes before rolling out.

YIELD: ENOUGH PASTRY FOR TWENTY 6-INCH CIRCLES OF DOUGH.

SWISS STEAK

2 pounds chuck steak in 1 slice (about	*⅓ cup lard or corn oil*
¾ inch thick)	*½ cup finely chopped onion*
½ cup flour	*1 cup water or beef broth*
Salt to taste, if desired	*1 cup crushed canned tomatoes*
Freshly ground pepper to taste	*¾ cup fresh or frozen green peas,*
1 teaspoon finely minced garlic	*optional*

1. Put the meat on a flat surface.
2. Combine the flour, salt, pepper, and garlic and blend well. Sprinkle the flour mixture on both sides of the meat. Start pounding the steak with the side of a mallet or the bottom of a heavy skillet. The meat must be pounded thoroughly all over on both sides, pounding in as much flour as the meat will hold.

3. Heat the lard or oil in a heavy casserole with a tight-fitting lid and brown the steak thoroughly on both sides. Lift up the steak and add the onion. Cook briefly without browning. Add the water or broth, tomatoes, and salt and pepper to taste. Turn the meat in the liquid. Cover closely and let simmer over moderate heat about 1½ hours, or until the meat is exceedingly tender. If the peas are used, cook the fresh peas briefly until barely tender. If frozen peas are used, put them in a sieve and run hot water over them for 30 seconds. Add the peas to the meat gravy and bring to the boil.

4. Cut the meat into individual servings and spoon the gravy over it. Serve, preferably with mashed potatoes.

YIELD: 4 TO 6 SERVINGS.

VENISON STEW

2 quarts Marinade for Game,
    approximately (see following recipe)
5 pounds shoulder of venison, cut into
    2-inch cubes
2 to 4 tablespoons peanut, vegetable, or
    corn oil
¼ cup flour
Salt to taste, if desired

Freshly ground pepper to taste
4 tablespoons currant jelly
⅓ pound lean salt pork
10 small white onions
1 teaspoon butter
1 teaspoon sugar
½ pound mushrooms, thinly sliced

1. Prepare the marinade and add the venison pieces. Stir and cover with foil. Refrigerate 4 or 5 days, no longer.

2. Preheat the oven to 400 degrees.

3. Remove the meat from the marinade and set it aside. Strain the marinade, reserving the solids and the liquid. There should be about 4 cups liquid.

4. Heat 2 tablespoons oil in a medium-size skillet. Brown one-third of the meat at a time. As the meat is browned, transfer it to a kettle. Use more oil as necessary to cook the meat. The total time for browning the meat should be about 10 minutes.

5. Add a little more oil to the skillet and cook the reserved solids over high heat about 5 minutes. Add this to the meat.

6. Sprinkle the flour over all and stir to coat the pieces more or less evenly. Cook about 3 minutes and add the reserved liquid. Add salt and pepper to taste. Bring to the boil and cover. Place the kettle in the oven and bake 2 hours.

7. Remove from the oven, tilt the kettle, and skim off the excess fat from the surface. Add the jelly and stir until dissolved. Simmer 5 minutes on top of the stove.

8. Meanwhile, cut the salt pork into matchlike sticks. Put them in a saucepan, cover with water, and bring to the boil. Simmer 1 minute and drain.

9. Peel the onions and combine them in a saucepan with water to barely cover, salt to taste, the butter and sugar. Cook until the liquid evaporates and the onions start to take on a brown glaze.

10. Heat a skillet and add the pieces of salt pork. When crisp, remove the pieces with a slotted spoon and set aside. Add the mushrooms to the rendered salt pork fat. Sprinkle with salt and pepper to taste and cook, stirring as necessary, about 10 minutes. Drain well and set aside.

11. Add the onions to a skillet and add the salt pork and mushrooms. Cook briefly, about 5 minutes. Sprinkle this mixture over the venison and cook 10 minutes.

12. Serve with buttered fine noodles.

YIELD: 12 OR MORE SERVINGS.

MARINADE FOR GAME

¼ cup red wine vinegar
½ teaspoon dried marjoram
4 juniper berries, crushed
1 bay leaf
1 teaspoon rosemary
2 whole cloves
¼ teaspoon dried thyme

10 peppercorns
4 cups dry red wine
1 cup coarsely chopped celery
1 cup thinly sliced carrots
1 cup quartered small onions
2 sprigs parsley
Salt to taste, if desired

1. Combine in a saucepan the red wine vinegar, marjoram, juniper berries, bay leaf, rosemary, cloves, thyme, and peppercorns. Bring to the boil and simmer about 5 minutes.

2. Empty the mixture into a stainless steel or enamel bowl and add the remaining ingredients. Use as a marinade for game.

YIELD: ABOUT 2 QUARTS, OR ENOUGH MARINADE FOR 5 POUNDS OF VENISON.

A SOUTHERN BARBECUE

It is, of course, possible to prepare one main dish of any given meal and call it authentic. When it comes to a Southern barbecue, however, I feel it essential that you also offer your guests all the "fixin's" as well. The barbecue recipe offered here is one that I created after a lengthy visit to numerous barbecue pits in North Carolina. My version is not made in a pit, but it is cooked for several hours in the oven and then, briefly, smoked in a home barbecue grill to give it more flavor. You serve it chopped or sliced (I prefer it chopped) on barbecue buns with coleslaw and a "dip" made with vinegar and spices. The dip is actually spooned onto the meat after it is placed on half a bun. You can either spoon on coleslaw or serve it separately, along with potato salad. I might add that, for the sake of "down-home" authenticity, you should use bottled mayonnaise rather than homemade.

To my mind, the perfect ending for a meal with barbecue as a main course is pecan pie or pecan pie topped with ice cream.

NORTH CAROLINA BARBECUE SANDWICH

8 hamburger buns
3 cups chopped Pork Barbecue (see following recipe)

¼ cup Lexington Barbecue Dip (page 173)
2 cups Goldsboro Coleslaw (page 233)

1. Open up the buns. Spoon equal portions of the chopped pork onto the bottom half of each bun.

2. Spoon a little of the barbecue dip on top of each serving.

3. Top with equal portions of coleslaw. Cover the sandwich and serve.

YIELD: 8 SERVINGS.

PORK BARBECUE

Several years ago I traveled for *The New York Times* to Lexington and Greensboro, North Carolina, to sample and explore the barbecues of each region. When I returned, I submitted a full account of my adventures, including the establishments in which I had dined, the techniques for barbecuing, a description of the professional ovens used, the woods burned, and so on. My editors requested recipes for preparing a barbecue in the home and I insisted that you cannot reproduce the same product in home ovens—it simply would not work because of the smoking conditions. They were insistent and I lay awake at night trying to find some compromise. At 6:00 A.M. I decided to experiment. I heated my home oven to 500 degrees, put in a batch of pork loins on a rack, and baked them 15 minutes. I reduced the oven heat to very low—250 degrees—and baked that pork 5 hours, until it was meltingly tender. I smoked it briefly on my barbecue grill to give it flavor, and chopped it to serve on hamburger buns. I have had numerous Southern cooks tell me that it is the best homemade barbecue they have ever sampled.

Speaking of Southern barbecues, each region or state of the South seems to differ as to the preferred meats to be cooked over hot coals. Quite generally speaking, North Carolinians seem to have a preference for pork; Georgians for fresh pork or chickens; Texans seem to prefer beef, and so on. The sauces, too, vary from place to place, although most of them are made with vinegar and ketchup with an emphasis on one or the other. In North Carolina the emphasis seems to be on vinegar; in Georgia on ketchup; and in Texas either one or the other, the sauce frequently spiced with a little chili powder. To tell the truth, the preferences vary from family recipe to family recipe.

2 boneless pork loins (about 2¼   Salt to taste, if desired
  pounds each), each tied with string   Freshly ground pepper to taste

1. Preheat the oven to 500 degrees.

2. Rub the pork lightly with salt and pepper.

3. Place a rack inside a baking dish. Place the pork loin on the rack and bake 15 minutes.

4. Immediately reduce the oven temperature to 250 degrees. Let the pork bake 5 hours. Turn the loin once each hour of baking time.

5. Meanwhile, heat a charcoal or gas grill. Arrange 2 handfuls of soaked wood chips—such as hickory, oak, or mesquite—used for smoking (available in hardware stores) on the coals, separating them so that they are not placed directly under the meat. Put the meat on the grill and cover. Let smoke at a low temperature about 10 minutes. Take care that the coals or hot surface does not flame up as the meat cooks. You can even scrape away the coals from directly beneath the meat, allowing it to cook away from intense heat. Or if there are double-burner units, turn off the heat of one unit and place the meat on this side. Let the other unit continue to heat.

6. The pork is now ready to be served. It may be served sliced, cut into chunks, or finely chopped. The finely chopped version is generally considered the best. Serve on platters or as fillings for sandwiches.

YIELD: ABOUT 2 POUNDS; 8 OR MORE SERVINGS.

LEXINGTON BARBECUE DIP

¾ cup distilled white or cider vinegar   ¾ teaspoon crushed dried hot red
¾ cup ketchup   pepper flakes
Salt to taste, if desired   1 teaspoon sugar
Freshly ground pepper to taste   ¼ cup water

1. Combine all the ingredients in a small saucepan and bring to a simmer. Cook, stirring, until the sugar dissolves.

2. Remove from the heat and let stand until cool. Spoon a small amount of the sauce over barbecued meats and poultry.

YIELD: ABOUT 1¾ CUPS.

TEX-MEX DISHES

In the home of my childhood in Mississippi, Tex-Mex cooking was very much a part of our "special occasion" food. It was certainly not served as often as barbecues and soul food, but when it did appear I reveled in it —mostly hot tamales, hot tamale pie, and chili con carne. The chili was invariably made with ground beef, and my mother's version was, to my young palate, "pure heaven." Many years later, I made the acquaintance of a magnificent cook, Margaret Field, of Eagle Pass and Uvalde, Texas, who assured me emphatically that no self-respecting Texan would ever use ground beef in chili con carne. She came into my home and prepared a kettle of her "authentic" chili. The beef is cut into small cubes by hand and the dish does not contain either tomatoes or beans. I learned why later. With the chili you serve a tomato-based table sauce plus small bowls of well-seasoned—and somewhat liquid—beans, and you may add these to your bowl of chili if you so desire. You may also serve, to be added at will, a separate bowl of pico de gallo, a fiery hot and spicy concoction of chopped jalapeño peppers, fresh coriander, a small portion of chopped fresh tomatoes, and cubes of avocado. In my own home, I also serve a fantastic *torta de masa,* or cornmeal cake, that goes extremely well with spicy Tex-Mex cuisine. The meal can be preceded with seviche, the uncooked fish or seafood appetizer.

CHILI CON CARNE WITH CUBED MEAT

5 pounds lean chuck roast
1/2 cup olive oil
1/2 cup flour
1/2 cup chili powder, more or less to
    taste
2 teaspoons ground coriander
2 teaspoons ground cumin
2 teaspoons dried oregano
6 to 10 garlic cloves, finely minced

5 cups fresh or canned beef broth
Salt to taste, if desired
Freshly ground pepper to taste
Pinto or Cowgirl Beans, optional (page
    231)
Mexican Table Sauce, optional (page
    272)
Guacamole (page 19)

1. Trim the meat of all fat and cut it into 1/2-inch cubes.

2. Heat the oil in a deep kettle and add the cubed meat. Cook, stirring, just until the meat loses its red color.

3. Sift together the flour and chili powder and sprinkle it over the meat, stirring constantly so that the pieces are evenly coated.

4. Place the coriander, cumin, and oregano in the palm of one hand. Rub the spices between the palms, sprinkling them over the meat. Add the garlic and stir. Add the broth, stirring the meat constantly. Add salt and pepper and bring to the boil. Partly cover and simmer 3 to 4 hours, or until the meat almost falls apart. If necessary, add more broth as the meat cooks. This chili should not be soupy, however.

5. Serve with pinto or cowgirl beans, Mexican table sauce, and guacamole.

YIELD: 12 TO 16 SERVINGS.

CHILI CON CARNE WITH GROUND MEAT

1/4 pound beef suet, or 3 tablespoons
   corn oil
3 tablespoons water
2 cups finely chopped onions
3/4 pound ground sirloin steak
3/4 pound ground pork
2 garlic cloves, finely minced
3 to 5 tablespoons chili powder, or

according to taste
1 tablespoon dried oregano
1 tablespoon cumin seeds
4 cups canned Italian plum tomatoes
Salt to taste, if desired
Freshly ground pepper to taste
1 tablespoon red wine vinegar
1 1/2 teaspoons sugar

1. Heat the suet and water in a deep skillet or casserole and cook, stirring, until much of the fat has been rendered. The water will evaporate. Remove and discard the piece of suet and pour off all but 2 tablespoons of the rendered fat.

2. Add the onions, and when wilted and translucent, add the beef and pork. Stir with the side of a kitchen spoon to break up the meat. Add the garlic and chili powder. Crush the oregano in the palm of the hand and add it. Crush the cumin seeds in a mortar or blender and add it. Add the tomatoes and stir to blend thoroughly. Bring to the boil and add the remaining ingredients. Partly cover and simmer about 1 hour, stirring occasionally. Skim off the fat as it accumulates.

YIELD: 6 SERVINGS.

VARIATIONS: Add a drained can of kidney or pinto beans to the chili. Serve the chili, if desired, with a dollop of sour cream on each serving or with lime wedges to be squeezed onto it.

FAJITAS

This is, to my taste, one of the greatest Tex-Mex dishes. I first sampled it at a backyard outing several years ago on a visit to San Antonio. The name of the dish is pronounced fah-HEAT-ahs. It consists of well-trimmed skirt steak, grilled quickly, and placed in the center of flour tortillas. You top the meat with a well-seasoned guacamole, a layer of Mexican table sauce, and the fiery hot garnish known as *pico de gallo,* or "rooster's beak." The latter is made with chopped jalapeño peppers and fresh coriander, and it does enliven the palate. You fold over the sides and bottom of the tortillas to enclose the filling. To balance this fiery dish, you serve a small portion of pinto beans cooked with tomatoes and fresh coriander on the side. Altogether it is a glorious combination of flavors to be eaten indoors or in the open air.

3 skirt steaks (about 3 pounds)
1 tablespoon finely minced garlic
1 1/2 tablespoons freshly squeezed
   lime juice
1 tablespoon water
Salt to taste, if desired
Freshly ground pepper to taste

12 homemade Flour Tortillas (page
   261) or storebought tortillas
Guacamole (page 19)
Mexican Table Sauce (page 272)
Pico de Gallo (see following recipe)
Pinto or Cowgirl Beans (page 231)

1. Preheat a charcoal fire.

2. The skirt steak should be as free of surface fat as possible. Place each steak on a flat surface and, using a sharp knife, carefully trim away most of the fat. Trim well on all sides.

3. Cut each steak crosswise into 3- or 4-inch pieces, each about 6 inches long.

4. Place each piece of meat on the flat surface and, holding a sharp slicing knife parallel to the cutting surface, cut each piece of meat, sandwich-style, into 2 thin rectangles. Count on 4 or 5 slices per person.

5. Blend the garlic, lime juice, water, salt, and pepper in a flat plate. Make layers of the meat slices, brushing a little of the sauce between each layer.

6. Brush the top of the grill with a little oil. Add the meat slices and cook about 2 minutes on each side, turning once. Meanwhile, heat a nonstick skillet and cook each flour tortilla briefly to heat through. The tortillas must remain soft.

7. To serve, let the guests help themselves. Arrange equal portions of the meat on each of 6 preheated plates. To assemble, the portion of meat is arranged in the center of a tortilla; a little guacamole is smeared on top of the meat; a small amount of Mexican table sauce is spooned on top of the guacamole, and a small amount of pico de gallo is spooned over all. The sides of the tortilla are folded over and the bottom of the tortilla is folded up to prevent dripping. Small bowls of the hot beans are served on the side.

YIELD: 6 SERVINGS.

PICO DE GALLO
(HOT CHILI SAUCE)

½ cup finely chopped fresh jalapeño peppers with the seeds
½ cup seeded, finely diced tomatoes
½ cup finely chopped red onion
3 tablespoons finely chopped fresh coriander

⅓ cup finely diced avocado
2 tablespoons freshly squeezed lime juice
Salt to taste, if desired
Freshly ground pepper to taste
1 teaspoon olive oil

Combine all the ingredients in a mixing bowl and serve at room temperature. Serve with any Tex-Mex food, such as fajitas and chili con carne.

YIELD: ABOUT 2½ CUPS.

STUFFED FLANK STEAK, TEXAS STYLE

4 cups crumbled Corn and Cheese
   Bread (page 245; this should be
   made at least 1 day in advance)
1 flank steak (1¾ to 2 pounds)
Salt to taste, if desired
Freshly ground pepper to taste
5 tablespoons safflower, corn, or peanut
   oil
2 cups finely chopped onions
1 cup finely chopped celery
1 cup finely chopped sweet green
   peppers

2 tablespoons finely minced garlic
2 eggs, lightly beaten
4 bottled pickled jalapeño peppers
2 tablespoons finely chopped parsley
2 tablespoons chili powder
1 teaspoon dried cumin
1 teaspoon crumbled dried oregano
1 cup drained, crushed canned
   tomatoes, preferably imported
1 cup fresh or canned beef broth
Mexican Table Sauce (page 272),
   optional

1. Preheat the oven to 350 degrees.

2. Put the crumbled corn bread in a large mixing bowl and set aside.

3. Place the flank steak on a flat surface. Hold a long, sharp carving knife parallel to the surface and cut the steak lengthwise in half to make 2 long rectangles of equal thickness. Or have the butcher do this. Sprinkle the meat with salt and pepper.

4. Heat 2 tablespoons oil in a skillet and add half the onions, half the celery, half the sweet green peppers, and half the garlic. Cook, stirring, until the mixture is wilted. Let cool briefly. Add this to the corn bread. Add salt, pepper, and eggs.

5. Remove and discard the stems of the jalapeño peppers. Chop the peppers and add them to the bowl. Add the parsley and blend well with the fingers.

6. Spoon equal portions of the corn bread mixture onto each half of the meat. Carefully roll the meat jelly-roll style, starting at the narrower end of each portion of the meat. It will be almost impossible to enclose the filling without a portion of it falling out. This is a minor problem. Continue to roll and enclose the filling as neatly as possible. Tie the meat with string in several places to secure it.

7. Heat the remaining 3 tablespoons oil in a skillet and add the stuffed meat rolls. Brown the meat as neatly as possible on all sides, turning it carefully. Once more, a portion of the filling will fall into the skillet, which is to be expected.

8. When the meat is browned, scatter the remaining onions, celery, sweet green peppers, and garlic around the rolls. Sprinkle the vegetables with the chili powder, cumin, and oregano. Stir to blend and add the crushed tomatoes, broth, salt, and pepper. Stir.

9. Bring to the boil, cover, and place in the oven. Bake about 1 hour. Transfer the meat to a serving dish and remove the strings. Pour the sauce into a saucepan and skim off the excess fat. Bring to the boil.

10. Cut the meat into rounds and serve hot with the sauce. Serve with Mexican table sauce on the side, if desired.

YIELD: 8 OR MORE SERVINGS.

TAMALE PIE

THE BEEF:

2 pounds very lean beef, preferably top
  sirloin
2 cups fresh or canned beef broth

3 cups water
2 garlic cloves, peeled but left whole

THE CORNMEAL MUSH:

2 cups cornmeal
Salt to taste, if desired

5 cups cold beef broth or water
1 1/2 tablespoons lard or vegetable oil

THE FILLING:

2 tablespoons bacon fat

1 cup finely chopped onion

3 tablespoons finely minced garlic

1 cup finely chopped sweet green or red peppers

3 tablespoons chili powder

1 teaspoon ground cumin

½ teaspoon dried oregano

½ teaspoon ground coriander

Salt to taste, if desired

Freshly ground pepper to taste

2 cups canned tomatoes

1 cup whole kernel corn, fresh or canned

2 tablespoons chopped hot canned chilies

1 tablespoon butter

1. To prepare the beef, put it in a large saucepan or small kettle. Add the broth, water, and the whole garlic. Bring to the boil and let simmer 2 hours, or until quite tender. Drain but reserve about ¼ cup of the cooking liquid. Shred the meat. If the meat is not tender enough, chop it in a food processor.

2. To prepare the cornmeal mush, put the cornmeal in a heavy saucepan and add the salt, broth, and lard. Bring to the boil, stirring constantly with a wire whisk. Cook until thickened. Continue cooking, stirring, about 5 minutes. Set aside. The mush should be slightly cooled, but do not let it get cold or it will not be manageable.

3. Preheat the oven to 400 degrees.

4. To make the filling, heat the bacon fat in a saucepan and add the onion, minced garlic, and chopped sweet peppers. Cook, stirring, until the vegetables are wilted. Add the shredded meat, chili powder, cumin, oregano, coriander, salt and pepper to taste, tomatoes, corn, and hot chilies. Add the reserved ¼ cup broth. Stir.

5. Butter a 10-cup baking dish.

6. Add enough of the cornmeal mush to coat the bottom and sides of the dish. Leave enough mush to cover the top. Spread the mush in the dish as neatly as possible over and around the bottom and sides. Add the filling. Smooth it over. Add the remaining mush and smooth it over. Dot the top with butter. Place the dish in the oven and bake about 45 minutes, until piping hot throughout and nicely browned on top.

YIELD: 8 SERVINGS.

SAN ANTONIO PICADILLO

½ pound ground beef or venison
½ pound ground pork
½ to ¾ cup water
1 cup peeled and chopped fresh or
    canned tomatoes
Salt to taste, if desired
Freshly ground pepper to taste
½ pound potatoes
1 teaspoon chopped garlic, or to taste

1 can (6 ounces) tomato paste
¾ cup diced pimientos
½ teaspoon dried crumbled oregano
2 to 4 canned jalapeño peppers
1 or 2 tablespoons jalapeño pepper
    liquid from the can
¾ cup toasted almonds, available in
    tins

1. Place the beef and pork in a saucepan and add just enough water to cover. Bring to the boil and break up the lumps with the side of a kitchen spoon. Cover and let simmer 30 minutes.

2. Add the tomatoes, salt, and pepper.

3. Peel the potatoes and cut them into ½-inch cubes. Add the potatoes to the saucepan. Add the garlic, tomato paste, pimientos, and oregano.

4. Split the jalapeño peppers in half and remove and discard the seeds. Dice or thinly slice the peppers and add them to the saucepan. Add the pepper liquid and cover.

5. Cook 15 minutes, or until the potatoes are tender. Add the toasted almonds.

6. Serve in individual bowls with tortilla chips on the side.

YIELD: 6 TO 8 SERVINGS.

TEXAS-STYLE MEATBALLS

1/2 pound ground sirloin, or a mixture
   of ground beef and pork
1 very small zucchini
2 tablespoons safflower, corn, or peanut
   oil
2 teaspoons finely minced garlic
1 1/4 cups finely chopped onions
1/4 cup finely chopped fresh coriander
   leaves, optional
1/4 teaspoon crumbled dried oregano
1/2 teaspoon ground cumin

1 egg
Salt to taste, if desired
Freshly ground pepper to taste
1 chile chilpotle, *available in
   Spanish markets,* or 2 tablespoons
   chili powder
2 cups chopped, peeled, and seeded ripe
   tomatoes or crushed imported canned
   tomatoes
Chopped coriander leaves for garnish,
   optional

1. Put the meat into a mixing bowl.

2. Trim off the ends of the zucchini and cut it into slices about 1/8 inch
thick. Stack the slices and cut them into strips about 1/8 inch wide. There
should be about 1/2 cup. Cut the strips into 1/8-inch cubes. Add this to the
meat.

3. Heat 1 tablespoon oil in a skillet and add 1 teaspoon garlic and 1/4
cup chopped onion. Cook, stirring, until the onion wilts. Let cook briefly
and add this mixture to the meat. Add the coriander, oregano, cumin, egg,
salt, and pepper to the meat. Using lightly oiled fingers and palms, shape
the mixture into 12 meatballs.

4. Heat the remaining 1 tablespoon oil in a saucepan and add the remaining garlic and onion. Cook, stirring, until wilted. If using the *chile
chilpotle,* add it. Otherwise, sprinkle the onion mixture with the chili powder and cook briefly, stirring. Add the tomatoes. Let simmer about 10
minutes, stirring often. Pour the mixture into the container of a food
processor and blend thoroughly. Return the tomato mixture to the saucepan.

5. Add the meatballs and let simmer about 20 minutes.

6. Serve garnished with chopped coriander.

YIELD: 4 SERVINGS.

STEAK STUFFED WITH CHILIES AND CHEESE

2 fresh poblano chilies (about 2 ounces each), or ¼ cup canned chilies
1 small onion (about ¼ pound)
2 tablespoons corn, peanut, or vegetable oil
1 small garlic clove, peeled and thinly sliced

6 ounces Cheddar cheese, cut into 1 piece about 1 inch thick
4 slices filet mignon (about 6 ounces each)
Salt to taste, if desired
Freshly ground pepper to taste
Salsa Picante (see following recipe)

1. If the whole, fresh chilies are used, put them over a gas flame or heat over charcoal, turning often, until the outsides are well burned or charred, 5 to 7 minutes. Wrap the chilies in a damp cloth and let cool.

2. Remove the chilies and peel. Discard the stems, veins, and seeds. Cut the chilies into fine shreds. If canned chilies are used, drain and shred them.

3. Peel the onion and cut it into lengthwise strips.

4. Heat the oil in a saucepan and add the onion and garlic. Cook, stirring, briefly. The onion must remain crisp. Add the chili pieces and stir. Remove from the heat.

5. Cut the cheese lengthwise into thin slices. Add the slices to the saucepan, still off the heat. Stir to blend. Do not cook.

6. Slice each piece of meat through the center, sandwich-fashion, but without cutting totally through. You want to butterfly the pieces. Open up the meat on a flat surface and pound lightly with a flat mallet. Sprinkle with salt and pepper.

7. Spoon a portion of the cheese mixture onto one side of each piece of meat. Fold over the second side to enclose the filling. Press around the edges with the fingers to seal.

8. When ready to cook, preheat a charcoal or gas-fired grill.

9. Add the beef. Cook 2 to 3 minutes on each side. Serve with salsa picante.

YIELD: 4 SERVINGS.

SALSA PICANTE
(TOMATO AND CHILI SAUCE)

1 cup finely cubed ripe tomatoes
1½ tablespoons finely chopped,
*   stemmed, seeded jalapeño or serrano*
*   chilies*

1 tablespoon lime juice
2 tablespoons cold water
½ teaspoon crumbled dried oregano
2 tablespoons finely chopped onion

Combine the ingredients in a small mixing bowl and crush. Set aside until ready to use.

YIELD: ABOUT 1½ CUPS.

HOPPIN' JOHN

Black-eye or black-eyed peas seem to figure ubiquitously on Southern tables, and Yankee visitors seem to look at them askance. They are not necessarily country fare, as many people claim them to be. They appear on the tables of rich and poor, the educated and uneducated alike, and are eaten with equal enthusiasm. They are a basis of the dish known as Hoppin' John, the origin of which name no one seems to be able to explain. The dish is made with either black-eyed peas or cow peas and rice, and it is certainly one of the most traditional of Southern dishes. It is served in many Southern homes on New Year's Day to bring all those assembled good luck throughout the year. I am amused to think that in South Carolina there is a dish made of okra and rice called Limping Susan. The first recipe for Hoppin' John is a modernized version demonstrated for me by Bill Neal, a fine young North Carolina chef.

¹/₈ pound streaky bacon or salt pork, cut into small cubes (about ¹/₂ cup)

¹/₃ cup diced carrots

¹/₂ cup finely chopped celery

²/₃ cup finely chopped onion

10 ounces fresh or frozen black-eyed peas

1 whole garlic clove

2 ³/₄ cups water, approximately

6 sprigs fresh thyme

1 bay leaf

Salt to taste, if desired

¹/₄ teaspoon dried hot red pepper flakes

1 cup rice

2 tablespoons butter

GARNISHES:

1 ripe tomato (about ¼ pound), cored
¼ pound sharp Cheddar cheese, finely
  grated
1 cup finely chopped scallions,
  including green part

1. Put the bacon or salt pork in a saucepan and cook, stirring often, until all the cubes are crisp. Add the carrots, celery, and onion and cook, stirring, about 1 minute.

2. Add the peas, garlic, about 1¼ cups water, or to barely cover, thyme, bay leaf, salt, and red pepper flakes. Bring to the boil and let simmer, uncovered, 30 to 40 minutes, until tender but not mushy. Remove from heat.

3. Put the rice in a saucepan and add 1½ cups water and salt to taste. Bring to the boil and let simmer 17 minutes. Stir in the butter.

4. Cut the unpeeled tomato into ¼-inch cubes; there should be about 1 cup.

5. Arrange the hot rice in the center of a platter. Spoon the hot pea mixture, including liquid, over the rice. Scatter the cheese over the peas. Place tomato cubes around the rice. Scatter the scallions over the tomatoes. Serve immediately.

YIELD: 4 TO 6 SERVINGS.

NEW YEAR'S DAY BLACK-EYED PEAS

2 pounds dried black-eyed peas
½ pound slab of lean bacon, cut into
  ¼-inch cubes (about 2 cups)
1 sweet green or red pepper, finely
  chopped (about ¾ cup)
½ cup finely chopped onion
½ cup finely chopped celery

2 teaspoons red wine vinegar
3½ cups Chicken Stock (page 275)
Salt to taste, if desired
Freshly ground pepper to taste
2 dried hot red peppers, crumbled
6 to 7 cups water, approximately

1. Rinse the peas and drain.

2. Put the bacon in a heavy kettle and cook, stirring, until rendered of fat and browned. Add the chopped sweet pepper, onion, and celery and cook, stirring, until wilted.

3. Add the peas, vinegar, stock, salt, pepper, and dried hot peppers. Bring to the boil. Cover closely and let simmer about 1 hour.

4. Add 6 cups water and return to the boil. Let simmer about 1 hour, stirring occasionally from the bottom. Check the peas and, if necessary, add more water. Continue cooking 30 minutes. The total cooking time is 2½ hours or longer.

YIELD: 16 OR MORE SERVINGS.

BLACK-EYED PEAS VINAIGRETTE

In days of yore, black-eyed peas were considered a basic ingredient in almost all Southern households, something taken for granted, a food to be cooked with fatback or hog jowls and cooked for hours, with collard greens and turnip greens simmering in separate pots. I had reached a certain adulthood when I discovered that they can be delectable when dressed with a vinaigrette sauce (always referred to in my childhood as a French dressing). Here is my version of a great Southern ingredient adapted *à la Francaise*.

1 pound dried black-eyed peas
8 cups water
Salt to taste, if desired
Freshly ground pepper to taste
1 onion stuck with 2 cloves
1 garlic clove, peeled
1 bay leaf
¼ teaspoon dried thyme

4 sprigs parsley
⅓ cup finely chopped onion
2 tablespoons finely chopped shallots
1 teaspoon finely minced garlic
¼ cup finely chopped parsley
3 tablespoons red wine vinegar
⅔ cup olive, peanut, or vegetable oil

1. Rinse and pick over the peas and place in a kettle. Add the water, salt, pepper, and onion stuck with cloves. Tie the garlic clove, bay leaf, thyme, and parsley sprigs in a cheesecloth bag, and add it. Bring to the boil and simmer until the peas are tender, about 1 hour and 15 minutes. Set aside for 15 minutes.

2. Remove the onion and cheesecloth bag. Drain the peas.

3. Put the peas in a mixing bowl. Add the chopped onion, shallots, minced garlic, chopped parsley, vinegar, and oil. Add salt and pepper to taste. Toss to blend well. Serve lukewarm or at room temperature.

YIELD: 12 OR MORE SERVINGS.

BUTTERNUT SQUASH WITH MINTED GREEN PEAS

2 butternut squash (about 1 1/2 pounds each)
3 tablespoons butter
1/4 cup brown sugar
1 teaspoon powdered ginger
1 package (10 ounces) frozen small green peas

2 teaspoons chopped fresh mint, or 1 teaspoon dried
Salt to taste, if desired
Freshly ground pepper to taste

1. Preheat the oven to 275 degrees.

2. Split the squash, lengthwise or crosswise, in half. Scrape out and discard the seeds. Cut off a thin slice from the bottom of each half so that it will rest firmly upright in a pan.

3. Melt 2 tablespoons butter and brush the rims and cavity of each squash with it.

4. Blend the sugar and ginger, and sprinkle each half, rim and cavity, with equal portions of the mixture. Arrange the halves on a baking sheet and bake 1 hour.

5. Meanwhile, put the peas into a sieve and run hot water over them for 15 seconds, or until defrosted. Put the peas in a small skillet. Add remaining 1 tablespoon butter, mint, salt, and pepper. Cook briefly until heated through. Do not overcook.

6. Fill the squash halves with the peas and serve immediately.

YIELD: 4 SERVINGS.

CHILES RELLENOS
(STUFFED CHILIES)

4 fresh poblano chilies
1 cup Bay Leaf Tea (see following
   recipe)
1/2 cup white wine vinegar
2 garlic cloves, thinly sliced
1 cup peeled, diced potato

1/2 cup peeled, trimmed, diced carrot
1/3 cup diced raw jicama, optional
2 tablespoons mayonnaise
Salt to taste, if desired
1/3 cup heavy cream
1/2 cup grated white Cheddar cheese

1. Put the chilies over a gas flame or heat them over charcoal, turning often, until the outsides are well burned or charred, 5 to 7 minutes. Dampen a cloth and wrap it around the chilies and let them cool.

2. Remove the chilies and peel. Make a lengthwise slit down one side. Leave the stems intact. Remove and discard the seeds and veins.

3. Blend the bay leaf tea, vinegar, and garlic in a small mixing bowl. Add the chilies and let stand at least 30 minutes. Drain, reserving the liquid.

4. Meanwhile, put the potatoes in a small saucepan and the diced carrot in another saucepan. Add cold water to cover. Bring to the boil. Let the diced carrot simmer about 3 minutes, or until crisp-tender. Let the potatoes cook about 5 minutes, or until crisp-tender. Drain both.

5. Add the potatoes and carrots to the reserved liquid. Let stand briefly.

6. Drain the vegetables. Put them in a mixing bowl and add the jicama and mayonnaise. Add salt to taste.

7. Whip the cream until it is almost but not quite stiff. Fold 2 tablespoons into the vegetables.

8. Spoon equal portions of the vegetable mixture into each of the chilies. Spoon an equal portion of the remaining whipped cream on top of each stuffed chili. Sprinkle with cheese and serve.

YIELD:　4 SERVINGS.

BAY LEAF TEA

4 large bay leaves
2 cups water

1. Combine the bay leaves and water in a saucepan and bring to the boil. Let cook over high heat 10 to 15 minutes, or until the water is reduced to 1 cup.
2. Strain, discarding the leaves.

YIELD:　ABOUT 1 CUP.

MIXED SOUTHERN GREENS

The standard item of soul food that appeared almost daily at my mother's table were one form of greens or another, always cooked with pieces of pork, sometimes salted, sometimes smoked. The greens were of a common garden variety, such as mustard greens, collard greens, and turnip greens. These would be put on to boil with a great quantity of water and salt and allowed to cook for hours. Once cooked, the liquid is much treasured by Southern palates. It is called "pot likker," and you sip it like soup with corn bread. If you want to be fancy, you can always make cornmeal dumplings to float on top of the cooking liquid.

7 pounds mixed greens (they may
 include collards, kale, and turnip
 greens)
3/4 pound slab of lean bacon, cut into
 1/4-inch cubes
1 cup finely chopped onion
1/2 cup finely chopped celery
3/4 cup chopped sweet green pepper

2 ham hocks (about 3/4 pound each)
Salt to taste, if desired
Freshly ground pepper to taste
2 tablespoons red wine vinegar
1 or 2 dried red hot peppers, broken
 into pieces
2 cups water

1. Pick over the greens to remove any tough stems and veins. Wash and drain thoroughly. Use only the tender leaves, cutting or breaking them into 2-inch pieces.

2. Put the bacon in a very large heavy kettle or casserole and cook, stirring, until rendered of fat and browned. Add the onion, celery, and sweet green pepper. Cook, stirring, about 5 minutes.

3. Add the greens, stirring. Cover closely and cook, stirring, until greens are wilted. Add the ham hocks, salt, pepper, vinegar, and dried hot pepper. Cover and cook about 15 minutes.

4. Add the water, cover, and let simmer about 1½ hours.

YIELD: 8 TO 12 SERVINGS.

COLLARD GREENS, SOUTHERN STYLE

4 1/2 pounds collard greens (about 3
 bunches)
6 cups ham hock liquid (see following
 recipe for Ham Hock Seasoning)
1 ham hock (2 pieces; see following

 recipe for Ham Hock Seasoning)
1/2 cup bacon fat drippings
Salt to taste, if desired
Freshly ground pepper to taste
3/4 teaspoon sugar

1. Cut off the bottoms of the stems of each bunch of greens 4 or 5 inches from the base. Break and pull off any remaining stems that may seem tough to the touch. Discard any blemished or yellow leaves.

2. Gather the leaves into small bunches and roughly cut. There should be about 36 cups, loosely packed. Rinse and drain thoroughly without patting dry.

3. Put the greens in a kettle and add the ham hock liquid, ham hock, bacon fat, salt, and pepper. Bring to the boil. Cover and cook about 1 hour. Add the sugar and continue cooking, covered, 45 minutes to 1 hour.

YIELD: 6 SERVINGS.

HAM HOCK SEASONING

2 ham hocks (about 1 1/2 pounds)
Water to cover (about 2 quarts)

1. Split or crack the ham hocks in half.
2. Put the ham hocks in a saucepan and add cold water to cover. Bring to the boil and cover. Cook 2 hours, or until the hocks are fork-tender. Add more water to the kettle as the liquid cooks down so that there will be about 6 cups of ham hock liquid in the saucepan when finished.

YIELD: 6 CUPS COOKING LIQUID AND 2 COOKED HAM HOCKS.

◆

CORN ON THE COB

The ideal way to cook corn on the cob, South or North, is to shuck it and remove as much of the silk as possible. Bring enough water to the boil to cover the corn when it is added. Add salt to taste, if desired. Drop the corn into the water and cover. Remove from the heat and let stand 5 minutes. Drain and serve.

CURRIED CORN WITH GREEN PEPPERS

4 ears corn on the cob, shucked
3 tablespoons butter
1/4 cup finely chopped sweet green
   pepper

1 teaspoon curry powder
Salt to taste, if desired
Freshly ground pepper to taste
1/4 cup heavy cream

1. Drop the corn into boiling water. When the water returns to the boil, cover and turn off the heat. Let the corn remain in the water 5 minutes. Drain and let the corn cool.

2. Cut and scrape the corn off the cob. There should be about 2 cups.

3. Heat 2 tablespoons butter in a skillet and add the green peppers. Cook, stirring, about 1 minute. Sprinkle with the curry powder and cook, stirring, about 30 seconds. Add the corn, salt, and pepper. Add the remaining 1 tablespoon butter and the heavy cream. Serve hot.

YIELD: 2 TO 4 SERVINGS.

CORN PUDDING

5 ears corn, shucked
1/2 cup heavy cream
2 egg yolks
2 whole eggs
1/2 cup grated Cheddar cheese, optional
1/8 teaspoon grated nutmeg

Salt to taste, if desired
Freshly ground pepper to taste
1 to 2 tablespoons diced mild or hot
   canned green chilies, optional
1 tablespoon butter

1. Preheat the oven to 375 degrees.

2. Grate and scrape the corn kernels from the cobs. There should be about 2½ cups. Put the corn pulp in a mixing bowl.

3. Add the cream, egg yolks, whole eggs, cheese, nutmeg, salt, pepper, and green chilies. Beat well.

4. Butter a baking dish with the butter (a 9-inch pie plate works well) and pour in the corn batter. Bake 25 minutes. Serve hot.

YIELD: 6 SERVINGS.

CORN, ZUCCHINI, AND CHEESE PUDDING

4 ears corn, shucked
1 tablespoon butter
½ cup finely chopped onion
1 teaspoon finely chopped garlic
3 zucchini (about 1 pound), trimmed
    and cut into ¼-inch-thick rounds
2 egg yolks
1 large egg

½ cup milk
½ cup heavy cream
Salt to taste, if desired
Freshly ground pepper to taste
⅛ teaspoon nutmeg
¼ pound grated Muenster or Cheddar
    cheese (about 1 cup)

1. Preheat the oven to 375 degrees.

2. Cut and scrape the corn off the cob. There should be about 2 cups. Set aside.

3. Melt the butter in a skillet and add the onion and garlic. Cook until wilted and add the zucchini. Cook, shaking the skillet, until the zucchini is slightly wilted. Remove from the heat.

4. Blend the yolks, egg, milk, cream, salt, pepper, and nutmeg. Add the corn and cheese and stir. Pour this over the zucchini and stir to blend.

5. Pour the mixture into a 4½- to 5-cup baking dish (an oval baking dish measuring about 1½ × 7 × 11½ inches is suitable). Set the dish in a shallow pan and pour about ½ inch boiling water around it. Place in the oven and bake about 25 minutes, or until the custard is set in the center.

YIELD: 4 TO 6 SERVINGS.

CORN FRITTERS

4 ears corn, or 2 cups frozen whole
   corn kernels, defrosted
2 eggs, separated
6 tablespoons flour
Salt to taste, if desired

Freshly ground pepper to taste
1/3 cup milk
4 tablespoons peanut, vegetable,
   or corn oil
2 tablespoons butter

1. If fresh corn is available, use it. Shuck the corn. Bring enough water to the boil to cover the corn and add the ears. Cover, and when the water returns to the boil, turn off the heat. Let the corn stand 5 minutes. Drain.

2. When the corn is cool enough to handle, cut off the kernels with a sharp knife. There should be 2 cups.

3. Put the corn kernels in a mixing bowl and add the egg yolks. Add the flour, salt, and pepper and blend with a spoon. Stir in the milk.

4. Beat the whites until stiff and fold them in.

5. Heat the oil and butter in a skillet, and when it is hot spoon about 4 mounds of batter into the fat. Add only enough at a time to fill the skillet. Cook 3 to 4 minutes, or until golden on one side. Turn with a spatula and cook until golden on the other side, 3 to 4 minutes. Transfer to paper towels, but serve quickly while they are still hot.

YIELD: ABOUT 16 FRITTERS.

SUCCOTASH WITH HOMINY

6 ears unshucked corn on the cob

8 tablespoons butter

½ cup finely chopped scallions

½ cup finely chopped sweet yellow pepper

½ cup finely chopped sweet red pepper

2 cups drained canned hominy

½ cup fresh or frozen baby lima beans

½ cup fresh or frozen field peas or lady peas, or use any tender, small white peas

¼ cup finely minced chives

1. Preheat the oven to 475 degrees.

2. Open up the tops of each corn cob to expose the cornsilks. Chop off and discard the top of each ear to remove most of the corn silks. Drop the corn into cold water to cover and let stand 5 minutes. Drain.

3. Reshape the husks and wrap 2 at a time in aluminum foil. Arrange them on a baking sheet and place in the oven. Bake 15 minutes.

4. Shuck the corn cobs, discarding any remaining cornsilks. Cut away the kernels and set aside.

5. Heat the butter in a casserole and add the scallions and peppers. Cook briefly, stirring, and add the hominy. If fresh lima beans and peas are used, add them and cook until tender. If frozen peas are used, run them under the hot water tap until defrosted. Drain and add them to the casserole. Cook, stirring, about 1 minute and stir in the chives.

YIELD: 6 SERVINGS.

MAQUE CHOUX

One of the most typically Cajun dishes is called maque choux, a name I have never heard explained. It is primarily a vegetable dish with corn as its principal ingredient.

16 ears fresh corn on the cob
4 tablespoons butter
1 tablespoon corn, peanut, or vegetable
  oil
1 cup finely chopped onion
1 cup finely chopped sweet green
  peppers
1 teaspoon freshly ground pepper,
  preferably white

1/2 teaspoon cayenne pepper
1/4 teaspoon dried thyme
2 cups cored, chopped, ripe tomatoes
Salt to taste, if desired
3 tablespoons heavy cream
1 teaspoon sugar

1. Cut the corn kernels from the cob using a sharp knife. Scrape the cobs to obtain the pulp. There should be about 8 cups.

2. Heat 1 tablespoon butter and the oil in a skillet and add the onion and green peppers. Cook, stirring, until wilted. Add the corn, ground pepper, cayenne, and thyme. Cook about 10 minutes, or until the corn starts to stick on the bottom.

3. Add the tomatoes, salt, cream, and sugar and stir. Cover and cook, stirring often, about 10 minutes. Stir in the remaining 3 tablespoons butter and serve hot.

YIELD: 10 OR MORE SERVINGS.

EGGPLANT STUFFED WITH SHRIMP
AND MUSHROOMS

1 eggplant (about 1 pound)
3 tablespoons olive oil
1/2 pound fresh mushrooms
5 tablespoons plus 1 teaspoon butter
1 lemon
Salt to taste, if desired
Freshly ground pepper to taste
1/3 cup finely chopped onion
1/2 cup finely chopped celery

1/2 cup finely chopped sweet green
  pepper
10 raw shrimp
1/8 teaspoon nutmeg
Cayenne pepper to taste
3/4 cup plus 2 tablespoons bread
  crumbs
1/3 cup heavy cream
1 egg yolk

1. Cut the eggplant in half lengthwise. Use a sharp paring knife and carefully trim around the inside edges, leaving a rim approximately ¼ inch thick. Score the center flesh almost but not down to the skin.

2. Heat the oil in a skillet and place the eggplant halves, scored side down, in the oil. Cover with a tight-fitting lid or aluminum foil. Cook over low heat until the eggplant is tender, 15 to 20 minutes.

3. Preheat the oven to 350 degrees.

4. Using a large spoon, scoop out the eggplant flesh, leaving a shell. Chop the flesh.

5. Rinse the mushrooms and drain them. Slice the mushrooms, then chop them fine. There should be about 2 cups.

6. Heat 2 tablespoons butter in a skillet and add the mushrooms, the juice of ½ lemon, and salt and pepper to taste. Cook, stirring, until the mushrooms give up their liquid. Continue cooking until almost all the liquid evaporates.

7. Heat 2 tablespoons butter in another skillet and add the onion. Cook, stirring, about 3 minutes, and add the celery and green pepper. Cook about 5 minutes and add this to the mushrooms.

8. Peel and devein the shrimp and chop them fine. Add them to the mushroom mixture. Add the chopped eggplant flesh, nutmeg, cayenne, salt and pepper to taste, and 1 teaspoon lemon juice. Add ½ cup bread crumbs, the heavy cream, and egg yolk. Fill the eggplant shells with the mixture. Sprinkle each half with equal parts of the remaining bread crumbs, and dot with equal amounts of the remaining butter. Place the shells in an oiled baking dish and bake 25 minutes, or until piping hot and bubbling. Run the eggplant briefly under the broiler until nicely golden. Serve piping hot.

YIELD: 6 SERVINGS.

EGGPLANT AU GRATIN

1 eggplant (about 1 pound)
Salt to taste, if desired
1/2 pound fresh mushrooms
3 1/2 tablespoons butter
Juice of 1/2 lemon
1 1/2 tablespoons flour
1/2 cup milk

1/4 cup heavy cream
Freshly ground pepper to taste
1/4 teaspoon nutmeg
Tabasco sauce to taste
1 egg, lightly beaten
2 tablespoons bread crumbs
2 tablespoons Parmesan cheese

1. Preheat the oven to 425 degrees.

2. Peel the eggplant and cut the flesh into 1-inch cubes, more or less. Drop the cubes into boiling salted water and cook about 5 minutes, just until cooked. Drain well.

3. Meanwhile, slice the mushrooms. There should be about 2 cups. Heat 1 tablespoon butter in a skillet and add the mushroom slices. Sprinkle with salt and about 1 teaspoon lemon juice. Cook, stirring and tossing, until the mushrooms give up their juice. Continue cooking until the liquid evaporates. Set aside.

4. Melt 1 1/2 tablespoons butter in a saucepan and add the flour, stirring with a wire whisk. Add the milk and cream, stirring rapidly with the whisk. When blended and smooth, add salt and pepper to taste, the remaining lemon juice, nutmeg, and Tabasco to taste. Stir in the mushrooms and eggplant. Stir in the egg. Spoon the mixture into a baking dish (an 8-inch pie plate works well). Sprinkle with a mixture of crumbs and cheese and dot with the remaining 1 tablespoon butter. Bake 30 to 40 minutes, and then brown under the broiler.

YIELD: 4 TO 6 SERVINGS.

EGGPLANT FRITTERS

1 eggplant (about 1 pound)

1/4 cup corn, peanut, or vegetable oil,
  plus more for deep-frying

Salt to taste, if desired

Freshly ground pepper to taste

1 cup finely chopped scallions

1 tablespoon finely minced garlic

2 eggs, lightly beaten

1 cup flour

1/3 cup milk

1 tablespoon baking powder

1/4 cup finely chopped chives

1. Peel the eggplant and cut it into 1/4-inch-thick slices. Stack the slices and cut them into 1/4-inch-wide strips. Cut the strips into 1/4-inch cubes. There should be about 4 cups.

2. Heat 1/4 cup oil in a skillet and add the eggplant, salt, and pepper. Cook, shaking the skillet and stirring, until the pieces are tender. Add the scallions and garlic. Cook, shaking the skillet and stirring, about 1 minute longer. Drain well in a colander.

3. Put the eggs in a mixing bowl and add the flour, stirring with a wire whisk. Add the milk, stirring. Stir in the baking powder and chives.

4. Add the eggplant and blend well.

5. Add oil to a skillet, preferably nonstick, to a depth of about 1/4 inch. When it is hot, drop the batter, about 2 tablespoons at a time, into the oil. Cook until browned on one side, about 1 minute. Turn the fritters and cook about 1 minute on the second side. Drain on paper towels. Continue cooking the fritters until all the batter is used, adding oil to the skillet as necessary. Serve hot.

YIELD: ABOUT 24 FRITTERS.

OYSTER-STUFFED EGGPLANT

1 firm, unblemished eggplant (about
   1 1/4 pounds)
Salt to taste, if desired
2 tablespoons butter
2 tablespoons flour
1 cup milk
1/3 cup finely chopped onion
3 tablespoons finely chopped shallots
1/4 pound fresh mushrooms, cut into
   fine cubes (about 1 1/4 cups)

Juice of 1/2 lemon
1/2 pint shucked oysters with their
   liquor
1/8 teaspoon freshly grated nutmeg
Pinch of cayenne pepper
Freshly ground black pepper to taste
3 tablespoons finely chopped parsley
1/2 cup finely grated Gruyère or Swiss
   cheese

1. Preheat the oven to 425 degrees.

2. Trim off the stem end of the eggplant. Cut the eggplant in half lengthwise. Run a sharp paring knife around the inside perimeter of each half, about 1/2 inch from the skin. Do not penetrate the skin. Score the insides of each half with the paring knife, running it to within about 1/2 inch of the bottom skin. The scoring should have a diamond pattern.

3. Sprinkle the top of each half with salt. Place the halves, cut side up, in a baking dish. Place in the oven and bake for about 20 minutes. Remove and let cool.

4. Meanwhile, heat 1 tablespoon butter in a saucepan and add the flour, stirring with a wire whisk. Add the milk, stirring rapidly with the whisk. When blended and smooth, remove from the heat.

5. Heat the remaining 1 tablespoon butter in a saucepan and add the onion and shallots. Cook, stirring, until they are wilted. Add the mushrooms and sprinkle with lemon juice. Cook, stirring, until the mushrooms give up their liquid. Cook until the liquid evaporates.

6. When the eggplant halves are cool enough to handle, scrape away the inside pulp, leaving a shell for stuffing. Chop the eggplant pulp. Add the pulp to the mushrooms and cook, stirring, over low heat, about 5 minutes.

7. Drain the oysters and reserve the liquor. There should be 3 to 4 tablespoons. Add this to the eggplant-and-mushroom mixture. Cook about 4 minutes. Pour and scrape the white sauce into the eggplant-and-mushroom mixture. Stir in the nutmeg, cayenne, salt, and pepper.

8. Add the shucked, drained oysters and parsley. Blend. Spoon an equal portion of the filling into each eggplant shell. Arrange the eggplant halves, stuffed side up, in a baking dish. Sprinkle the top of each with an equal portion of the cheese. Place in the oven and bake 25 minutes.

9. Cut each eggplant half crosswise into serving pieces.

YIELD: 4 TO 6 SERVINGS.

EGGPLANT WITH HAM STUFFING

4 tablespoons butter
1 1/2 cups finely chopped onions (about 1/2 pound)
1 garlic clove, finely minced
1 pound fresh mushrooms, finely chopped (about 4 cups)
Juice of 1 lemon
Salt to taste, if desired
Freshly ground pepper to taste
3 tablespoons finely chopped parsley
1/2 teaspoon dried thyme
2 tablespoons finely chopped fresh basil

1/2 pound sliced boiled ham, finely chopped
10 tablespoons fresh bread crumbs
7 tablespoons freshly grated Parmesan cheese
2 large or 3 medium eggplants (about 2 1/2 pounds)
Flour for dredging
1 cup peanut, vegetable, or corn oil, approximately
Tomato Sauce (page 271)

1. Heat the butter and add the onions and garlic. Cook, stirring, until onions are wilted, about 5 minutes. Add the mushrooms, lemon juice, salt, pepper, parsley, thyme, and basil. Cook over relatively high heat, stirring frequently, until the liquid has almost completely evaporated, 8 to 10 minutes.

2. Add the ham and cook, stirring, about 4 minutes. Add 6 tablespoons bread crumbs and 3 tablespoons Parmesan cheese.

3. Trim off the ends and cut each eggplant into ½-inch slices. You should have about 16 slices.

4. Pour the flour into a baking dish and add salt and pepper to taste. Dredge the eggplant slices in the flour mixture on both sides, shaking off the excess.

5. Heat about ¼ cup oil in a large heavy skillet and add as many eggplant slices as the skillet will hold. Cook until golden brown on one side, 1½ to 2 minutes, adding more oil, little by little. The point is to add as much oil as necessary but as little as possible. Turn the slices, cook until golden on that side, and drain on paper towels. Continue adding eggplant slices and oil as necessary until all the slices have been cooked on both sides. The total cooking time for all the slices should be about 15 minutes.

6. Select a rectangular, square, or oval baking dish. (A No. 6 Pyrex glass dish that measures 11¾ × 7½ × 1¾ inches works well.) Arrange the smaller slices of eggplant, sides touching, on the bottom of the dish. Spoon the filling in the center, spreading it out almost but not quite to the edges and mounding it in the center. Cover with the remaining eggplant slices, overlapping as necessary.

7. Blend the remaining bread crumbs and cheese and sprinkle over all.

8. When ready to cook, preheat the oven to 400 degrees.

9. Place the dish in the oven and bake 35 to 40 minutes. Remove the dish and pour off the fat that will have accumulated on top and around the edges. Let cool slightly.

10. Serve with tomato sauce.

YIELD: 6 TO 10 SERVINGS.

BEEF-STUFFED EGGPLANT

2 medium to large eggplants (about
   1¼ pounds each)
Salt to taste, if desired
1 tablespoon olive oil
1 teaspoon finely chopped garlic
1½ cups finely chopped onions
1¼ pounds ground lean beef

¾ cup cubed fresh tomatoes
½ cup raw rice
Juice of 1 lemon
¼ cup chopped parsley
Freshly ground pepper
4 tablespoons grated Parmesan cheese

1. Preheat the oven to 400 degrees.

2. Split the eggplants in half lengthwise. Run a sharp paring knife around the inside perimeter of each half, about 1 inch from the skin. Do not penetrate the skin. Score the insides of each half with the paring knife, running it to within about ½ inch of the bottom skin. The scoring should have a diamond pattern.

3. Sprinkle the tops of each half with salt. Place the halves, cut side up, in a baking dish and place in the oven. Bake about 25 minutes.

4. Heat the oil in a skillet and add the garlic and onions. Cook until the onions wilt, about 5 minutes. Add the beef, stirring and chopping down with the side of a heavy metal spoon to break up any lumps.

5. Add the tomatoes and cover. Continue cooking about 10 minutes. Uncover.

6. Meanwhile, bring about 4 cups of water to the boil. Add the rice and cook, stirring occasionally, about 10 minutes. Drain.

7. When the eggplants are ready, remove from the oven. Using a spoon, scoop out the center scored portion, leaving the ½-inch-thick shell. Chop the center pulp. There should be about 1½ cups.

8. Add the pulp to the beef mixture and continue cooking about 1 minute. Add the drained rice and stir. Add the lemon juice, parsley, and salt and pepper to taste.

9. Arrange the eggplant shells on a baking dish. Fill with the beef mixture, piling it up until all is used. Sprinkle the top of each eggplant half with 1 tablespoon grated Parmesan cheese.

10. When ready to cook, preheat the oven to 375 degrees.

11. Place the dish in the oven and bake for 30 minutes.

YIELD: 4 SERVINGS.

STUFFED MIRLITONS, CREOLE STYLE

Mirlitons are, to my mind, one of the most delectable of vegetables, a member of the squash family, and I find it curious that in America they are cooked and enjoyed almost exclusively in Louisiana. They are notably popular throughout the Caribbean, where they are known principally as chayote, but also as chocho, choko, and chuchu. In America they are also referred to as vegetable pears. They resemble pale green quince, although they are often likened in physical shape to an avocado or a pear. They have dozens of uses—stuffed, served cooked and chilled in salads, and so on.

7 mirlitons (chayotes) (about ¾ pound each)

Salt to taste, if desired

½ pound butter

½ teaspoon cayenne pepper

Freshly ground black pepper to taste

½ teaspoon dried thyme

1 teaspoon dried basil

¾ cup finely chopped onion

½ cup finely chopped sweet green pepper

1 cup finely chopped celery

1 cup Fish Stock (page 274)

2½ cups bread crumbs made from toasted bread

1 cup flour, for dredging

24 medium-size shrimp (about ¾ pound), peeled and deveined

½ pound crabmeat, preferably lump

Oil for deep-frying

1½ cups milk

2 eggs, lightly beaten

1. Put the unpeeled mirlitons in a kettle and add water to cover and salt to taste, if desired. Bring to the boil and cook about 45 minutes, or until the flesh is tender when pierced with a fork. Drain.

2. When the mirlitons are cool, peel and cut them in half. Remove the inner pit or pit coating. Reserve 6 of the halves for stuffing. Cut the remaining halves into ½-inch cubes. There should be about 4 cups.

3. Heat ¼ pound butter in a skillet and add the cubed mirliton. Cook over moderately high heat, stirring often, about 12 minutes. Sprinkle with salt, if desired, and add the cayenne, black pepper, thyme, and basil.

4. Add the onion, green pepper, celery, and 4 tablespoons butter. Cook, stirring often, about 5 minutes.

5. Add the fish stock and continue cooking over moderately high heat, stirring often, about 30 minutes. When ready, the mixture will be sticking to the bottom of the skillet and will be well browned. Add 1¼ cups bread crumbs and stir to blend, mashing down.

6. Put the flour on a plate and the bread crumbs on another plate. Set aside.

7. Add the raw shrimp and crab to the mirliton in the skillet. Cook, stirring gently and often, until the shrimp lose their raw look. Stir in the remaining 4 tablespoons butter.

8. Heat the oil to 360 degrees.

9. Combine the milk and eggs. Blend well.

10. Dip the mirliton halves in the flour and shake off the excess. Dip the flour-coated halves in the milk mixture to coat thoroughly. Drain off the excess. Dip the halves in the bread crumbs to coat well.

11. Drop the halves, 2 at a time, into the hot oil and cook until nicely browned and crisp, 3 to 4 minutes. Drain on paper towels. Continue until all the halves are fried.

12. Fill each hot mirliton half with an equal portion of the shrimp filling, piling it up. If desired, you may pick out the shrimp and arrange them neatly over the top. Serve immediately.

YIELD: 6 SERVINGS.

MIRLITONS STUFFED WITH SHRIMP

3 mirlitons (chayotes) (³/₄ to 1 pound each)
Salt to taste, if desired
³/₄ pound raw shrimp in the shell
4 tablespoons butter
1 cup finely chopped onion
1 teaspoon finely minced garlic
2 tablespoons flour

1 cup milk
¹/₄ cup finely chopped scallions
1 egg yolk
Freshly ground pepper to taste
¹/₂ cup fine fresh bread crumbs
¹/₄ cup finely chopped parsley
¹/₂ cup grated Cheddar cheese

1. Split the mirlitons in half lengthwise. Put in a kettle of cold water and add salt to taste. Bring to the boil and simmer about 10 minutes. Do not overcook or the mirlitons will become mushy. Drain and run briefly under cold water. Drain again.

2. Using a spoon or melon-ball cutter, scoop out the flesh and seeds of each half, leaving a shell about ¹/₈ inch thick or slightly thicker. Set the shells aside. Chop flesh and seeds fine. There should be about 1 cup. Set aside.

3. Peel and devein the shrimp and coarsely chop. There should be about 1¹/₄ cups. Set aside.

4. When ready to cook, preheat the oven to 425 degrees.

5. Heat 2 tablespoons butter in a saucepan and add the onion and garlic. Cook, stirring, until wilted. Sprinkle with flour and stir to distribute evenly. Add the milk, stirring rapidly with a wire whisk.

6. When the sauce is thickened and smooth, add the chopped pulp. Bring to the boil, stirring, and add the scallions.

7. Remove from the heat and stir in the egg yolk. Let stand to room temperature. Stir in the shrimp, salt, pepper, ¼ cup bread crumbs, and parsley.

8. Stuff the mirliton halves with the mixture, piling it up and smoothing it over.

9. Blend the remaining ¼ cup bread crumbs and the cheese. Sprinkle over the stuffing, patting to help it adhere. Dot with remaining 2 table-spoons butter.

10. Arrange stuffed halves in a lightly buttered baking dish and place in the oven. Bake 20 minutes.

YIELD: 6 SERVINGS.

MIRLITONS STUFFED WITH CHEESE

3 mirlitons (chayotes) (³/₄ to 1 pound each)
Salt to taste, if desired
1 ¹/₂ cups fine fresh bread crumbs
2 ¹/₂ cups finely grated Muenster cheese
1 egg, lightly beaten

2 teaspoons finely minced garlic
¹/₄ cup finely chopped scallions
¹/₄ teaspoon dried hot red pepper flakes
Freshly ground pepper to taste
2 tablespoons butter

1. Split the mirlitons in half lengthwise. Put them in a kettle of cold water with salt to taste. Bring to the boil and let simmer about 10 minutes. Do not overcook or the mirlitons will become mushy. Drain and run briefly under cold water. Drain again.

2. Using a spoon or melon-ball cutter, scoop out the flesh and seeds of each half, leaving a shell about ⅛ inch thick or slightly thicker. Set the shells aside. Chop the flesh and seeds fine. There should be about 1 cup.

3. When ready to cook, preheat the oven to 425 degrees.

4. In a mixing bowl, combine the chopped pulp with 1 cup bread crumbs, 2 cups cheese, the egg, garlic, scallions, red pepper flakes, salt, and pepper.

5. Use this mixture to fill the mirliton halves. Pile the filling up and smooth it over.

6. Combine the remaining ½ cup cheese with remaining ½ cup bread crumbs. Sprinkle the tops with the mixture, patting to help it adhere. Dot the tops of each half with butter.

7. Arrange stuffed halves on a lightly buttered baking dish. Place in the oven and bake 20 minutes.

YIELD: 6 SERVINGS.

OKRA WITH TOMATO SAUCE

One of the best okra dishes I have ever sampled came about during a visit to Chapel Hill, North Carolina, where it was difficult to find a soul-food restaurant. I discovered Dip's Country Kitchen, and enjoyed this simply made but delectable dish of okra with tomato sauce.

2 pounds fresh baby okra, or 2 packages (10 ounces each) frozen whole okra
4 cups canned tomatoes

4 tablespoons butter
Salt to taste, if desired
Freshly ground pepper to taste

1. Wash the okra well in cold water, whether fresh or frozen. If frozen is used, continue rinsing until the okra is defrosted. Drain well.

2. Put the okra in a saucepan and add about ½ cup cold water. Bring to the boil and cover. Let cook about 7 minutes.

3. Meanwhile, blend the tomatoes thoroughly in the container of a food processor or electric blender.

4. Drain the okra and add the tomatoes, butter, salt, and pepper. Bring to the boil, partly cover, and cook until the okra is tender, about 10 minutes.

YIELD: 4 TO 6 SERVINGS.

ONIONS AU GRATIN

1 1/2 pounds small white onions (36 to 48)
Salt to taste, if desired
2 tablespoons butter
2 tablespoons flour
1/2 cup heavy cream

1/8 teaspoon grated nutmeg
Freshly ground black pepper to taste
1/2 teaspoon dried thyme
1/8 teaspoon cayenne pepper
1/2 cup freshly roasted peanuts, optional

1. Do not peel the onions but put them in a saucepan and add water to cover and salt to taste. Bring to the boil and simmer until tender, 15 to 20 minutes. Drain, but reserve 1 cup of the cooking liquid. Peel the onions.

2. Heat the butter in a saucepan and add the flour, stirring with a wire whisk. When blended, add the reserved onion liquid, stirring rapidly with the whisk. When blended and smooth, add the cream, nutmeg, salt, black pepper, thyme, and cayenne. Add the onions.

3. Just before serving, bring to the boil and stir in the peanuts, if desired. Serve immediately.

YIELD: 12 SERVINGS.

SAUSAGE-STUFFED PEPPERS

Sausage-stuffed peppers were a staple in my home and they were generally made with country sausage produced by one or another fine, amateur sausage-maker in my small hometown. It is easy to make your own sausage and there are various recipes for sausage-making listed in this book.

If you can't obtain or make your own sausage, I recommend hot or sweet Italian sausages, the meat removed from the casings.

6 large, firm, unblemished sweet green peppers

1 pound hot or sweet Italian sausages

2 cups finely chopped onions

1 garlic clove, finely minced

1 1/4 pounds fresh mushrooms, cut into tiny cubes or chopped (about 3 1/2 cups)

1 cup finely chopped parsley

2 cups fine fresh bread crumbs

2 eggs

Salt to taste, if desired

Freshly ground pepper to taste

3/4 cup Tomato Sauce (page 271)

3/4 cup freshly grated Parmesan cheese

1. Preheat the oven to 425 degrees.

2. Split the peppers in half lengthwise. Remove and discard the seeds and veins.

3. Remove the meat from the sausage skins and put it in a skillet. Cook, stirring and cutting down with the side of a heavy kitchen spoon to break up any lumps in the meat.

4. When cooked through, add the onions and garlic. Cook about 5 minutes and add the mushrooms. Cook about 2 minutes and spoon the mixture into a mixing bowl. Let cool slightly.

5. Add the parsley, bread crumbs, eggs, salt, and pepper. Blend well. Spoon equal portions of the mixture into the pepper halves and smooth it over.

6. Arrange the pepper halves in a buttered baking dish. Spoon 1 tablespoon of the tomato sauce on top of each half. Sprinkle with cheese. Bake 40 to 45 minutes, or until piping hot throughout and nicely browned.

YIELD: 6 TO 12 SERVINGS.

PEPPERS STUFFED WITH PORK AND TARRAGON

4 large sweet green peppers
Salt to taste, if desired
Freshly ground pepper to taste
1 pound leftover cooked roast pork
¼ pound fresh mushrooms, rinsed and
    drained
½ bay leaf
6 tablespoons butter
1½ cups finely chopped onions
2 garlic cloves, finely minced
2 sprigs fresh thyme, finely chopped, or
    ½ teaspoon dried
2 tablespoons finely chopped parsley

1 tablespoon finely chopped fresh
    tarragon, or 1 teaspoon dried,
    crushed
1 cup cooked rice
2 eggs
½ cup pine nuts, optional
¼ cup fine fresh bread crumbs
¼ cup grated Parmesan cheese
2 cups chopped peeled tomatoes,
    preferably Italian plum tomatoes if
    canned
½ cup chicken broth

1. Split the peppers in half lengthwise. Sprinkle the insides with salt and pepper.

2. Put the meat through a meat grinder fitted with a coarse blade, or chop it fine. There should be about 4 cups. Put the meat in a mixing bowl.

3. Put the mushrooms through the grinder and set aside.

4. Chop the bay leaf with a knife or in a small, clean coffee grinder.

5. Melt 1 tablespoon butter in a skillet or saucepan and add the mushrooms, 1 cup chopped onion, and half the garlic. Cook, stirring, until the mushrooms give up most of their liquid. Cook until most of the liquid evaporates. Add the thyme, bay leaf, parsley, and tarragon.

6. Add the mushroom mixture to the pork. Add the rice, eggs, salt and pepper to taste, and the pine nuts. Blend well.

7. Stuff the pepper halves with the mixture and sprinkle with bread crumbs and cheese.

8. Grease a flameproof baking dish large enough to hold the peppers with 3 tablespoons butter. Add the remaining ½ cup chopped onion and garlic and sprinkle with salt and pepper. Arrange the peppers in the dish.

9. Blend the tomatoes in an electric blender and pour them around the peppers. Add the chicken broth. Sprinkle salt and pepper over all. Melt the remaining 2 tablespoons butter and dribble it over the peppers.

10. Preheat the oven to 350 degrees.

11. Bring the dish to the boil on top of the stove, then place it in the oven. Bake 45 minutes. Serve the peppers with the tomato sauce in the pan.

YIELD: 8 SERVINGS.

TAMALE-STYLE STUFFED PEPPERS

4 sweet red or green peppers
1 cup chopped ripe tomatoes or drained
    imported canned tomatoes
¼ cup yellow cornmeal
3 tablespoons olive oil
1 cup finely chopped onion
1 tablespoon finely minced garlic
1 pound ground lean beef
¼ cup chili powder, more or less to
    taste

1 teaspoon ground cumin
½ teaspoon ground coriander
Salt to taste, if desired
Freshly ground pepper to taste
1 cup cooked corn cut from the cob or
    drained canned whole-kernel corn
2 tablespoons chopped fresh coriander
    leaves, optional
½ cup grated Cheddar cheese

1. Preheat the oven to 350 degrees.

2. Split the peppers in half lengthwise. Remove and discard the seeds and veins. Drop the peppers into a saucepan or kettle of boiling water. When the water returns to the boil, drain the peppers.

3. Put the tomatoes in a saucepan and cook them about 3 minutes, stirring and breaking up lumps. Add the cornmeal, stirring constantly. Let cook over low heat about 10 minutes, stirring often to prevent lumping.

4. Heat 2 tablespoons olive oil in a saucepan and add the onion and garlic. Cook, stirring, until onion is wilted. Add the beef and cook, chopping down with a heavy metal spoon to break up any lumps. Add the chili powder, cumin, ground coriander, salt, and pepper. Add the tomato mixture, the corn, and the chopped fresh coriander. Blend well.

5. Select a baking dish large enough to hold the peppers in one layer. Rub with the remaining 1 tablespoon olive oil.

6. Stuff the pepper halves with equal portions of the filling. Sprinkle each stuffed pepper with 1 tablespoon grated cheese. Bake 30 minutes.

YIELD: 4 SERVINGS.

RUTABAGA AND SWEET POTATO CASSEROLE

2 pounds rutabaga (yellow turnips)
3/4 pound sweet potatoes
Salt to taste, if desired
Freshly ground pepper to taste

3 tablespoons butter, at room
  temperature
1/4 teaspoon grated nutmeg
1/3 cup heavy cream

1. Preheat the oven to 350 degrees.

2. Peel the rutabaga and sweet potatoes. Cut both in half, then into 2-inch chunks.

3. Place the rutabaga in a saucepan and the potatoes in another saucepan. Cover both with cold water and add salt. Bring to the boil and cook until tender. The potatoes will require less cooking than the rutabaga. Drain well.

4. While hot, put the vegetables through a food mill into a mixing bowl. Stir in salt and pepper to taste, 2 tablespoons butter, nutmeg, and cream.

5. Spoon the mixture into a baking dish, dot with remaining butter, and bake 20 minutes. At the last minute, run the dish under the broiler to glaze.

YIELD: 4 TO 6 SERVINGS.

MASHED RUTABAGA

1 rutabaga (about 2 pounds)
Salt to taste, if desired
Freshly ground pepper to taste

2 tablespoons butter
1/8 teaspoon freshly grated nutmeg
1/2 cup heavy cream

1. Peel the rutabaga carefully. Cut it into 1-inch cubes. There should be about 8 cups. Put the cubes in a saucepan or kettle and add water to cover and salt. Bring to the boil and cover. Cook 15 minutes, or until tender.

2. Drain and put the cubes into the container of a food processor. Add salt, pepper, butter, and nutmeg. Start processing while gradually adding the cream. Serve piping hot.

YIELD: 4 SERVINGS.

TOMATOES STUFFED WITH HAM AND RICE

6 firm, ripe tomatoes (about 3 1/2
  pounds)
6 tablespoons butter
1/2 cup finely chopped onion
1 garlic clove, finely minced
1/2 cup finely chopped sweet green
  pepper
1 pound cooked ham, ground (about 3
  cups)

2 cups cooked rice
2 eggs
1/2 cup heavy cream
Salt to taste, if desired
Freshly ground pepper to taste
1 teaspoon ground turmeric
1/4 cup finely chopped parsley
1/4 cup fine fresh bread crumbs

1. Preheat the oven to 425 degrees.

2. Cut away and discard the core from each tomato. Slice the tomatoes in half to prepare them for stuffing. Cut out a small portion from the center of each tomato half. Squeeze the tomato halves gently to remove some of the seeds. Set aside.

3. Melt 2 tablespoons butter in a skillet and add the onion, garlic, and green pepper. Cook until wilted.

4. Combine the ham, rice, eggs, cream, salt, pepper, and turmeric in a mixing bowl. Add the parsley and the onion mixture. Blend well.

5. Mound equal amounts of the filling on each tomato half. Using the fingers, smooth over the mounds of filling.

6. Sprinkle with bread crumbs. Arrange the tomatoes on a buttered baking dish. Melt the remaining 4 tablespoons butter and pour it over the stuffed tomatoes. Bake 40 to 45 minutes, or until piping hot throughout and nicely browned.

YIELD: 6 SERVINGS.

FRIED GREEN TOMATOES

Green tomatoes have always seemed to me to be one of the most curious of foods to be cooked. I have always wondered if they were first plucked and cooked because some gardener simply could not wait for the summer harvest when they were sweet, red, and luscious. I, personally, love fried green tomatoes, particularly those that are coated with cornmeal before cooking.

1 ½ pounds green tomatoes
Tabasco sauce to taste
6 tablespoons flour
6 tablespoons cornmeal
Coarse salt to taste, if desired

Freshly ground black pepper to taste
½ teaspoon cayenne pepper
¾ cup peanut or vegetable oil,
  approximately

1. Cut the tomatoes in slices about ¼ inch thick. Sprinkle the slices with Tabasco.

2. Combine the flour and cornmeal with salt, black pepper, and cayenne pepper. Put in a plastic bag. Add the tomato slices, a few at a time, and toss to coat with the flour mixture. Shake off the excess.

3. Heat about ¼ inch of oil in a skillet and fry the tomatoes, adding them a few at a time, without overcrowding, until golden brown on each side. Drain on paper towels.

4. Serve immediately. If kept, the tomatoes will turn soggy.

YIELD: 4 SERVINGS.

BROILED TOMATOES

2 ripe tomatoes (about ¾ pound)
Salt to taste, if desired
Freshly ground pepper to taste
2 garlic cloves, cut into thin slivers

1 tablespoon olive oil
1 tablespoon finely chopped fresh basil,
  optional

1. Preheat the broiler to high.

2. Cut the core from each tomato. Cut each tomato crosswise in half. Arrange the halves, cut side up, on a rack and sprinkle with salt and pepper. Stud each tomato half with equal portions of the garlic slivers. Sprinkle with oil.

3. Place the tomatoes under the broiler and broil about 5 minutes, or until the garlic slivers start to burn. Discard the garlic slivers and sprinkle with chopped basil.

YIELD: 4 SERVINGS.

CANDIED SWEET POTATOES

4 medium-size sweet potatoes (about
  1 ½ pounds)
⅔ cup plus 1 tablespoon firmly packed
  brown sugar

¼ cup water
3 tablespoons butter
1 teaspoon pure vanilla extract

1. Put the unpeeled potatoes in a saucepan and add cold water to cover. Bring to the boil and cook until barely soft, about 15 minutes. Drain.

2. Cool the potatoes and peel them. Slice them and arrange the slices, slightly overlapping, in a buttered baking dish.

3. Preheat the oven to 350 degrees.

4. In a saucepan, combine ⅔ cup brown sugar, water, and butter. Bring to the boil and let simmer 5 minutes, stirring occasionally. Add the vanilla.

5. Pour the syrup evenly over the potatoes and sprinkle with the remaining brown sugar. Place in the oven and bake 30 minutes, basting several times with the syrup.

YIELD: 4 TO 6 SERVINGS.

ORANGE AND SWEET POTATO CASSEROLE

6 sweet potatoes (about 2 pounds)
4 tablespoons butter
6 tablespoons firmly packed brown
    sugar
3 tablespoons dark rum
Salt to taste, if desired

¾ cup sectioned mandarin oranges,
    regular oranges, or tangerines, seeds
    and membranes removed and
    discarded
2 tablespoons coarsely chopped pecans

1. Put the potatoes in a kettle with water to cover and bring to the boil. Cook until tender, 30 minutes or longer. Cooking time will depend on the size of the potatoes. Drain.

2. Preheat the oven to 375 degrees.

3. Peel the potatoes and cut them into cubes. Put them through a food mill or potato ricer into a mixing bowl. Add 2 tablespoons butter, 4 tablespoons sugar, the rum, and salt. Beat thoroughly.

4. Add half the oranges to the mixture and fold them in. Turn this mixture into a buttered 2-quart casserole. Smooth over the top. Arrange the remaining orange pieces neatly over the top.

5. Combine the remaining butter, sugar, and pecans and sprinkle this over the top.

6. Place in the oven and bake 30 minutes.

YIELD: 6 SERVINGS.

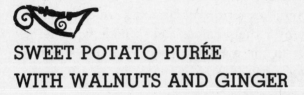

SWEET POTATO PURÉE
WITH WALNUTS AND GINGER

6 to 8 sweet potatoes (about 3 pounds)
½ cup ginger preserves
3 tablespoons dark rum
2 tablespoons butter

1 cup chopped walnuts, preferably
*   black walnuts*
¾ cup milk

1. Preheat the oven to 350 degrees.

2. Put the potatoes in a baking dish and place in the oven. Bake 1 to 2 hours, depending on the size of each potato. Press with the fingers and remove each potato as it becomes soft.

3. When all the potatoes are cooked, let them rest until cool enough to handle. Split each potato in half and scoop out the flesh.

4. Put the flesh through a fine sieve or potato ricer. There should be about 3 cups. Put this in a saucepan.

5. Combine the preserves and rum in a small saucepan. Bring to the boil, stirring. Add this to the potatoes. Add the butter, walnuts, and milk and heat to the boiling point, stirring.

YIELD: 6 TO 8 SERVINGS.

Side Dishes

RED BEANS AND RICE

1 1/2 pounds red kidney beans
1 tablespoon olive oil
1 large onion, finely chopped
1 ham steak (about 1 pound), cut into
   1/2-inch pieces
3 garlic cloves, finely chopped
1 1/2 teaspoons dried thyme
1 1/2 teaspoons dried oregano
1 bay leaf
1/2 pound salt pork, cut into small
   pieces
1 ham bone or ham hock

3 tablespoons tomato paste
Salt to taste, if desired
Freshly ground pepper to taste
1 teaspoon Tabasco sauce, or to taste
1 pound chorizo, linguica, or a mixture
   of linguica and pepperoni, cut into
   1/2-inch pieces
2 cups raw rice, cooked separately and
   steamed until dry
1 red or Bermuda onion
Olive oil, optional
Red pepper vinegar, optional

1. Wash the beans carefully and discard the broken ones. Do not, in spite of the instructions, soak them. (The modern bean has been overprocessed and needs no soaking.)

2. Heat the olive oil in a large pot and sauté the chopped onion until it is soft but not brown. Add the beans and all the remaining ingredients except the chorizo or linguica, the rice, and the purple onion.

3. Add enough water to just cover the beans. Bring to the boil, cover tightly, and lower the heat to a simmer. Stir every 10 minutes or so and add more water as needed. It is difficult to give an exact cooking time. It depends on whether the beans are purchased in a Spanish store—they taste better and will take a little longer to cook—or whether regular American red beans are used. Usually, the beans take 1½ to 2 hours to become soft yet remain whole. The sauce should be quite thick.

4. About 15 minutes before the beans have fully cooked, add the chorizo or linguica.

5. Meanwhile, cook the rice separately, making sure it is quite dry when finished.

6. Chop the red or Bermuda onion into small pieces.

7. Serve the beans on a bed of rice and offer the chopped onion separately, to be sprinkled on top of the beans. Place a cruet of olive oil and a cruet of hot pepper vinegar on the table for guests to add to the dish to their taste.

YIELD: 4 TO 6 SERVINGS.

HOMINY AND GRITS

One of the staples of my childhood was whole hominy in one form or another. There is a good deal of confusion in the minds of those who were not raised on it as to the difference between whole hominy and hominy grits. Whole hominy is made from the whole dried kernels of corn with the hull and germ removed. The kernels may be white or yellow. If dried kernels are used, they must be soaked or well simmered before using. Originally, the dried kernels were soaked in wood-ash lye and then well washed. That is why it is sometimes referred to as lye hominy. Canned hominy is excellent, and a lot more expedient to use than dried hominy. If you enjoy the flavor of tortillas, you will like the flavor of hominy, for they are both corn products and the flavors are very much akin.

Hominy grits are the whole grains of dried corn that have been ground and milled.

The largest producer of grits in this country and the brand most commonly found in America is Quaker Oats. That's the brand I grew up on. A spokesman at Quaker told me that 140 million pounds of grits are sold industry-wide each year in the United States. That's a silo-full.

I do not know of any other dish, including buttermilk biscuits and red-eye gravy, that is more down-home Southern than grits. If you are Southern born, it is something that becomes addictive from the cradle. It is a dish that I serve on special occasions when I am at home in the Hamptons on Long Island. It is a food for which I will arise mighty early when I find myself in a home or hotel in the South. Breakfast in the South without grits borders on the unthinkable, preferably served as a side dish with an egg or eggs over light, fried country ham, and red-eye gravy.

HOMINY AND CHEESE CASSEROLE

1 can whole white or yellow hominy
1 cup grated Cheddar cheese
1 can (4 ounces) chopped green chilies
1/2 cup sour cream

Salt to taste, if desired
Freshly ground pepper to taste
1/4 cup heavy cream

1. Preheat the oven to 350 degrees.

2. Drain the hominy. There should be about 3 cups. Set aside 1/4 cup cheese for the topping.

3. Put a layer of hominy on the bottom of a 4-cup casserole. Start forming layers of chilies, sour cream, the remaining 3/4 cup cheese, salt, and pepper. Pour on the heavy cream.

4. Sprinkle the reserved 1/4 cup cheese on top and bake 25 minutes.

YIELD: 4 SERVINGS.

GRITS ARE (OR IS) GOOD

As a child of the South (and one who has not infrequently been described as having cornmeal mush in his mouth), I feel notably secure in stating that grits, that celebrated Southern cereal, constitutes a plural noun. I staunchly defend this opinion, but I do feel moved to give the opposition a moment of self-defense.

A fellow Mississippian, who shall go nameless, has written to me as follows:

"I wonder whether you have quietly fallen victim of a Yankee malaise, one that causes even editors of dictionaries, alas, to refer to grits as a plural noun. Never mind what these Yankee dictionaries say, come back home where grits is IT, not them. Do Yankees refer to those oatmeal? Does one eat one grit or many? Isn't it supposed, at least by tradition, to be a singularly singular noun? Please say it's so.

"I remember, growing up on the Mississippi Gulf Coast, laughing with smirking pleasure over Yankees' references to grits as 'them' and 'those.' I do not recall whether any of them referred to the finer-ground cousin of grits, cornmeal, as 'them' or 'those' cornmeal, but maybe I was not listening.

"Until I hear better, I am going to assume that you remain well, and the dictionary usage for grits was insinuated (or were insinuated) into your otherwise impeccable article by some scurrilous (Yankee) copy editor.

"P.S.: Now, repeat after me: 'I like grits. It is good. I eat it (not them) whenever possible.' "

FRIED GRITS

2 cups water	3 eggs
2 cups plus 2 tablespoons milk	1 cup fine fresh bread crumbs
Salt to taste, if desired	2 tablespoons butter, or more
1 cup regular or quick-cooking grits	

1. In a saucepan, combine the water and 2 cups milk with salt, and gradually add the grits, stirring often. Cook until done, according to package directions.

2. Remove from the heat. Lightly beat 2 eggs, then beat them into the grits. Pour the mixture into an 8-inch-square pan. Chill until firm.

3. Cut the mixture into 1½-inch squares.

4. Beat the remaining egg and dip each square into it. Coat with the bread crumbs.

5. Heat the butter in a skillet and cook the grits squares until golden brown on both sides, turning once.

YIELD: 8 SERVINGS.

GRITS CASSEROLE

1 quart milk
½ cup plus ⅓ cup butter
1 cup regular grits
1 teaspoon salt, if desired

½ teaspoon freshly ground pepper
1 cup chopped Gruyère cheese
½ cup grated Parmesan cheese

1. Preheat the oven to 350 degrees.

2. Bring the milk just to the boil in a heatproof casserole and add ½ cup butter. Stir in the grits and continue to cook until it is the consistency of cereal.

3. Remove from the stove and add salt and pepper. Beat with an electric beater and add the remaining ⅓ cup butter.

4. Stir in the Gruyère until melted. Sprinkle Parmesan on top. Place in the oven and bake 1 hour, until crusty on top.

YIELD: 8 SERVINGS.

BAKED GRITS

1 cup regular or quick-cooking grits
1/2 pound grated sharp Cheddar cheese
8 tablespoons butter

3 eggs, well beaten
1/3 cup plus 1 tablespoon milk

1. Preheat the oven to 350 degrees.

2. Cook the grits according to package directions. Regular grits require 25 to 30 minutes of slow cooking; quick-cooking grits will take 3 to 5 minutes.

3. Stir in the cheese, butter, eggs, and milk, and pour into a buttered 3-cup baking dish. Bake 40 minutes or longer, or until set.

YIELD: 6 TO 8 SERVINGS.

BAKED GARLIC-CHEESE GRITS

1 cup quick-cooking grits
1 roll (6 ounces) garlic cheese (see note)
8 tablespoons butter
1/2 cup chopped scallions, including
    green part, optional

2 eggs, lightly beaten
3/4 cup milk

1. Cook the grits according to package directions. Stir in the cheese, butter, and scallions. Pour the mixture into a buttered 2-quart casserole. Let cool.

2. Preheat the oven to 375 degrees.

3. Blend the eggs and milk and pour over the grits. Bake about 1 hour.

YIELD: 4 TO 6 SERVINGS.

NOTE: If garlic cheese, a commercially packaged product, is not available, use 1 1/2 cups grated Cheddar cheese and 1 teaspoon finely chopped garlic.

CHEESE AND GRITS CASSEROLE

2 1/2 cups water
1/2 cup grits, preferably stone-ground
Salt to taste, if desired
2 cups grated sharp Cheddar cheese
1/2 teaspoon finely chopped garlic

3 tablespoons finely chopped jalapeño
  peppers, more or less to taste
4 eggs, lightly beaten
2 teaspoons Worcestershire sauce

1. Bring the water to the boil in a saucepan and gradually add the grits, stirring. Add salt to taste. Cover and cook about 25 minutes.

2. Meanwhile, preheat the oven to 350 degrees.

3. Add 1¾ cups cheese to the grits and stir. Add the garlic, jalapeño peppers, eggs, and Worcestershire. Blend well.

4. Pour the mixture into a 2-quart casserole and sprinkle the top with the remaining ¼ cup cheese. Place in the oven and bake 25 minutes.

YIELD: 6 SERVINGS.

BAKED RICE

2 1/2 tablespoons butter
2 tablespoons minced onion
1/4 teaspoon minced garlic
1 cup long-grain rice
1 1/2 cups Chicken Stock (page 275)
2 sprigs parsley

1 sprig fresh thyme, or 1/4 teaspoon
  dried
1/2 bay leaf
1/8 teaspoon cayenne pepper, or Tabasco
  sauce to taste

1. Preheat the oven to 400 degrees.

2. Melt 1 tablespoon butter in a heavy saucepan and cook the onion and garlic, stirring with a wooden spoon, until the onion is translucent. Add the rice and stir briefly over low heat, until all the grains are coated with butter.

3. Stir in the stock, making sure that there are no lumps in the rice. Add the parsley, thyme, bay leaf, and cayenne or Tabasco. Cover with a tight-fitting lid and place in the oven.

4. Bake the rice exactly 17 minutes. Remove the cover and discard the parsley and thyme sprigs. Using a two-pronged fork, stir in the remaining butter. If the rice is not to be served immediately, keep covered in a warm place.

YIELD: 4 SERVINGS.

RICE CREOLE

6 cups water
Salt to taste, if desired
1 1/2 cups long-grain rice

1 1/2 tablespoons butter
Freshly ground pepper to taste
1 1/2 teaspoons lemon juice

1. Bring the water to the boil in a saucepan and add salt and rice. When the water returns to the boil, let rice boil vigorously until tender, 14–17 minutes.

2. Drain in a colander. Run hot water over the rice; drain again.

3. Add the butter, salt, and pepper. Sprinkle with lemon juice and toss until the grains are coated.

YIELD: 6 TO 8 SERVINGS.

DIRTY RICE

One of the most humorous names ever applied to a dish, Southern or otherwise, is "dirty rice," a well-known Louisiana dish of Cajun inspiration. It is called that because of the darkened color of the rice, once the dish is made. The color comes from the other ingredients, which include the chopped-up livers and gizzards of a chicken. I find this dish absolutely delectable.

1 pound chicken livers

1 pound chicken gizzards

10 tablespoons peanut, vegetable, or corn oil

6 cups peeled eggplant cut into 1-inch cubes

1 pound ground pork

1 1/2 cups finely chopped sweet green peppers

1 cup finely chopped celery

1 cup finely chopped onion

1 teaspoon cayenne pepper

Salt to taste, if desired

1 teaspoon white pepper

1 1/2 teaspoons black pepper

6 1/2 cups Chicken Stock (page 275)

1 cup long-grain rice

1 cup chopped scallions

1. Put the livers and gizzards in separate piles on a flat surface and chop until fine, or use a food processor but do not blend to a purée. The gizzards and livers must retain their character.

2. Heat the oil in a skillet until it is almost smoking. Add the eggplant and cook, stirring, about 5 minutes.

3. Add the pork and stir with a heavy metal spoon, chopping down with the sides of the spoon to break up lumps. Add the gizzards. Cover closely and cook about 10 minutes.

4. With the spoon, mash down on the eggplant pieces. Add green peppers, celery, and onion. Cover and continue cooking over high heat about 10 minutes. Stir from the bottom to scrape up the brown particles. Add the cayenne, salt, white pepper, and black pepper. Cook, stirring always from the bottom to incorporate the dark brown matter that sticks to the bottom of the skillet, about 10 minutes.

5. Add the broth and stir to clean the bottom. Cover and cook about 20 minutes. Uncover and stir in the livers and gizzards. Cook about 5 minutes. Add the rice and cover. Cook 15 to 20 minutes, or until the rice is tender. Stir in the scallions, and serve.

YIELD: 10 TO 12 SERVINGS.

SAVANNAH RED RICE

No one seems to know precisely why red rice is so firmly associated with Savannah. The connection, however, is as traditional as New England and clam chowder, Philadelphia and scrapple, San Francisco and that regional fish stew known as cioppino. Oddly enough the rice, cooked with onions, celery, green peppers, and tomatoes, is referred to in other sections of the country as "Spanish rice."

¼ pound lean bacon
1 cup finely chopped onion
1 cup finely chopped celery
1 cup finely chopped sweet green
 peppers
3½ cups long-grain rice

4 cups canned tomatoes with their
 liquid
Salt to taste, if desired
Freshly ground pepper to taste
1½ teaspoons sugar
¼ teaspoon Tabasco sauce

1. Preheat the oven to 325 degrees.

2. Cut the bacon into small cubes. Put the cubes into a skillet and cook, stirring, until the pieces are crisp and browned. Remove the pieces using a slotted spoon. Set the bacon aside and leave the fat in the skillet.

3. To the fat remaining in the skillet, add the onion, celery, and green peppers. Cook, stirring, until the onion is wilted. Add the rice and stir.

4. Put the tomatoes with their liquid in the container of a food processor and blend thoroughly. Add this to the rice and stir. Add the salt, pepper, sugar, and Tabasco.

5. Bring to the boil, stirring, and cook for about 5 minutes.

6. Pour and scrape the rice mixture into a casserole and cover. Bake, stirring occasionally, about 1 hour, or until the rice is tender and the liquid is absorbed.

YIELD: 12 TO 16 SERVINGS.

PINTO OR COWGIRL BEANS

1 1/4 cups pinto beans (about 1/2
    pound)
6 1/2 cups water, approximately
Salt to taste, if desired
3/4 cup finely chopped onion
1 tablespoon safflower, corn,
    or peanut oil

2 teaspoons finely chopped seeded fresh
    jalapeño peppers
3/4 cup finely diced tomatoes
6 tablespoons chopped fresh coriander

1. Pick over the beans and wash them well. Put them in a kettle and add
the water. Bring to the boil, partly covered, and let simmer 1 hour.

2. Add salt and half the onion. Continue cooking, uncovered, about 30
minutes longer.

3. Heat the oil in a small skillet and add the remaining onion and the
jalapeño peppers. Cook briefly until the onion is wilted. Add the tomatoes
and coriander and cook, stirring, about 3 minutes.

4. Scoop out 1 cup beans, plus a little of their liquid, and place them in
the container of a food processor or electric blender. Blend until as fine as
possible. Return this to the beans.

5. Add the tomato mixture to the beans and continue to simmer, about
5 minutes.

YIELD: 6 TO 8 SERVINGS.

LENTIL AND SCALLION SALAD

2 small smoked pork hocks, or 1/2
    pound smoked pork
6 cups water, approximately
1 pound lentils
Salt to taste, if desired

1/4 cup chopped scallions
4 to 6 tablespoons olive oil
2 to 3 tablespoons wine vinegar
Freshly ground pepper to taste
1/4 to 1 teaspoon dry mustard

1. Put the pork hocks in a large saucepan and add the water. Bring to the boil and cover. Simmer 1½ hours.

2. Remove the pork from the saucepan and skim off any fat. Add the lentils and salt. Bring to the boil and simmer, covered, about 25 minutes, or until tender. It may be necessary to add more water to the saucepan. The lentils, as they cook, should be almost but not quite covered with the boiling liquid. When the lentils are tender, drain them. They must not be cooked to a mushy stage.

3. Let the lentils cool.

4. Cut the meat off the pork hocks and add it to the lentils. Add the remaining ingredients with salt to taste. Blend well and let stand for several hours to develop the flavor.

YIELD: 6 OR MORE SERVINGS.

GOLDSBORO POTATO SALAD

6 potatoes (about 1¾ pounds)
Salt to taste, if desired
3 hard-cooked eggs

½ cup finely chopped red onion
1 cup mayonnaise (see note)
¼ cup chopped sour pickles

1. Put the potatoes in a kettle and add cold water to cover and salt to taste. Bring to the boil and cook until quite tender when tested with a fork. Drain and let cool.

2. Peel the potatoes and cut into ½-inch cubes. Put into a bowl.

3. Coarsely chop the eggs and add to the potatoes. Add the onion, mayonnaise, and pickles. Toss to blend thoroughly.

YIELD: 8 OR MORE SERVINGS.

NOTE: *Though homemade mayonnaise may be used in the preparation of this potato salad and the Goldsboro Coleslaw, most of the barbecue restaurants in North Carolina use Hellmann's mayonnaise.*

POTATO SALAD WITH BACON AND ONION

2 pounds small new red-skinned
   potatoes
Salt to taste, if desired
6 slices of lean bacon
4 tablespoons finely chopped onion
3 tablespoons finely chopped parsley

Freshly ground pepper to taste
1 tablespoon wine or herb vinegar
5 tablespoons peanut, vegetable, or corn
   oil
Romaine lettuce leaves or other greens
   for garnish

1. Put the potatoes in a kettle and add cold water to cover and salt to taste. Bring to the boil and cook until tender, 15 to 20 minutes. Remove from the heat and drain.

2. As soon as the potatoes are cool enough to handle, peel them. Cut them into ¼-inch-thick slices and put them in a mixing bowl.

3. Meanwhile, cook the bacon until crisp. Drain on paper towels. Chop coarsely. Set aside.

4. To the potatoes, add the onion, parsley, and salt and pepper to taste. Add the vinegar and oil and half the bacon and toss.

5. Spoon into a salad bowl and garnish with the remaining bacon bits and small heart of romaine lettuce leaves or other greens.

YIELD: 6 TO 8 SERVINGS.

GOLDSBORO COLESLAW

1 small cabbage (about 1½ pounds)
1½ cups mayonnaise
1 cup finely chopped onion

Salt to taste, if desired
Freshly ground pepper to taste

1. Remove the core of the cabbage and the tough or blemished outer leaves. Cut the head in half and shred fine. There should be 6 cups. Coarsely chop the shreds and put them into a mixing bowl.

2. Add the mayonnaise, onion, salt, and pepper and toss to blend well.

YIELD: 8 TO 12 SERVINGS.

MY MOTHER'S 1930s PARTY SALAD

In all my years at *The New York Times,* I never printed a recipe for commercially packaged, fruit-flavored gelatin salads—not until I wrote a nostalgic piece about my mother's cooking. She was, many years ago, interviewed by a then-well-known and now defunct magazine called *Liberty.* The author called her "the best cook in town" and printed a few of her most admired recipes. My mother was a great bridge player, and when she entertained, one of her party dishes was a three-layered gelatin affair. The bottom layer was green and made with lime-flavored gelatin. The middle layer was white and made with cream cheese flavored with grated onion and lemon. The top layer was red, a jellied, well-seasoned tomato aspic. It is not the most sophisticated dish on earth, but it sure smacks of my childhood.

FIRST LAYER:

1 box (3 ounces) lime-flavored gelatin

SECOND LAYER:

2 packages (3 ounces each) cream cheese, at room temperature
¼ cup milk
1 teaspoon finely grated raw onion
1 tablespoon lemon juice

Salt to taste, if desired
1 envelope unflavored gelatin
¼ cup boiling water
1 cup heavy cream, whipped

THIRD LAYER:

2 cups tomato juice
1 envelope unflavored gelatin
Salt to taste, if desired
Freshly ground pepper to taste

2 tablespoons fresh lemon juice
1/2 teaspoon Worcestershire sauce
Tabasco sauce to taste
1 large celery rib

THE GARNISH:

1/4 cup Mayonnaise (page 263)

1. Prepare the lime gelatin according to package directions. Pour the mixture into a cake pan measuring 8 × 8 × 2 inches. Refrigerate until set.

2. For the second layer, put the cream cheese and milk into a deep mixing bowl. Beat with an electric mixer on low speed. When thoroughly blended and smooth, add the onion, lemon juice, and salt.

3. Put the gelatin and water in a heatproof cup and set the mixture in a small pan of boiling water. Stir until gelatin dissolves and becomes clear. Pour this into the cream cheese mixture. Fold in the whipped cream. Do not refrigerate or allow to set.

4. When the lime gelatin is chilled and set, pour the cream cheese mixture on top, smoothing it over. Refrigerate.

5. For the third layer, put 1/4 cup tomato juice in a heatproof cup and stir in the gelatin. Set the cup in a small pan of boiling water. Stir until gelatin dissolves.

6. Put the remaining tomato juice in a mixing bowl and add salt, pepper, lemon juice, Worcestershire, and Tabasco. Add the gelatin.

7. Grate the celery very fine and add it to the tomato juice mixture.

8. When the cream cheese layer is set, pour the tomato mixture over all. Chill until set.

9. When ready to serve, run a knife around the outside of the layers. Turn the pan upside down on a large plate. Run a towel under very hot water and squeeze well. Place the hot towel over bottom of pan. Repeat until the salad can be shaken loose from the pan.

10. Run a long sharp carving knife under hot water. Wipe dry. Cut the salad into 8 to 12 squares. Serve, topping each square with a dab of mayonnaise.

YIELD: 8 TO 12 SERVINGS.

CORN RELISH

8 ears cooked corn
1/2 pound cabbage, finely chopped
   (about 2 cups)
1 cup finely chopped onion
1/2 cup chopped celery
2 tablespoons finely chopped fresh
   ginger, or more
2 cups chopped, cored, seeded sweet red
   and green peppers
2 tablespoons dry mustard

2 tablespoons salt, if desired
1 teaspoon freshly ground black pepper
2 teaspoons turmeric
1 teaspoon celery seeds
1 1/2 teaspoons mustard seed
3/4 cup water
2 cups distilled white vinegar
1 whole dried red chili pepper
1 cup sugar

1. Slice and scrape the kernels from the cob. There should be at least 4 cups.

2. Combine the corn with the remaining ingredients in a saucepan and bring to the boil, stirring. Cook 20 minutes. Remove and discard the dried red pepper.

3. Pack the relish boiling hot into 6 hot half-pint jars or 3 hot pint jars, leaving 1/4-inch space at the top before capping. Process in a boiling-water bath for 10 minutes.

YIELD: 3 PINTS.

CHOW-CHOW RELISH

1 quart chopped cabbage (about 1
  small head)
3 cups chopped cauliflower (about 1
  medium head)
2 cups chopped green tomatoes (about 4
  medium)
2 cups chopped onions
2 cups chopped sweet green peppers
1 cup chopped sweet red peppers

3 tablespoons salt
2 1/2 cups distilled white vinegar
1 1/2 cups sugar
2 teaspoons celery seed
2 teaspoons dry mustard
1 teaspoon mustard seed
1 teaspoon turmeric
1/2 teaspoon ground ginger

1. Combine the chopped vegetables and sprinkle with salt. Let stand 4 to 6 hours in a cool place. Drain well.

2. In a saucepan, combine the vinegar, sugar, and spices and simmer 10 minutes. Add the vegetables and simmer 10 minutes more. Bring to the boil.

3. Pack, boiling hot, into hot pint jars, leaving 1/4-inch headspace. Adjust the caps. Process 10 minutes in a boiling-water bath.

YIELD: ABOUT 4 PINTS.

DILLY BEANS

2 pounds green beans, trimmed
1 teaspoon cayenne pepper
4 garlic cloves
4 large dill sprigs

1/4 cup salt
2 1/2 cups vinegar
2 1/2 cups water

1. Pack the beans, lengthwise, into 4 hot pint jars, leaving ¼-inch headspace. To each pint, add ¼ teaspoon cayenne pepper, 1 garlic clove, and 1 dill sprig.

2. Combine the remaining ingredients and bring to the boil. Pour, boiling hot, over the beans, leaving ¼-inch headspace. Remove air bubbles. Adjust caps. Process 10 minutes in a boiling-water bath.

YIELD: ABOUT 4 PINTS.

WATERMELON RIND PRESERVES

1 watermelon (about 9 pounds)   4 cups sugar
4 tablespoons salt   ¼ cup lemon juice
1 tablespoon ground ginger   1 thinly sliced lemon

1. To prepare the rind, trim the green skin and pink flesh from thick watermelon rind; cut the rind into 1-inch pieces.

2. Dissolve the salt in 2 quarts of cold water and pour over rind. Let stand 5 to 6 hours. Drain, rinse, and drain again. Cover with cold water and let stand 30 minutes.

3. Drain the rind. Sprinkle ginger over it, cover with water, and cook until fork-tender, 8 to 10 minutes. Drain.

4. Combine the sugar, lemon juice, and 7 cups water. Boil 5 minutes, add the rind, and boil gently for 30 minutes. Add the sliced lemon and cook until the melon rind is clear.

5. Pack the rind, boiling hot, into 6 hot half-pint or 3 hot pint jars, leaving ¼-inch headspace. Adjust the caps. Process 20 minutes in a boiling-water bath.

YIELD: ABOUT 6 HALF-PINTS.

HOT PEPPER JELLY

I am persuaded that Southerners (including those of the Southwest) have a much greater addiction to hot or spicy foods than those of any other region. This is true of other nations; the hotter the climate, the greater the craving for foods that enliven the tongue and stomach—India, Mexico, China, or wherever. This is true even for certain sweet foods such as Hot Pepper Jelly, which is made with hot red or green chilies cooked with sugar and vinegar. It is a delectable "snack" food when spooned onto crackers spread with a relatively soft Brie cheese.

1 cup cored and ground sweet red or green peppers, with the seeds
1/2 cup cored and ground long hot red or green peppers (see note)
6 1/2 cups sugar

1 1/2 cups white vinegar
1/4 teaspoon salt, if desired
1 bottle (6 ounces) fruit pectin
Red or green food coloring, optional

1. Combine the sweet peppers, hot peppers, sugar, vinegar, and salt in a saucepan. Simmer about 10 minutes, stirring occasionally.

2. Strain or not, as desired, and return mixture to the saucepan. If strained, the solids are good as a relish. Pour in the pectin and bring to the boil. Stir in the food coloring. Pour into sterilized half-pint jars and seal with paraffin. Store in a cool place.

YIELD: 8 TO 10 HALF-PINTS.

NOTE: *If long hot peppers are not available, drained tinned jalapeño peppers, available in many supermarkets, may be substituted according to taste.*

PEPPER RELISH

12 sweet red peppers (about 4 1/2
  pounds)
12 sweet green peppers (about 4 1/2
  pounds)
1 onion (about 1/3 pound)

4 cups boiling water
2 cups cider vinegar
2 cups sugar
Salt to taste, if desired

1. Rinse the peppers and pat dry. Cut each in half, discard the seeds and the white inside veins. Outfit a food chopper or grinder with a coarse blade. Put the peppers through the food chopper or grinder. There should be 7 cups of each. Put them in a mixing bowl.

2. Peel the onion and cut it into cubes. Put the cubes through the food chopper or grinder. Add this to the peppers.

3. Pour boiling water over all and let stand 10 minutes.

4. Line a mixing bowl with cheesecloth and pour the pepper mixture into it. Bring up the edges of the cloth and tie with string to make a bag. Let the pepper mixture hang overnight to drain, or for a minimum of 8 hours. Discard the liquid.

5. Put the pepper mixture into a kettle and add the vinegar, sugar, and salt. Bring to the boil and cook 20 minutes. Pour into 4 hot pint-size sterile jars and seal at once.

YIELD: 4 PINTS.

PICKLED OKRA

3 1/2 pounds small, unblemished okra
  pods
4 or 5 whole garlic cloves, peeled
4 or 5 dried whole small hot red
  peppers

4 or 5 teaspoons dill seeds
6 teaspoons salt
4 1/2 cups white vinegar
1 1/2 cups water

1. Leave a small portion of the stem end on each okra pod. Rinse the okra and drain well.

2. Pack enough okra into 4 or 5 pint jars to pack them firmly, but leave 1/4 inch headspace. Insert 1 garlic clove, 1 hot red pepper, and 1 teaspoon of dill seeds into each jar as you go along.

3. Combine the salt, vinegar, and water and bring to the boil. Pour equal amounts of the boiling liquid over the okra to cover, leaving 1/4 inch headspace. Seal tightly with screw-top lids. Process 10 minutes in a boiling-water bath.

YIELD: 4 OR 5 PINTS.

JERUSALEM ARTICHOKE PICKLES

1 pound (8 to 10) Jerusalem artichokes
  (sunchokes)
4 cups water
1/2 cup coarse salt
2 to 6 whole, very small white onions,
  peeled
2/3 cup white wine vinegar
2 tablespoons brown sugar

4 whole allspice
4 whole cloves
1 teaspoon whole mustard seeds
1/2 teaspoon celery seeds
1/4 teaspoon turmeric
1/2 teaspoon dry mustard
1/2 teaspoon peppercorns

1. Peel the artichokes with a swivel-bladed vegetable peeler. If they are very large, cut them in half or even into quarters.

2. Combine the water and salt in a mixing bowl and stir until the salt dissolves. Add the artichokes and let stand in a cool place overnight.

3. Drain the artichokes and put them in a 1-pint sterilized glass preserving jar. Add the small white onions. Press down firmly.

4. Combine the vinegar, sugar, allspice, cloves, mustard seeds, celery seeds, turmeric, dry mustard, and peppercorns in a saucepan. Bring to the boil.

5. Pour the liquid and spices over the artichokes. Seal tightly and let stand about 2 months before using.

YIELD: 1 PINT.

OLD-FASHIONED APPLE BUTTER

6 pounds apples, unpeeled but cut into
eighths
2 cups fresh apple cider
5 cups sugar, approximately

1 teaspoon ground cloves
1 teaspoon ground cinnamon
1/2 teaspoon ground allspice

1. Put the cut-up apples in a large heavy kettle. Add the cider and cover, cooking over low heat until the apples are very tender. Stir occasionally and watch carefully so that they do not burn.

2. Cool slightly and run through a food mill or sieve.

3. Measure the apple mixture and combine with half as much sugar. Stir in the spices and simmer over low heat until dark and thick, about 2 hours. Be sure to stir frequently to avoid scorching.

4. Remove from the heat and pour into hot, sterilized jars, leaving about 1/4-inch headroom. Adjust lids, and process pints in a boiling-water bath for 10 minutes. The apple butter will thicken as it stands.

YIELD: APPROXIMATELY 5 PINTS.

Breads & Batters

SOUTHERN CORN BREAD

There are more recipes for corn bread than there are magnolia trees in the South. This is a family standard.

1/3 cup sifted flour
1 1/2 cups sifted cornmeal
1 teaspoon baking soda
1/2 teaspoon salt, if desired

2 eggs
1 cup buttermilk
2 cups whole milk
1 1/2 tablespoons butter

1. Preheat the oven to 350 degrees.
2. Sift the flour, cornmeal, baking soda, and salt into a mixing bowl. Beat the eggs until foamy and stir them into the dry mixture. Stir in the buttermilk and 1 cup whole milk.
3. Heat the butter in a 9 × 2-inch black skillet, and when it is very hot but not brown, pour in the batter. Carefully pour the remaining 1 cup whole milk on top of the batter without stirring. Place the dish in the oven and bake 50 minutes, or until set and baked through. Slice into wedges.

YIELD: 8 SERVINGS.

NOTE: *If this is to be used as a stuffing, it is best if it is made a day or so ahead.*

CORN STICKS

½ cup yellow cornmeal
½ cup flour
2 tablespoons sugar
1½ teaspoons baking powder
Salt to taste, if desired
¾ cup plus 3 tablespoons heavy cream

2 tablespoons melted butter
1 egg, separated
1 tablespoon butter
½ cup corn kernels freshly cut from
  the cob

1. Preheat the oven to 425 degrees.

2. Select a standard mold for making corn sticks. Place it in the oven until thoroughly heated.

3. Meanwhile, combine the cornmeal, flour, sugar, baking powder, and salt in a mixing bowl. Blend well.

4. Blend the cream, melted butter, and egg yolk. Add this to the cornmeal mixture, stirring to blend.

5. Melt the 1 tablespoon butter in a small skillet and add the corn. Cook, stirring, just until heated through. Stir this into the batter.

6. Beat the egg white, and fold it into the mixture.

7. Brush the corn stick mold lightly with oil. Spoon an equal portion of the filling inside each corn stick mold.

8. Bake 15 to 20 minutes. Serve hot.

YIELD: 6 TO 8 CORN STICKS.

CORN AND CHEESE BREAD

1 cup canned cream-style corn
1 cup yellow cornmeal
3 eggs
Salt to taste, if desired
1/2 teaspoon baking soda

3/4 cup buttermilk
*1/3 cup melted vegetable shortening or
    oil*
3/4 cup grated sharp Cheddar cheese
2 tablespoons butter

1. Preheat the oven to 400 degrees.
2. In a mixing bowl, combine the corn, cornmeal, eggs, salt, baking soda, and buttermilk. Stir well and add the shortening and 1/2 cup cheese. Stir to blend.
3. Meanwhile, put the butter in a 9-inch skillet, preferably of black iron. Place it in the oven and heat until the butter melts without browning.
4. Pour the batter into the skillet. Sprinkle with the remaining cheese and bake 30 minutes, or until the bread is firm and golden brown on top.

YIELD: 8 SERVINGS.

JALAPEÑO CORN BREAD

I have no earthly idea how or when I came by this recipe for a corn bread made with jalapeño peppers, Cheddar cheese, and cream-style corn. It is, however, to my mind one of the great adventures in taste. It is excellent when used as a replacement for regular corn bread in a poultry stuffing.

1 can (8 1/2 ounces) cream-style corn
1 cup yellow cornmeal
3 eggs
1 teaspoon salt, if desired
1/2 teaspoon baking soda

3/4 cup milk
1/3 cup corn oil
1 cup grated sharp Cheddar cheese
1/4 cup chopped jalapeño peppers
2 tablespoons butter

1. Preheat the oven to 400 degrees.

2. In a mixing bowl, combine the corn, cornmeal, eggs, salt, baking soda, milk, oil, ½ cup cheese, and the jalapeño peppers. Blend well.

3. Meanwhile, put the butter in a 1½-quart casserole (preferably a glazed Mexican earthenware casserole) or a 9-inch skillet. Place the casserole in the oven until the butter is hot but not brown. Immediately pour in the corn bread mixture. Sprinkle with the remaining ½ cup cheese, and bake 40 minutes.

YIELD: 8 SERVINGS.

HOT-WATER CORN BREAD

1 cup white cornmeal
4 teaspoons sifted flour
2 teaspoons baking powder
½ teaspoon salt, if desired

1 tablespoon sugar
1¼ cups boiling water
Fat for deep-frying

1. Put the cornmeal in a mixing bowl and add the flour, baking powder, salt, and sugar.

2. It is imperative that the water be boiling before it is added. Stir the mixture well while adding the boiling water. Blend thoroughly.

3. Meanwhile, heat the fat to 360 degrees. Drop the batter by spoonfuls (about 1½ tablespoons) into it. Cook until golden brown and crisp, turning the pieces as they cook.

YIELD: ABOUT 30 PIECES.

TORTA DE MASA

This is a fine-grained, sweet corn bread, to be served with Tex-Mex food.

1 cup masa harina (see note)
Salt to taste, if desired
1½ teaspoons baking powder
8 tablespoons sugar

10 tablespoons butter, at room
temperature
½ cup cold water
6 eggs, separated

1. Preheat the oven to 375 degrees.
2. Butter a loaf pan measuring 9 × 5 × 3 inches. It is not essential but it is recommended that you line the bottom of the pan with a rectangle of parchment paper, neatly cut to fit.
3. Sift together the *masa harina,* salt, baking powder, and sugar into the bowl of an electric mixer.
4. Start beating on low speed, while slowly adding the butter. As you go along, gradually increase the speed to high.
5. Reduce the speed to low and beat in the water. Add the 6 egg yolks, beating on medium speed until well blended.
6. Beat the whites until stiff and fold them in, carefully lifting from the bottom. Pour and scrape the mixture into the prepared loaf pan. Place in the oven and bake 45 minutes.
7. Unmold the loaf while it is still hot. Serve sliced, hot or lukewarm.

YIELD: 8 TO 10 SERVINGS.

NOTE: *Masa harina is a fine-grained cornmeal available where Mexican specialties are sold. This dish may be made with regular white or yellow cornmeal, but it is imperative that you add ¾ cup of all-purpose flour. Sift together the cornmeal, flour, salt, baking powder, and sugar into the bowl of an electric mixer. Proceed with step 4.*

SALT-RISING BREAD

Salt-rising bread is one of the greatest inventions, which I think of as peculiarly Southern. It smells and tastes a little bit "cheesy" and is not to everyone's liking, but it makes excellent sandwiches and toast. Because of the timing and temperature, it takes a little practice to make a perfect loaf.

2 medium-size potatoes, peeled and thinly sliced
2 tablespoons cornmeal
1/2 tablespoon sugar
1 teaspoon salt
2 cups boiling water

2 cups milk, scalded and cooled to lukewarm
1/8 teaspoon baking soda
8 cups sifted flour, approximately
4 tablespoons shortening or butter, at room temperature

1. Place the potatoes, cornmeal, sugar, and salt in a 3-quart bowl. Add the boiling water and stir until the sugar and salt are dissolved. Cover with plastic wrap or foil. Set the bowl in a pan of warm water over the pilot light of a stove, or where it will stay at about 120 degrees, until small bubbles show in the surface, 24 hours or longer.

2. Remove the potatoes to a sieve and press out the excess moisture. Add this liquid to the potato water still in the bowl. Discard the potatoes.

3. Add the milk, baking soda, and 4 cups flour to the bowl. Stir until smooth. Set the bowl again in the pan of warm water and let it stand for about 2 hours, until the dough is almost doubled in bulk.

4. Cut the shortening or butter into 1 cup of the remaining flour. Add this to the dough. Add enough additional flour, about 3 cups, to make a moderately stiff dough. Knead on a floured surface quickly and lightly. Do not let the dough get cold.

5. Return the dough to the bowl, grease the surface of the dough, and let it rise for about 2 hours, until doubled in bulk.

6. Turn the risen dough out on a lightly floured surface and shape into 2 loaves. Place in greased loaf pans (9 × 5 × 3 inches) and grease the tops of the loaves. Let rise again for about 2 hours, until almost doubled in bulk or slightly above the tops of the pans. Sprinkle the tops with cornmeal, if desired.

7. About 15 minutes before the loaves have finished rising, preheat the oven to 400 degrees.

8. Bake the loaves for 15 minutes, then lower the oven temperature to 350 degrees and bake for about 35 minutes longer, or until the bread shrinks from the sides of the pans and is well browned. Cool on a rack.

YIELD: 2 LOAVES.

CRACKLIN' BREAD

When I was a child in Mississippi, my family owned an enormous cast-iron pot with four small "legs". It was used in my infancy to render pork fat, which was used for almost all the frying needs in the kitchen. When the fat was rendered, the crisp, crunchy, solid pieces were broken into pieces and eaten, to the great delight of young and old alike. These pieces were known as *cracklin's* or, to use the dictionary spelling, *cracklings*. One of the greatest uses for them was in the preparation of cracklin' bread. Cracklin's are sold today in plastic bags, but they taste awfully commercial. You can make acceptable cracklin's by rendering store-bought pork fat in your home.

1 1/2 cups cornmeal, preferably stone-
* or water-ground*
Salt to taste, if desired
1 teaspoon baking powder
1 1/2 cups buttermilk

1 egg, lightly beaten
1/2 cup Cracklin's (see following
* instructions)*
4 tablespoons butter

1. Preheat the oven to 450 degrees.

2. Sift together the cornmeal, salt, and baking powder into a mixing bowl. Start stirring with a wire whisk while gradually adding the buttermilk. Stir in the beaten egg. When well blended, stir in the cracklin's.

3. Put the butter into a 9-inch black iron skillet and heat on top of the stove until it is quite hot but not brown. Pour half the butter into the batter and stir to blend. Pour the batter immediately into the hot skillet and place on the center rack of the oven. Bake 30 to 35 minutes, or until the crust is golden brown.

4. Cut into wedges and serve.

YIELD: 8 SERVINGS.

CRACKLIN'S

These crisp pieces are not the real McCoy, which are made with fresh pork fat used at hog-killing time in the South. They are, however, an acceptable substitute and work far better than the store-bought, plastic-wrapped variety. Fatback is available at supermarket meat counters.

½ pound fatback

1. Cut the fatback into slices and cut the slices into thin strips. Stack or align the strips and cut them into small cubes. There should be about 1 cup.

2. Put the cubes in one layer in a small skillet and barely cover with water. Bring to the boil and cook until the water evaporates. Continue cooking until the pieces are totally rendered of fat, until they are quite crisp and browned. Do not allow to burn.

3. Drain the pieces in a sieve and pour them onto paper towels to drain further.

YIELD: SLIGHTLY MORE THAN 1 CUP.

HUSH PUPPIES

There is a well-known legend about the fried corn bread known as hush puppies. Legend has it that in the days during the Civil War, Southerners would sit beside a campfire out-of-doors to prepare their meals. They would fry their cornmeal batter, and if Yankee soldiers came close, they would toss one or more of the fried cakes to their yapping dogs with the command, "Hush, puppies."

2 cups cornmeal, preferably water- or
   stone-ground
1 tablespoon flour
1/2 teaspoon baking soda
1 teaspoon baking powder
1 teaspoon salt, if desired

3 tablespoons finely chopped scallions
1 cup plus 3 tablespoons buttermilk
1 egg, lightly beaten
Corn, peanut, or other vegetable oil for
   deep-frying

1. Sift together the cornmeal, flour, baking soda, baking powder, and salt into a mixing bowl. Add the scallions, buttermilk, and egg. Stir until thoroughly mixed.

2. Heat the oil to 375 degrees and drop the batter by spoonfuls (about 2 teaspoons) into the hot oil. Fry until golden brown. Drain and serve hot.

YIELD: 6 SERVINGS.

SPOONBREAD

This recipe was served in my home with sliced, home-cured ham or with butter to be added according to taste.

3 cups milk
1 1/2 cups sifted yellow cornmeal
8 tablespoons butter, melted

Salt to taste, if desired
4 eggs, separated
2 teaspoons baking powder

1. Preheat the oven to 350 degrees.

2. Bring 2 cups milk to the boil and gradually add the cornmeal in a steady stream, stirring rapidly with a wire whisk. Stir in the butter and salt. Cook over low heat, stirring almost constantly, about 10 minutes.

3. Scrape the mixture into a mixing bowl and let cool to lukewarm.

4. Beat the yolks until light, and stir them into the mixture. Blend the baking powder with the remaining 1 cup milk and stir it into the mixture.

5. Beat the egg whites until stiff and fold them into the mixture.

6. Butter a 1½-quart casserole and pour the mixture into it. Bake 40 minutes, or until a knife inserted in the center comes out clean. Serve immediately, with butter on the side.

YIELD: 6 TO 8 SERVINGS.

SOUTHERN BISCUITS

3 cups sifted flour
3/4 teaspoon salt, if desired
1/2 teaspoon baking soda

4 teaspoons baking powder
2/3 cup lard
1 cup plus 2 tablespoons buttermilk

1. Preheat the oven to 450 degrees.

2. Combine the flour, salt, baking soda, and baking powder. Sift them together into a mixing bowl.

3. Add the lard and mix it with a pastry blender or the fingers, until it has the texture of coarse cornmeal.

4. Add the buttermilk all at once, pouring it all around and over the flour mixture.

5. Stir vigorously with a heavy wooden spoon. It will be quite soft at first, but will stiffen after a brief period. Continue beating 1 or 2 minutes longer.

6. Scrape dough from the sides of the bowl and shape it into a ball. Turn it out onto a lightly floured surface. Dust lightly with flour to prevent sticking. Flatten the dough gently with the hands into a thick round cake. Knead for a minute, folding the outer edge of the dough into the center of the circle, giving a light knead as you fold the sides in, overlapping each other.

7. Dust a rolling pin and the surface of the dough with flour. Roll the dough out to a ½-inch thickness. Prick the surface of the dough with the tines of a fork. Use a biscuit cutter (pressing directly down into the dough instead of wiggling it) and cut out the biscuits. Cut the biscuits as close together as possible. The scraps of dough may be gathered together and rolled out again, but the texture will not be as good.

8. Select a baking sheet, preferably one with a shiny surface. Arrange the biscuits, ½ inch apart, on the baking sheet as they are cut.

9. Place in the oven and bake 13 minutes. Remove from the oven and let the biscuits rest 3 or 4 minutes before serving. Serve hot.

YIELD: 18 TO 24 BISCUITS.

SOUTHERN BISCUIT MUFFINS

The finest biscuits I have ever eaten were not made from a family heirloom recipe. They were not rolled out and cut with a biscuit cutter and they weren't made from a dough dropped from a spoon. They were, rather, buttermilk biscuits baked in muffin tins. This is my adaptation of that recipe.

2 ¼ cups flour
Salt to taste, if desired
3 tablespoons sugar
1 ½ teaspoons baking powder

10 tablespoons butter, at room
  temperature
1 cup buttermilk

1. Preheat the oven to 350 degrees.
2. Sift together the flour, salt, sugar, and baking powder into a mixing bowl.

3. Cut the butter into small pieces and add it. Using the fingers or a pastry cutter, work the butter into the dry ingredients until it has the texture of coarse cornmeal. Add the buttermilk and stir to blend without overmixing.

4. Spoon the mixture into a muffin-tin pan with twelve indentations, each with a ⅓-cup capacity. Place in the oven and bake 40 to 45 minutes, until crusty and golden brown on top.

YIELD: 12 BISCUITS.

BEATEN BISCUITS

My family adored homemade beaten biscuits, and in the back of my mind I can still hear the pounding of that dough out-of-doors atop an old tree trunk. The dough was made and placed on a heavy flat surface. It was beaten vigorously (one book I know instructs the cook to "use boys to do it") at least 200 times, until the dough was very white and stiff. It was then rolled out until thin, cut into small circles, and baked. Ideally, each biscuit should be filled with very thin slices of Southern ham. No modern cookbooks, for obvious reasons, give a serious recipe for these biscuits. I do here, for the record. But I also offer a modernized version made in a food processor. The results are fair but cannot compare with those beaten with anguish.

4 cups flour
1 teaspoon sugar
¾ teaspoon salt, if desired
1 teaspoon baking powder
4 tablespoons cold butter

¼ cup cold lard
½ cup milk
½ cup water
Melted butter for brushing

1. Sift together the flour, sugar, salt, and baking powder into a mixing bowl.

2. Using a pastry blender, cut the butter and lard into the dry mixture, until it has the texture of coarse cornmeal. Add the milk and water and blend until it yields a stiff dough.

3. Knead for 20 minutes. Turn the dough out onto a flat, heavy surface and start beating with a heavy paddle, mallet, or rolling pin. As you work, fold the dough over in half. Continue beating at least 200 times, or for 20 to 30 minutes.

4. Meanwhile, preheat the oven to 350 degrees.

5. Roll out the dough to ¼-inch thickness, and use a biscuit cutter with a 1½-inch diameter to cut the dough into rounds. Prick the top of each biscuit with 3 rows, using the tines of a fork. Arrange the biscuits on a baking sheet and place in the oven. Bake 30 to 40 minutes, until firm but not browned. They must not be soggy when they are split in half.

6. Serve hot or cold. Serve split, if desired, with thin slices of Smithfield ham nestled between the halves.

YIELD: ABOUT 4 DOZEN.

FOOD PROCESSOR BEATEN BISCUITS

2 cups flour　　　　　　　　　　　*8 tablespoons very cold butter*
1 teaspoon salt, if desired　　　　　*½ cup ice water*

1. Preheat the oven to 350 degrees. Place the oven rack in the center position.

2. Put the flour and salt in the container of the food processor. Turn the machine on and off twice to aerate the mixture. Cut the butter into small pieces and add it. Process until the mixture has the consistency of coarse cornmeal.

3. With the machine still running, pour the water through the funnel in a small stream. Process until mixture forms a ball.

4. Continue processing 2 minutes longer.

5. Turn the dough out onto a lightly floured board. Roll the dough into a rectangle about ⅛ inch thick. Fold the dough over itself to make 2 layers.

6. Use a biscuit cutter 1½ inches in diameter to cut out rounds of dough. As the dough is cut, arrange the biscuits on an ungreased cookie sheet.

7. Bake 25 to 30 minutes, until golden brown. Split the biscuits. If they are still soft in the center, return the biscuit halves briefly to the oven to crisp.

YIELD: ABOUT 10.

PEARL'S SWEET POTATO BISCUITS

One of the principal cooks in my mother's boardinghouse over the years was named Pearl Hutchins. He not only cooked but acted as my personal part-time nurse. It never occurred to me in my childhood to wonder if Pearl was his given name or a nickname. One of his many fine Southern specialties was his sweet potato biscuits.

2 cups sifted flour
2 teaspoons baking powder
1/2 teaspoon baking soda
Salt to taste, if desired
1/4 to 1/2 teaspoon sugar

12 tablespoons butter
1 cup mashed, freshly cooked or canned
   sweet potatoes
1/3 cup heavy cream, approximately

1. Preheat the oven to 450 degrees.
2. Sift together the flour, baking powder, baking soda, salt, and sugar into a mixing bowl. Add the butter and cut it in with a pastry cutter until it has the texture of coarse cornmeal. Stir in the mashed sweet potatoes.
3. Add the cream, a little at a time, stirring. Add only enough to make a soft dough.
4. Roll the dough out on a lightly floured board to 1/2-inch thickness. Cut the dough into rounds using a 2-inch biscuit cutter. Arrange the biscuits close together but not touching on a lightly greased baking sheet. Place in the oven and bake about 15 minutes, or until lightly browned.

YIELD: ABOUT 3 DOZEN.

2
POCKETBOOK ROLLS

Throughout my childhood, pocketbook rolls were served hot from the oven at Sunday dinner (the meal taken at midday) and on holidays and other special occasions. They are called "pocketbook" because the dough is folded over before baking and the rolls resemble small purses or pocketbooks. These rolls are not of Southern origin, although they figure largely throughout the South. They are basically Parker House rolls and were first created at the Parker House in Boston.

2 cups milk
4 tablespoons butter
4 tablespoons sugar
Salt to taste, if desired
1 tablespoon (2 packages) granular
  yeast

1/4 cup lukewarm water
5 to 6 cups sifted flour
Melted butter for brushing rolls

1. Bring the milk to the simmer. Add the butter, sugar, and salt and let stand until lukewarm.

2. Soften the yeast in the lukewarm water and add this to the milk mixture. Add enough flour to make a soft dough.

3. Turn the dough out onto a lightly floured board and let rest 10 minutes. Knead until smooth, about 10 minutes.

4. Lightly grease the inside of a mixing bowl and add the dough, shaped into a ball. Grease the surface of the dough and cover. Let stand in a warm place until double in bulk.

5. Turn the dough out onto a lightly floured surface and knead lightly until the surface of the dough is smooth.

6. Roll the dough out to a 1/2-inch thickness. Lightly flour the cutting edge of a 3-inch biscuit cutter and cut out rounds. Dip the back of a table knife in flour and use this to make a crease slightly off center across each roll, taking care not to cut through the roll. Brush each roll with melted butter, and fold the larger portion over the smaller half.

7. Arrange the rolls 1 inch apart on a lightly greased baking sheet. Brush with melted butter, cover with a towel, and let stand until double in bulk, 30 to 40 minutes.

8. About 10 minutes before the rolls are ready to be baked, preheat the oven to 375 degrees.

9. Brush the rolls with a little additional melted butter and place in the oven. Bake 15 to 20 minutes until golden brown.

YIELD: ABOUT 3 DOZEN.

SAVANNAH CRISPY WAFERS

These wafers, easily made with flour and yogurt, are one of the most delightful "breads" I have ever sampled in the South. They are delectable served with soups or salads or served with different dips.

1 1/2 cups flour
1/4 teaspoon baking soda
Salt to taste, if desired
4 tablespoons chilled butter, cut into
   small cubes

1/2 cup yogurt
2 tablespoons sugar or grated Parmesan
   cheese

1. Combine the flour, baking soda, and salt in the container of a food processor. Start blending while adding the butter cubes. Continue blending while adding the yogurt. Remove the dough and wrap it in wax paper or plastic wrap. Chill thoroughly.

2. Preheat the oven to 400 degrees.

3. Lightly flour a clean surface. Break off pieces of the dough and roll them into 10 to 12 rounds, each about 1 inch thick. Place each round on the floured surface and roll until paper-thin. Sprinkle with sugar or Parmesan cheese. Transfer the rounds to a baking sheet and bake 5 minutes. Turn off the heat and let stand until the wafers are crisp and lightly browned. Remove from the oven and let cool before serving.

YIELD: 10 TO 12 WAFERS.

CORNMEAL WAFFLES

Waffles were never a part of our daily "bread" in Mississippi. They were, as a matter of fact, a novelty to be served on special occasions, generally for Sunday-morning breakfast, which was a bit more elaborate than most first-meals-of-the-day. They were served with a variety of sweet liquids, including maple syrup, honey, or my father's favorite, sorghum molasses. Even as a child I had a loathing for maple syrup, one of my few food prejudices.

*1 cup cornmeal, preferably
    stone-ground
1 1/2 cups boiling water
Salt to taste, if desired
1/4 cup solid vegetable shortening
2 eggs, separated*

*1 cup flour
1/2 teaspoon baking soda
2 teaspoons baking powder
1/2 cup milk
1 cup buttermilk*

1. Put the cornmeal in a saucepan and pour the boiling water over it. Stir in the salt and shortening. Set the saucepan in a basin of simmering water and cover. Let cook, stirring occasionally, about 10 minutes. Remove from the heat.

2. Beat the egg yolks and add them to the cornmeal mixture, stirring.

3. Sift together the flour, baking soda, and baking powder. Blend the milk with the buttermilk and alternately add this and the flour mixture to the cornmeal mixture. Beat the egg whites until stiff and fold them into the mixture. There should be about 4 1/2 cups.

4. Pour the mixture, an appropriate amount at a time, on the surface of an electric waffle iron. The volume will depend on the size of the iron. Cover and cook according to the manufacturer's instructions.

YIELD: UP TO 14 WAFFLES, DEPENDING ON THE SIZE OF THE WAFFLE IRON.

PECAN WAFFLES

1 1/2 cups flour
Salt to taste, if desired
2 teaspoons baking powder
2 whole eggs

1 cup plus 6 tablespoons milk
4 tablespoons butter, melted
1/2 cup finely ground pecans
2 egg whites, stiffly beaten

1. Sift together the flour, salt, and baking powder.

2. Beat the whole eggs and gradually beat in the milk and butter. Add the flour mixture and beat with a wire whisk until smooth. Add the pecans. Beat until thoroughly blended. Fold in the egg whites. There should be about 4 1/4 cups.

3. Pour the mixture, an appropriate amount at a time, on the surface of an electric waffle iron. The volume will depend on the size of the iron. Cover and cook according to the manufacturer's instructions.

YIELD: UP TO 14 WAFFLES, DEPENDING ON THE SIZE OF THE WAFFLE IRON.

KATHLEEN CLAIBORNE'S HOTCAKES

1/2 cup cornmeal
1 tablespoon sugar
1/2 teaspoon salt, if desired
1 cup boiling water
2 eggs, separated

1 cup flour
1 tablespoon baking powder
1 cup milk
1/4 cup peanut, vegetable, or corn oil
Syrup, preserves, jams, or jellies

1. Combine the cornmeal, sugar, and salt in a saucepan.

2. Pour the boiling water over it, stirring constantly with a whisk. Cook, stirring, about 2 minutes and let cool. Beat in the egg yolks.

3. Sift together the flour and baking powder and stir it into the batter. Add the milk and oil.

4. Beat the egg whites until stiff and fold them in.

5. Lightly oil a griddle. Ladle about ⅓ cup batter onto the griddle for each pancake. Cook until browned on one side. Turn and cook on the other side. Continue ladling and cooking until all the batter is used.

6. Serve with syrup, preserves, jams, or jellies.

YIELD: 10 PANCAKES.

FLOUR TORTILLAS

Flour tortillas are becoming increasingly popular in America, gaining equal status with the more familiar tortillas made with cornmeal or *masa harina*. They are used, of course, as wrappers for various fillings, such as beef with sauces in fajitas. They are widely available fresh or frozen in specialty food markets. They are also easy to make in the home.

1 pound flour (about 3 ¼ cups)
½ cup solid white vegetable shortening
  or lard
Salt to taste, if desired

1 cup warm water (slightly hotter than
  lukewarm but not unpleasantly hot
  to the touch)

1. The volume of flour varies so it is best to measure by weight. Put the flour in a mixing bowl. Cut the shortening into bits and add it. Rub the mixture between the fingers to blend.

2. Dissolve the salt in the water and add to the flour mixture, stirring. Knead the dough well for about 3 minutes.

3. Shape the dough into a ball and put in a small bowl. Cover and let stand for 2 hours at room temperature.

4. Knead the dough once more for about 2 minutes. Pull off pieces of dough, one at a time, and shape into balls roughly 1½ inches in diameter. Press each ball with the palm of the hand onto a floured board or pastry cloth. Roll out into a circle about ⅛ inch thick and about 7 inches in diameter. As each tortilla is made, put it in a hot skillet or griddle and cook for about 20 seconds on one side, or until bubbles appear on the surface and the underside is lightly browned and speckled. Turn and cook briefly on the other side. Continue until all the flour mixture is used.

YIELD: ABOUT 2 DOZEN 7-INCH TORTILLAS.

Sauces & Stocks

MAYONNAISE

1 egg yolk
1 tablespoon lemon juice, or more to
   taste
1 teaspoon Dijon or other imported
   mustard, or more to taste

Salt to taste, if desired
Freshly ground pepper to taste
1/2 cup olive oil
1/2 cup peanut, vegetable, or corn oil
Tabasco sauce to taste

1. Put the yolk into a mixing bowl and add 1 tablespoon lemon juice, 1 teaspoon mustard, salt, and pepper.

2. Gradually add the oils, beating rapidly with a wire whisk. As the mixture starts to thicken, the oil may be added more rapidly. Add a touch of Tabasco, more salt, pepper, lemon juice, and/or mustard to taste.

YIELD: 1 CUP.

DILL MAYONNAISE

1 cup Mayonnaise (see preceding
   recipe)
1/4 cup finely chopped fresh dill
1/2 cup finely chopped heart of celery

1/4 cup finely chopped onion
Salt to taste, if desired
Freshly ground pepper to taste

Blend all the ingredients in a mixing bowl, and chill until ready to use.

YIELD: ABOUT 1½ CUPS.

TARTAR SAUCE

½ cup Mayonnaise (page 263)
1 hard-cooked egg
1 tablespoon finely chopped shallots
2 tablespoons finely chopped parsley
2 tablespoons finely chopped chives

2 tablespoons capers, drained and
    pressed to extract excess liquid
1 teaspoon lemon juice
¼ teaspoon Tabasco sauce

1. Put the mayonnaise in a mixing bowl.
2. Put the egg through a fine sieve and add it to the mayonnaise. Add the shallots, parsley, chives, and capers. Add the lemon juice and Tabasco sauce and blend.

YIELD: ABOUT ¾ CUP.

RUSSIAN DRESSING

½ cup Mayonnaise (page 263)
1 tablespoon chili sauce or ketchup
1 teaspoon finely chopped onion
½ teaspoon prepared horseradish

¼ teaspoon Worcestershire sauce
1 tablespoon finely chopped parsley
1 tablespoon black or red caviar,
    optional

Combine all the ingredients in a mixing bowl. Blend well.

YIELD: ABOUT ¾ CUP.

SAUCE GRIBICHE

1 cup Mayonnaise (page 263)
1 tablespoon finely chopped shallots
1 tablespoon finely chopped onion
1 tablespoon finely chopped chives
1 tablespoon water

2 hard-cooked eggs, pressed through a
sieve
Salt to taste, if desired
Freshly ground pepper to taste
1 tablespoon chopped parsley

Combine all the ingredients in a mixing bowl and blend well. Serve with cold or lukewarm fish or meats.

YIELD: ABOUT 2 CUPS.

HOLLANDAISE SAUCE

½ pound butter
2 egg yolks
1 tablespoon water
Salt to taste, if desired

⅛ teaspoon cayenne pepper
1 tablespoon freshly squeezed lemon
juice

1. Put the butter in a heatproof bowl or glass measuring cup and set it in a basin of simmering water. Let it heat until the butter is melted.

2. Carefully spoon off the white residue from the top of the clear yellow liquid. Carefully pour off and reserve the yellow liquid. Discard the milky bottom portion.

3. Combine the egg yolks and water in a saucepan, beating rapidly with a wire whisk. Place the saucepan in a larger basin of simmering water, beating constantly. Gradually add the clear yellow liquid, beating constantly while heating the mixture in the simmering water. Do not overheat. Beat and heat until the sauce has the consistency of a thin mayonnaise.

4. Add the salt, cayenne pepper, and lemon juice and blend thoroughly.

YIELD: ¾ CUP.

BÉARNAISE SAUCE

½ pound butter
2 tablespoons finely chopped shallots
2 tablespoons tarragon vinegar
1 teaspoon crushed black peppercorns

1 teaspoon dried tarragon
2 egg yolks
1 tablespoon cold water

1. Put the butter in a small heavy saucepan and let it melt slowly. Skim off the white foam that rises to the top. Carefully pour off and reserve the clear yellow liquid. Discard the milky residue at the bottom.

2. Heat the shallots, vinegar, peppercorns, and tarragon in another small heavy saucepan and cook until all the liquid evaporates. Remove from the heat and let the saucepan cool slightly.

3. Add the egg yolks and water to the shallot mixture.

4. Return the saucepan to the stove and vigorously stir the yolk mixture over very low heat. Do not overheat or the eggs will curdle. Remove the saucepan from the heat and place it on a cold surface. Add the melted butter, ladleful by ladleful, stirring vigorously after each addition. Do not add the butter too rapidly.

YIELD: ABOUT 1 CUP.

MUSTARD SAUCE

2 eggs
2 dashes Tabasco sauce
8 tablespoons cold butter
Juice of ¹/₂ lemon

1 tablespoon prepared mustard
Salt to taste, if desired
Freshly ground pepper to taste

1. Put the eggs in a heavy saucepan and add the Tabasco sauce.

2. Pour about 1 inch of water into a skillet large enough to hold the saucepan comfortably. Bring the water to the simmer.

3. Beat the eggs off the heat. Cut the butter into 6 pieces and add 2 pieces to the eggs. Set the saucepan in the hot water. Stir constantly with a whisk. The important thing about this sauce is that it must not become too hot or the eggs will curdle.

4. When the butter melts, remove the skillet from the heat but continue beating constantly. Add another piece of butter and beat until melted. Continue adding butter, 1 piece at a time, beating constantly until all the butter is used. When thickened and smooth, remove the saucepan from the skillet. Add the lemon juice, mustard, salt, and pepper.

5. Serve with fish.

YIELD: 4 SERVINGS.

HOT MUSTARD

¹/₄ cup dry mustard
2 tablespoons water, beer, milk, or dry
   white wine

Salt to taste, if desired
¹/₂ teaspoon sugar

1. Place the mustard in a mixing bowl and gradually add the water or other liquid, stirring with a fork.

2. Stir in the salt and sugar and let stand at least 10 minutes. This is essential because the mustard is bitter when it is first made. After standing it loses its bitter taste and develops flavor. The mustard may, of course, be diluted as desired with additional liquid.

YIELD: ABOUT 3½ TABLESPOONS.

NOTE: *The quantities in this recipe may, of course, be doubled, tripled, quadrupled, and so on. But do not make the mustard in large batches to save. It is best to make a fresh batch before each use.*

BASIC WHITE SAUCE

2 tablespoons butter
2 tablespoons flour
1 to 1½ cups milk

Salt to taste, if desired
Freshly ground pepper to taste,
    preferably white

1. Melt the butter in a medium-size saucepan. Add the flour and immediately start stirring with a wire whisk.
2. Add the milk all at once, stirring rapidly with the whisk. Add the salt and pepper. Cook, stirring frequently, about 5 minutes.

YIELD: 1 TO 1½ CUPS.

BASIC CREAM SAUCE

6 tablespoons butter
½ cup flour
4 cups Chicken Stock (page 275)

1½ cups heavy cream
Salt to taste, if desired
Freshly ground pepper to taste

1. Melt the butter in a 1½- to 2-quart saucepan and add the flour, stirring with a wire whisk. When blended and smooth, add the stock, stirring rapidly with the whisk. When thickened, let simmer about 5 minutes, stirring often.

2. Add the cream, salt, and pepper. Let simmer 5 minutes longer.

YIELD: ABOUT 5 CUPS.

MUSHROOM SAUCE

1 tablespoon butter
2 tablespoons finely minced onion
4 medium-size mushrooms (about ¼ pound), cut into small cubes (about 1 cup)
Salt to taste, if desired

Freshly ground pepper to taste
2 tablespoons flour
1 cup Chicken Stock (page 275) or canned chicken broth
½ cup heavy cream

1. Melt the butter in a saucepan and add the onion. When wilted, add the mushrooms and cook until they give up their liquid. Cook until the liquid evaporates. Sprinkle with salt and pepper.

2. Sprinkle with flour, stirring with a wire whisk. When blended, add the stock, stirring rapidly with the whisk. When blended and smooth, continue cooking, stirring occasionally, about 15 minutes. Add the cream and simmer about 5 minutes longer.

YIELD: ABOUT 2 CUPS.

SALAD DRESSING WITH GARLIC

¼ cup wine vinegar
2 teaspoons Dijon or other imported mustard
2 teaspoons finely chopped garlic

1 teaspoon paprika
Salt to taste, if desired
Freshly ground pepper to taste
1 cup olive oil

1. Put the vinegar, mustard, garlic, paprika, salt, and pepper in a mixing bowl.

2. Gradually add the oil, beating rapidly with a wire whisk. Stir this sauce vigorously prior to each use.

YIELD: 1¼ CUPS.

FRENCH DRESSING

2 tablespoons red wine vinegar
6 to 8 tablespoons peanut, corn, or
  olive oil

Salt to taste, if desired
Freshly ground pepper to taste

Combine all the ingredients in a small jar. Close and shake until thoroughly blended. Serve over salad greens.

YIELD: ABOUT ½ CUP.

THOUSAND ISLAND DRESSING

A Thousand Island dressing is not of Southern origin. Legend has it that it was created many years ago by the executive chef of the Drake Hotel in Chicago. He concocted the mayonnaise dressing with many chopped foods such as olives, pickles, and egg, and when his wife saw it she remarked that it looked like the Thousand Islands, near Ontario, New York, that they had recently visited. Whatever its origins, I cannot imagine a Southern home without it.

1 cup mayonnaise
1/4 cup chili sauce or ketchup, or equal
  parts of each
1 hard-cooked egg, chopped
1 tablespoon finely chopped onion
2 tablespoons finely chopped
  pimiento-stuffed green olives

1/2 cup finely chopped heart of celery
2 tablespoons finely chopped sweet
  pickles
Lemon juice to taste
Salt to taste, if desired
Freshly ground pepper to taste
2 teaspoons finely chopped parsley

Combine all the ingredients in a mixing bowl and blend well. Serve on wedges of iceberg lettuce, on hard-cooked egg halves, seafood, and so on.

YIELD: ABOUT 1½ CUPS.

TOMATO SAUCE

2 tablespoons butter
1 1/2 tablespoons finely chopped onion
1/2 teaspoon finely minced garlic
2 cups canned tomatoes that have been

blended or sieved
1/4 bay leaf
Salt to taste, if desired
Freshly ground pepper to taste

1. Melt 1 tablespoon butter in a saucepan and add the onion and garlic, stirring. When the onion is wilted, add the tomatoes, bay leaf, salt, and pepper. Cook, stirring occasionally, about 30 minutes.

2. Swirl in the remaining 1 tablespoon butter and serve hot.

YIELD: ABOUT 2 CUPS.

TOMATO SAUCE WITH MUSHROOMS

3 tablespoons butter
1/2 cup finely chopped celery
1/2 cup finely chopped onion
1/2 cup finely chopped sweet green
   pepper
1/2 teaspoon finely chopped garlic
1/4 pound mushrooms, thinly sliced

Salt to taste, if desired
Freshly ground pepper to taste
1 tablespoon flour
2 cups crushed tomatoes
1/2 bay leaf
Tabasco sauce to taste

1. Melt 1 tablespoon butter and add the celery, onion, green pepper, and garlic. Cook, stirring, about 5 minutes. Add the mushrooms, salt, and pepper. Cook about 3 minutes and sprinkle with flour. Stir to blend well.

2. Add the tomatoes and stir. Add the bay leaf and simmer over low heat, about 45 minutes. Stir in the remaining butter and more salt and pepper, if desired. Add a few drops of Tabasco sauce and serve hot.

YIELD: ABOUT 3 CUPS.

MEXICAN TABLE SAUCE

2 cups well-drained canned tomatoes,
   preferably imported
1/2 cup finely chopped red onion
2 tablespoons finely chopped fresh
   coriander

1 bottled pickled jalapeño pepper,
   drained
1 whole fresh jalapeño pepper (see note)
Salt to taste, if desired
Freshly ground pepper to taste

1. Put the tomatoes into the container of a food processor or electric blender. Blend until they are coarsely chopped. The tomatoes should not become too soupy. Pour the mixture into a bowl.

2. Add the chopped onion and coriander.

3. Trim off the ends of each jalapeño pepper. Do not remove the seeds. Chop the peppers and add them to the bowl. Add salt and pepper. Blend thoroughly.

YIELD: ABOUT 2½ CUPS.

NOTE: *If fresh jalapeños are not available, use 2 bottled jalapeños in this recipe.*

SOUTHERN BARBECUE SAUCE

2 tablespoons butter
6 tablespoons cider vinegar
¼ cup water
1½ cups ketchup
2 tablespoons Worcestershire sauce
¼ teaspoon Tabasco sauce, or more to taste
1 teaspoon finely chopped garlic
3 tablespoons peanut, vegetable, or corn oil

Salt to taste, if desired
Freshly ground pepper to taste
¼ teaspoon dried hot red pepper flakes
½ bay leaf
2 tablespoons sugar
1 teaspoon paprika
1 lemon

1. Combine all the ingredients except the lemon in a saucepan. Add the juice of the lemon. Cut the lemon into quarters and add it.
2. Heat thoroughly without boiling.
3. Use the sauce to baste chicken, fish, spareribs, and so on as they are grilled.

YIELD: ABOUT 2¾ CUPS.

NOTE: *This sauce will keep for days, tightly sealed in the refrigerator.*

MARYLAND-STYLE BARBECUE SAUCE

3/4 cup red wine vinegar
1 teaspoon freshly ground black pepper
2 teaspoons salt, if desired
1 teaspoon sugar
1 bay leaf

2 teaspoons chili powder
1 teaspoon dry mustard
1 teaspoon paprika
1 teaspoon ground cumin

Combine all the ingredients in a flat dish and blend well. Use the sauce both as a marinade and to baste meat and poultry, especially very fatty meats, such as duck or spareribs, when charcoal-grilled.

YIELD: ABOUT 3/4 CUP.

FISH STOCK

2 pounds bones from a white-fleshed,
*   nonoily fish, including heads, if*
*   possible, but with gills removed*
6 cups water
1 cup dry white wine
1 cup coarsely chopped celery

1 cup coarsely chopped onion
3 sprigs fresh thyme, or 1 teaspoon
*   dried*
1 bay leaf
10 peppercorns
Salt to taste, if desired

Run the bones under cold running water. Place the bones in a kettle or deep saucepan and add all the remaining ingredients. Bring to the boil and simmer for 20 minutes. Strain. Discard solids.

YIELD: ABOUT 7 CUPS.

NOTE: *Leftover stock can be frozen.*

CHICKEN STOCK

5 pounds meaty chicken bones
2 cups coarsely chopped onions
1/2 pound carrots, coarsely chopped
   (about 2 cups)
1 cup coarsely chopped celery
1 garlic clove, peeled

10 sprigs fresh parsley
1 bay leaf
1/2 teaspoon dried thyme
10 whole black peppercorns
16 cups water

1. Put the chicken bones in a large stockpot and cover with water. Bring to the boil and drain, discarding the water. Rinse the bones thoroughly and return to the stockpot.

2. Add the remaining ingredients, including 16 cups water, and bring to the boil. Reduce the heat so the stock simmers slowly. Cook for 2 hours, skimming fat and scum from the surface every 15 or 20 minutes.

3. Strain the stock though a fine sieve into a large bowl. Let cool, and then cover and refrigerate.

4. Remove the fat from the top of the stock with a slotted spoon. Use the clear stock as needed.

YIELD: 10 CUPS.

NOTE: *The stock can be frozen in convenient-size containers.*

Desserts & Candy

COCONUT CAKE

One of my earliest recollections was watching my mother or one of the servants tediously grating coconut in large quantities, sometimes for ice cream, sometimes for a curried dish, but more often than not for coconut cake, which was one of Kathleen Craig Claiborne's great specialties. It was a personal favorite of mine and generally appeared on Sundays or on special holidays.

THE CAKE:

2 1/2 cups sifted cake flour
1 2/3 cups sugar
1 teaspoon salt, if desired
3 1/2 teaspoons baking powder

2/3 cup solid vegetable shortening
1 1/4 cups milk
3 eggs
1 teaspoon pure vanilla extract

THE COCONUT FROSTING:

Boiled Frosting (see following recipe)
2 1/2 cups Grated Fresh Coconut (page 279)

1. Preheat the oven to 350 degrees.
2. Lightly butter the bottom and sides of two 9-inch layer cake pans. Line the bottoms with rounds of wax paper. Lightly butter the paper. Set the pans aside.

3. In the bowl of an electric mixer, combine the flour, sugar, salt, and baking powder.

4. Add the shortening and start beating vigorously. While beating, add ¾ cup milk. Beat 2 minutes.

5. Add the eggs, the remaining ½ cup milk, and vanilla. Beat 2 minutes longer.

6. Pour equal amounts of the batter into the prepared pans. Bake 35 to 40 minutes.

7. Remove the pans to a rack and let stand 5 minutes. Unmold the cakes. Remove the wax paper.

8. Spread the top of the first layer with frosting and coat generously with grated coconut. Place the second layer on top of the first. Frost the top and sides of the cake, and coat with the remaining coconut.

YIELD: 12 OR MORE SERVINGS.

BOILED FROSTING

Do not attempt this recipe on a rainy day or any other day with high humidity.

2½ cups sugar
5 tablespoons light corn syrup
½ cup water

2 egg whites
1½ teaspoons pure vanilla extract

1. In a saucepan, combine the sugar, corn syrup, and water. Bring to the boil and cook to 242 degrees on a candy thermometer, or to the firm-ball stage (the syrup, when dropped into very cold water, forms a firm ball that does not flatten when removed). Remove from the heat.

2. Beat the egg whites in a mixing bowl until stiff but not dry. Gradually add the syrup while beating. Add the vanilla and continue beating until the mixture holds its shape.

YIELD: ENOUGH TO FROST A 2-LAYER 9-INCH CAKE.

GRATED FRESH COCONUT

Use 1 or 2 coconuts. It is best to use 2 in case 1 isn't sweet enough. Select large coconuts that are heavy and contain a lot of liquid. You can determine the amount of liquid when you shake the coconut.

Pierce the eyes of the coconut with an ice pick. Crack the shell of the coconut in several places, using a hammer or hatchet.

Pry out the flesh with a blunt knife. Pare away the dark skin. Grate the coconut using the coarse blade of a grater or a food processor.

ANGEL FOOD CAKE

If I had to name my absolutely favorite dessert at about the time I reached puberty or before, it would be, without question, angel food cake. To me it was divine, celestial, and manna from heaven. It is still cause for celebration—or something to celebrate with.

1 1/3 cups twice-sifted sugar
1 cup sifted cake flour
1/4 teaspoon salt, if desired
1 1/2 cups egg whites (11 or 12 whites)

1 1/4 teaspoons cream of tartar
1 teaspoon pure vanilla extract
1/2 teaspoon almond extract

1. Preheat the oven to 350 degrees.
2. In a sifter, combine 1/3 cup sugar, the cake flour, and salt. Sift the mixture three times.
3. Put the egg whites into the bowl of an electric mixer and beat until foamy. Add the cream of tartar. Continue beating until the whites hold soft peaks.
4. While still beating, gradually add the remaining 1 cup sugar, about 1 tablespoon at a time.
5. Fold in the vanilla and almond extracts. Sift approximately one-quarter of the flour mixture over the whites. Fold this in with a rubber spatula. Continue adding the flour mixture, one-quarter at a time, folding in after each addition.

6. Pour the batter into an ungreased 9-inch tube pan. Bake 45 minutes, or until the top of the cake springs back when lightly touched.

7. Immediately invert the cake onto a wire rack and let stand in the pan until cool, about 1½ hours.

YIELD: ABOUT 10 SERVINGS.

CHARLESTON TRUFFLE CAKE

This is a recipe given to me by friends in Charleston, South Carolina. It is one of the finest and most devastatingly rich desserts I have ever sampled.

THE NUT CRUST:

3 cups finely chopped pecans
1 cup not-too-firmly packed brown sugar

⅛ teaspoon freshly grated nutmeg
½ pound butter, at room temperature

THE FILLING:

1½ pounds bittersweet chocolate, preferably imported from Belgium
9 large eggs
½ pound butter, melted

1 cup heavy cream
1¼ cups loosely packed confectioners' sugar

1. The pecans may be chopped in the food processor but not too fine. Blend them in a mixing bowl with the brown sugar, nutmeg, and butter. Press the mixture as evenly as possible over the bottom and up the sides of a 9-inch springform pan. It should have the shape of a tall pie shell. Chill.

2. For the filling, put the chocolate in a saucepan and set it in a slightly larger pan containing simmering water.

3. Put the eggs into the bowl of an electric mixer and start beating. Scrape the chocolate into the eggs while beating. Add the melted butter, cream, and confectioners' sugar. Continue beating on medium speed for 3 minutes. Pour the filling into the crust and chill.

4. Unmold and cut into wedges. Serve, if desired, with sweetened whipped cream on the side.

YIELD: 8 OR MORE SMALL PORTIONS.

BUTTERCUP CAKE WITH LEMON CURD

THE CAKE:

2 cups flour
2 teaspoons baking powder
1/4 teaspoon salt, if desired
6 tablespoons solid vegetable shortening
6 tablespoons butter

1 1/4 cups granulated sugar
4 eggs
3/4 cup half-and-half
1 teaspoon pure vanilla extract

THE FILLING:

2 large lemons
3 large eggs
1 cup granulated sugar

3 tablespoons butter
1/4 teaspoon salt, if desired

THE GARNISH:

6 thin lemon slices
2 tablespoons confectioners' sugar

1. Preheat the oven to 350 degrees.
2. To make the cake batter, sift together the flour, baking powder, and salt. Set aside.

3. Using an electric mixer, cream together the shortening, butter, and granulated sugar. Add the eggs, 1 at a time, beating well after each addition. Alternately fold in thoroughly the flour mixture and the half-and-half. Add the vanilla.

4. Line the bottoms of two 8-inch layer cake pans with parchment or buttered wax paper. Pour equal amounts of the batter into the pans and place them in the oven. Bake about 30 minutes, or until a cake tester inserted into the center of each cake comes out clean.

5. Remove the pans and set them on racks. Let cool. Unmold the layers.

6. Meanwhile, prepare the filling. Grate the rind of 1 lemon and set aside. Squeeze the juice from both lemons and set aside. Discard the shells.

7. In a saucepan, combine the eggs, sugar, lemon rind, lemon juice, butter, and salt. Blend well and set the pan over very low heat (preferably using a metal Flame Tamer) or in a basin of simmering water. Cook, stirring often, 30 minutes or less, until thickened and smooth. Let cool, and use as a filling to spread between the cake layers and on top.

8. Garnish with lemon slices and sprinkle with confectioners' sugar, using a sieve.

YIELD: 8 OR MORE SERVINGS.

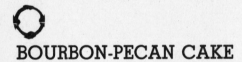

BOURBON-PECAN CAKE

8 tablespoons butter, at room
   temperature
1/2 cup dark brown sugar
2 large eggs
2 1/2 teaspoons baking powder
2 cups flour

Salt to taste, if desired
1/2 cup maple syrup
1/2 cup bourbon, rum, or Cognac
1 1/2 cups coarsely chopped pecans
Confectioners' sugar for garnish

1. Preheat the oven to 350 degrees.

2. Put the butter into the bowl of an electric mixer. Start beating and gradually add the sugar, beating on high. Add the eggs, 1 at a time, beating well after each addition.

3. Sift together the baking powder, flour, and salt. Beat the flour mixture, maple syrup, and bourbon into the creamed butter, adding the ingredients alternately. Stop beating. Stir in the pecans.

4. Butter a small tube pan (one that measures 9½ inches in diameter is suitable), loaf or Bundt pan and spoon in the mixture, smoothing it over on top.

5. Bake 45 to 50 minutes. Let cool 10 minutes. Remove from the pan and let cool.

6. Serve sprinkled with confectioners' sugar.

YIELD: 8 OR MORE SERVINGS.

CHOCOLATE-PECAN CAKE
WITH CHERIMOYA CUSTARD SAUCE

Cherimoyas are also known as custard apples. They have an outer greenish to greenish-black skin and are eaten with the seeds discarded. They have a sweet flavor that resembles a blend of strawberries and pineapple. For desserts they must have achieved a perfect ripeness.

1 cup heavy cream

4 tablespoons butter

2 ounces (squares) unsweetened
   chocolate, chopped

10½ ounces (squares) semisweet
   chocolate, chopped

5 large eggs

⅓ cup sugar

1 teaspoon pure vanilla extract

¾ cup toasted or roasted pecans,
   chopped

Cherimoya Custard Sauce (see
   following recipe)

1. Preheat the oven to 350 degrees.

2. Butter the inside of a 9-inch cake pan. Place a round of parchment or wax paper, cut to fit, in the bottom of the pan. Butter the round of paper. Add about 1 tablespoon flour to the buttered pan and shake it around to coat the bottom and sides of the pan. Shake out excess.

3. Combine the cream and 4 tablespoons butter and bring to the simmer. When the mixture starts to bubble, add the chocolate and stir around the bottom and sides until the chocolate melts. Remove from the heat and let stand.

4. Break the eggs into a heatproof earthenware or metal mixing bowl. Stir in the sugar and vanilla. Place the bowl over—not in—a basin of simmering water, beating the egg mixture vigorously with a wire whisk.

5. After about 1 minute, when the eggs are warm and not overly heated, remove the bowl from the basin of simmering water and start beating with an electric mixer. Continue beating until the mixture is tripled in volume and reaches room temperature, 7 to 10 minutes.

6. Scrape about one-third of the chocolate mixture into a large mixing bowl. Add about one-third of the egg mixture and blend well with a spatula. Add the remaining egg mixture and fold it in. Fold in the remaining chocolate mixture and stir in the nuts.

7. Pour the batter into the prepared pan and smooth over the top. Set the cake pan into a larger pan and pour boiling water around the cake pan. Place in the oven and bake 45 to 50 minutes, or until a cake tester inserted in the center of the cake comes out clean.

8. Remove the cake from the oven and let it sit in its water bath about 30 minutes. Remove the cake from the water bath and wipe off the bottom of the pan. Invert the cake onto a platter, remove the round of paper, and let stand to room temperature. Serve with cherimoya custard sauce.

YIELD: 10 TO 12 SERVINGS.

CHERIMOYA CUSTARD SAUCE

3 very ripe cherimoyas (custard apples)
  (about 1 1/2 pounds)
1 cup milk
1 teaspoon pure vanilla extract

3 large egg yolks
1/3 cup sugar
1/3 cup heavy cream or, preferably,
  crème fraîche

1. Peel the cherimoyas and discard the skins. The flesh should be quite soft. Put the flesh into a food mill and turn the handle to strain the pulp. Discard the seeds. There should be slightly more than 1 cup pulp. Put the pulp into the container of a food processor and blend thoroughly. Set aside.

2. Put the milk into a saucepan and add the vanilla. Bring to the boil.

3. Meanwhile, put the egg yolks in another saucepan and add the sugar. Beat rapidly with a wire whisk or electric mixer. Beat until light and fluffy. Gradually add the hot milk, beating vigorously. Pour this mixture into a clean saucepan and continue beating. Cook over low to medium heat (it is best if you use a heat pad), beating constantly. Have ready a bowl of ice in which to chill the sauce. Cook the sauce, stirring, until it reaches 185 degrees on a candy thermometer, or until it coats a wooden spoon. It must be thickened and custardlike.

4. Remove from the heat and set the saucepan in the bed of ice. Stir occasionally, until cooled.

5. Stir in the cream or crème fraîche and the cherimoya purée.

6. Serve with chocolate-pecan cake.

YIELD: ABOUT 2 CUPS.

MY MOTHER'S ORANGE CAKE

1/2 pound butter
3 cups sugar
4 cups sifted flour
1 teaspoon baking soda
4 eggs

1 1/3 cups buttermilk
2 tablespoons finely grated orange rind
1 1/2 cups chopped pitted dates
1 cup finely chopped pecans
1 1/2 cups freshly squeezed orange juice

1. Preheat the oven to 350 degrees.

2. Cream together the butter and 2 cups sugar, until light and fluffy. Sift together the flour and baking soda and add it to the butter mixture, stirring until well blended. Beat in the eggs, buttermilk, 1 tablespoon grated orange rind, the dates, and pecans.

3. Pour and scrape the mixture into a 4-quart tube pan and bake 1 hour and 10 minutes, or until a cake tester inserted in the cake comes out clean. Do not unmold the cake.

4. Combine the remaining 1 cup sugar with the orange juice and remaining 1 tablespoon grated orange rind. Bring to the simmer, stirring until the sugar is dissolved. Gently plunge an ice pick or skewer in several spots on top of the cake and pour the orange juice mixture overall. Let stand 30 minutes or longer, until it is absorbed and the cake is cool. Unmold and serve cut into wedges.

YIELD: 10 OR MORE SERVINGS.

LADY BALTIMORE CAKE

I am indebted to a Yankee for information pertaining to the origins of some of the recipes in this book. He is John Mariani, the author of *The Dictionary of American Food and Drink.* He states that there are various stories as to the origin of the famed Lady Baltimore Cake. One has it that it was first conceived by a Southern belle named Alicia Rhett Mayberry of Charleston, South Carolina. It is said that she created it for Owen Wister, the novelist, who described the cake in his "next book" and named the novel itself—published in 1906—*Lady Baltimore.* Alicia Rhett Mayberry, Mariani notes, maintained in a book titled *200 Years of Charleston Cooking* that the recipe came from the Woman's Exchange at the time Wister wrote his novel.

12 tablespoons butter, at room temperature	2 1/2 teaspoons baking powder
1 1/2 cups sugar	1 cup milk
1 1/2 teaspoons pure vanilla extract	4 large or 5 small egg whites
1 teaspoon almond extract	Fruit Filling, with almonds (page 288)
2 3/4 cups sifted cake flour	Seven-Minute Frosting (page 289)

1. Preheat the oven to 350 degrees.

2. Butter the bottom of two 8-inch layer cake pans. Cover the bottom of each with a round of wax paper and brush the top of the paper with melted butter.

3. Put the 12 tablespoons butter into the bowl of an electric mixer and beat on high speed while gradually adding 1 cup sugar. Beat until light and lemon-colored. Beat in the vanilla and almond extracts.

4. Sift together the flour and baking powder. Sift a second time.

5. To the butter mixture, beat in alternately one-third of the flour and one-third of the milk, until all the flour and milk are used. Set the batter aside.

6. Beat the whites until they stand in peaks. Do not beat them until they are dry. Beat the remaining ½ cup sugar into the whites to make a meringue.

7. Fold the meringue into the batter, using large folding strokes. Pour equal portions of the batter into the prepared cake pans. Tap the bottom of each pan on a flat surface to remove air bubbles.

8. Place the pans on the center rack of the oven and bake 35 to 40 minutes, or until a cake tester inserted in the cake comes out clean. Let stand briefly, then invert the cakes onto a rack. Let cool.

9. Place 1 layer on a flat surface or plate and cover with the fruit filling, smoothing it over. Cover with the second layer. Smear the top and sides with the frosting.

YIELD: 8 TO 12 SERVINGS.

LORD BALTIMORE CAKE

No authority I have encountered has ever proposed the origins of the cake known as the Lord Baltimore. It may be that some good cook decided that if the Lady Baltimore cake was made with a goodly number of egg whites, it would be logical to prepare a related cake using similar fillings and a seven-minute frosting, but made with all egg yolks. That is pure conjecture.

1 cup milk
8 tablespoons butter
11 egg yolks
2 cups sugar
2 1/4 cups sifted cake flour
2 teaspoons baking powder

Salt to taste, if desired
1 1/2 teaspoons pure vanilla extract
Fruit Filling, with macaroons (see
    following recipe)
Seven-Minute Frosting (page 289)

1. Preheat the oven to 350 degrees.

2. Butter the bottom of two 8-inch layer cake pans. Cover the bottom of each with a round of wax paper and brush the top of the paper with melted butter.

3. Combine the milk and butter in a saucepan and bring barely but not quite to the simmer. Remove from the heat.

4. Put the yolks in the bowl of an electric mixer and start beating on high speed while gradually adding the sugar. Beat until light.

5. Sift together the cake flour, baking powder, and salt. Add the flour mixture alternately with the milk-and-butter mixture to the yolks. Mix only until the batter is smooth.

6. Pour equal portions of the batter into the prepared pans. Bake 30 to 35 minutes. Let stand briefly, then invert the cakes onto a rack. Let cool.

7. Place 1 layer on a flat surface or plate and cover with the fruit filling, smoothing it over. Cover with the second layer. Smear the top and sides with the frosting.

YIELD: 8 TO 12 SERVINGS.

FRUIT FILLING FOR CAKES

3 large or 4 small egg yolks
1/2 cup sugar
Salt to taste, if desired
1/4 pound butter, melted
1/4 cup macaroon crumbs or chopped
    blanched almonds (see note)

1/4 cup chopped seeded dates
1/4 cup chopped pecans
1/2 cup chopped mixed candied fruits,
    such as pineapple, angelica, and
    cherries
1 teaspoon pure vanilla extract

1. Put the yolks into the bowl of an electric mixer. Start beating on high speed while gradually adding the sugar and salt. When light and lemon-colored, add the melted butter.

2. Pour and scrape the mixture into a saucepan and cook, stirring constantly, over hot water 20 to 25 minutes, or until thickened. Remove the saucepan from the heat and stir in the remaining ingredients. Let cool before using.

YIELD: ENOUGH FILLING FOR A 2-LAYER CAKE.

NOTE: *The macaroon crumbs are traditional in a Lord Baltimore cake; the chopped almonds are used in the Lady Baltimore filling.*

SEVEN-MINUTE FROSTING

1 cup confectioners' sugar	*Salt to taste, if desired*
3 tablespoons hot water	*¼ teaspoon cream of tartar*
1 egg white	*1 teaspoon pure vanilla extract*

1. Put the sugar and water into a saucepan and cover. Bring to the boil and cook until the sugar is dissolved.

2. Put the egg white into the bowl of an electric mixer. Add the salt and cream of tartar and start beating on high speed while gradually adding the syrup. Beat 4 or 5 minutes, or until the frosting is spreadable. Beat in the vanilla.

YIELD: ABOUT 2 CUPS.

LANE CAKE

One of the most Southern of cakes is a creation known as a Lane cake. It was named after Emma Rylander Lane of Clayton, Alabama. It was published in 1898 in her book titled *Some Good Things to Eat,* and the original recipe title was Prize Cake. It is a white layer cake with a bourbon-flavored filling made with egg yolks.

THE CAKE:

2 cups sugar
1/2 pound plus 4 tablespoons butter
1 1/2 teaspoons pure vanilla extract
3 1/2 cups flour
4 teaspoons baking powder

1 teaspoon salt, if desired
1 1/4 cups milk
8 egg whites, beaten until stiff but not
    dry

THE FILLING:

9 egg yolks
1 1/4 cups sugar
1 teaspoon grated orange rind
1/3 cup bourbon
3/4 teaspoon pure vanilla extract
1/2 teaspoon ground mace

1 cup chopped pecans
1 cup shredded coconut, preferably fresh
    (see page 279)
1 cup candied cherries, cut into
    quarters
1 cup raisins

THE ICING:

2 egg whites
1 cup sugar
1/2 cup water

1/4 teaspoon cream of tartar
1/8 teaspoon salt, if desired
1 teaspoon pure vanilla extract

1. Preheat the oven to 375 degrees.

2. Butter the bottom and sides of three 9-inch layer cake pans. Add a little flour and shake to coat the bottom and sides. Shake out the excess. Set the pans aside.

3. To make the cake batter, beat the sugar and butter together until light and fluffy. Beat in the vanilla extract.

4. Sift together the flour, baking powder, and salt. Sift a second time.

5. Add the flour mixture alternately with the milk to the batter. Add one-fourth of the egg whites and beat them in. Fold in the remaining egg whites. Spoon equal portions of the batter into each of the prepared pans. Bake 20 to 25 minutes. Place on a rack and let stand 10 minutes. Turn the cake layers out onto a rack to cool.

6. Meanwhile, prepare the filling. Combine the yolks, sugar, and orange rind in the top of a double boiler and place it in a basin of simmering water. Cook gently, stirring constantly, until the mixture thickens enough to coat a wooden spoon. Do not let the mixture boil or the yolks will curdle.

7. Remove from the heat and beat in the bourbon, vanilla, mace, pecans, coconut, cherries, and raisins. Let cool to room temperature. Spread the filling between the cake layers.

8. To prepare the icing, beat the whites until stiff and set aside.

9. In a saucepan, combine the sugar, water, cream of tartar, and salt and bring to the boil, stirring. Cook 5 minutes over moderate heat. Add the vanilla. Pour the mixture over the whites, beating constantly. Use this mixture to frost the top and sides of the cake.

YIELD: 10 OR MORE SERVINGS.

MUD HENS

8 tablespoons butter, at room
   temperature
1 cup sugar
2 eggs, separated (do not combine the
   whites)
1 1/2 cups flour

1 teaspoon baking powder
1/2 teaspoon salt, if desired
1 teaspoon pure vanilla extract
1 cup coarsely chopped pecans
1 cup dark brown sugar

1. Preheat the oven to 325 degrees.

2. Put the butter into the bowl of an electric mixer and add the sugar. Beat until light and lemon-colored. Beat in 2 egg yolks and 1 egg white.

3. Sift together the flour, baking powder, and salt. Sift this mixture over the butter-and-sugar mixture and fold it in. Beat in the vanilla.

4. Butter a baking tin measuring about 9 × 13 inches. Pour and scrape in the dough and smooth it over. Sprinkle evenly with the pecans.

5. Beat the remaining egg white until stiff. Gradually beat in the brown sugar. Pour and scrape this over the batter and smooth it over.

6. Place the pan in the oven and bake 30 minutes or longer, until the cake is set. Cool on a rack and cut the cake into 1½-inch squares.

YIELD: ABOUT 40 SQUARES.

GERMAN CHOCOLATE CAKE

German chocolate cake became a staple in many Mississippi homes during my childhood. The recipe used by my mother was clipped from a newspaper and pasted in the manuscript cookbook she compiled for me many years ago. It is an excellent cake, the layers coated on top with a coconut-pecan frosting.

THE CAKE:

½ pound sweet chocolate
½ cup boiling water
½ pound butter
2 cups sugar
4 egg yolks
1 teaspoon pure vanilla extract

2½ cups sifted cake flour
1 teaspoon baking soda
½ teaspoon salt, if desired
1 cup buttermilk
4 egg whites, stiffly beaten

THE FROSTING:

1 cup half-and-half
1 cup sugar
3 egg yolks
¼ pound butter

1 teaspoon pure vanilla extract
1⅓ cups canned flaked, sweetened
    coconut
1 cup chopped pecans

1. Preheat the oven to 350 degrees.

2. Combine the chocolate and boiling water in a saucepan. Heat, stirring, until the chocolate melts. Let cool.

3. Using an electric mixer, cream together the butter and sugar until light and fluffy. Add the yolks, 1 at a time, beating well after each addition. Add the vanilla extract and the chocolate mixture, beating to blend.

4. Sift together the flour, baking soda, and salt. Add these ingredients alternately with the buttermilk, beating after each addition until the batter is smooth. Fold in the beaten egg whites.

5. Line the bottoms of three 8-inch cake pans with parchment or buttered wax paper and pour equal amounts of the batter inside each. Bake 30 to 40 minutes, or until a cake tester inserted in the center of each layer comes out clean. Let stand until cool. Unmold.

6. Meanwhile, prepare the frosting. Combine the half-and-half, sugar, egg yolks, butter, and vanilla extract in a saucepan. Cook, stirring constantly, over medium heat, 12 minutes, or until the mixture thickens. Add the coconut and pecans and beat thoroughly until cool and of a spreadable consistency. Cover the top of each layer with the frosting and stack the layers. Do not coat the sides.

YIELD: 10 OR MORE SERVINGS.

CARROT CAKE

1 pound carrots, approximately
2 cups sugar
1 1/2 cups corn or peanut oil
4 eggs
2 cups flour
2 teaspoons baking powder

2 teaspoons baking soda
1 teaspoon salt, if desired
1/2 cup coarsely chopped pecans
Cream Cheese Frosting (see following
    recipe)

1. Preheat the oven to 325 degrees.

2. Trim, scrape, and grate the carrots, then measure them; there should be about 3 cups. Set aside.

3. Combine the sugar and oil in the bowl of an electric mixer. Start beating. Add the eggs, 1 at a time, beating well after each addition.

4. Sift together the flour, baking powder, baking soda, and salt. Add this to the oil mixture while beating. Add the grated carrots and nuts and blend well.

5. Lightly oil three 9-inch cake pans. Line the bottoms with circles of wax paper; oil the paper. Pour the batter into the pans and bake 45 minutes.

6. Turn the cakes onto wire racks and let cool. Remove the paper liners. Frost with cream cheese frosting.

YIELD: 8 OR MORE SERVINGS.

CREAM CHEESE FROSTING

2 cups confectioners' sugar
1 package (8 ounces) cream cheese
4 tablespoons butter, at room
   temperature

2 teaspoons pure vanilla extract

1. Sift the sugar into the bowl of an electric mixer.

2. Add the cream cheese, butter, and vanilla. Beat until smooth and creamy.

YIELD: ENOUGH FROSTING FOR A 3-LAYER CAKE.

RED VELVET CAKE

THE CAKE:

1/2 cup vegetable shortening
1 1/2 cups sugar
2 eggs
2 to 4 tablespoons unsweetened cocoa
1 ounce red food coloring, or up to 1/4
   cup if you want a really red cake

1 teaspoon salt, if desired
1 teaspoon pure vanilla extract
1 cup buttermilk
2 1/2 cups sifted flour
1 tablespoon vinegar
1 teaspoon baking soda

THE FILLING:

8 tablespoons butter

1 cup sugar

8 egg yolks

1 cup chopped pecans or walnuts

2 tablespoons bourbon or rum

1 cup raisins

1. Preheat the oven to 350 degrees.

2. To make the cake batter, cream together the shortening and sugar in the bowl of an electric mixer until fluffy. Add the eggs, 1 at a time, beating well after each addition. Beat 1 minute on medium speed.

3. Blend the cocoa and red food coloring to make a paste, and add it and the salt to the creamed mixture. Blend the vanilla and buttermilk. Alternately add the buttermilk and the flour to the creamed mixture, beating constantly. Blend the vinegar and baking soda and beat this in.

4. Meanwhile, butter and flour two 9-inch cake pans. Shake out the excess. Pour and scrape the cake batter into each pan and bake 25 to 30 minutes.

5. Remove the cake layers and let cool on a rack, then turn out onto the rack.

6. For the filling, combine the butter, sugar, and egg yolks in a saucepan. Set the saucepan in a skillet of boiling water and beat with a wire whisk until thickened. Add the remaining ingredients and blend. Let cool. As the filling stands it will thicken more. Spread the filling between the cake layers and on the top and sides.

YIELD: 8 OR MORE SERVINGS.

MISSISSIPPI CHRISTMAS CAKE

¾ pound butter

2 cups sugar

6 eggs

4 cups flour

1 cup bourbon, brandy, or rum

½ cup dark corn syrup

1 cup Fig Preserves (see following
    recipe)

6 cups raisins

8 cups broken pecan halves

1 teaspoon freshly grated nutmeg

2 teaspoons ground cinnamon

1 teaspoon ground cloves

1. Preheat the oven to 275 degrees.

2. Cream together the butter and sugar until light and fluffy. Beat in the eggs, 1 at a time, and fold in the flour. Combine the bourbon, corn syrup, and preserves and stir in.

3. Add the raisins, pecans, nutmeg, cinnamon, and cloves and fold to blend thoroughly. Pour and scrape the batter into a buttered 4-quart tube pan and bake 2½ hours, or slightly longer. Let stand until cool. Unmold.

YIELD: 12 OR MORE SERVINGS.

FIG PRESERVES

7 cups sugar

¼ cup lemon juice

6 cups water

8 cups ripe but firm figs (about 4½
    pounds)

2 lemons, sliced or coarsely chopped,
    seeds removed

1. In a kettle combine the sugar, lemon juice, and water. Bring to the boil and stir until the sugar dissolves.

2. If the figs are young, leave the stems intact. Add the figs to the syrup and cook 10 minutes, stirring occasionally to prevent sticking. Add the sliced or chopped lemons and continue cooking until the figs are almost translucent, 10 to 15 minutes. If the syrup becomes too thick, add a little boiling water, about ¼ cup at a time.

3. Remove from the heat and cover. Let stand in a cool place overnight, or for up to 24 hours. Pack the figs and their syrup in hot, sterilized half-pint jars, leaving ¼ inch headspace. Process in a boiling-water bath for 30 minutes.

YIELD: ABOUT 10 HALF-PINTS.

MY MOTHER'S "PAST PERFECT" FRUITCAKE

4 cups shelled pecans, coarsely chopped
2 cups whole candied cherries
5 slices candied pineapple, each slice
   cut into 8 pieces
1 cup flour

1 ½ teaspoons baking powder
⅛ teaspoon salt, if desired
4 large eggs
1 cup sugar
1 teaspoon pure vanilla extract

1. Preheat the oven to 250 degrees.
2. Butter the bottom and sides of an 8-cup cake pan and line the bottom with parchment paper cut to fit neatly. Set aside.
3. In a large mixing bowl, combine the pecans, cherries, and pineapple pieces.
4. Combine the flour, baking powder, and salt in a sifter, and sift the mixture over the pecans and fruits.
5. Combine the eggs, sugar, and vanilla in another bowl and beat well. Pour this over the pecan-and-fruit mixture and beat with a wooden spoon to blend thoroughly.
6. Pour the batter into the prepared cake pan and bake 1½ hours. Set the pan in a larger pan and pour boiling water around it. Continue baking 15 minutes longer.

7. Let cool on a rack, then slice and serve. Or wrap the fruitcake in several layers of cheesecloth and store in a cool place.

YIELD: 12 OR MORE SERVINGS.

MISSISSIPPI MUD PIE

Although I was born and raised in the Mississippi Delta, I never heard of a Mississippi mud pie or a Mississippi mud cake until I moved North and became food editor of *The New York Times.* It is conceivable that they existed, but no amount of research has revealed to me whether they did, or if these are recent creations that came about during my adulthood. Nevertheless, they are both rich as Croesus and many people find them delectable.

Pastry for a 9-inch Pie (page 308)
1/4 pound butter
3 ounces (squares) unsweetened
* chocolate*
3 eggs

3 tablespoons light corn syrup
1 1/2 cups sugar
1 teaspoon pure vanilla extract
Vanilla ice cream, optional

1. Preheat the oven to 350 degrees.
2. Line a 9-inch pie plate with the pastry.
3. Combine the butter and chocolate in a saucepan. Heat gently, stirring often, until melted and blended.
4. Beat the eggs until light and frothy. Stir in the corn syrup, sugar, and vanilla. Pour in the chocolate mixture, stirring.
5. Pour the filling into the prepared pie plate. Bake 35 to 40 minutes, or until the top is slightly crunchy and the filling is set. Do not overcook. The filling should remain soft inside.
6. This is best served warm with a spoonful of vanilla ice cream on top, but it is excellent served at room temperature or cold.

YIELD: 6 TO 8 SERVINGS.

MISSISSIPPI MUD CAKE

THE CAKE:

1/2 pound butter

2 cups sugar

4 eggs

1 1/2 cups flour

1/3 cup unsweetened cocoa

1 cup coarsely chopped pecans

1 teaspoon pure vanilla extract

3 cups miniature marshmallows or
    large marshmallows cut into
    1/2-inch pieces

THE ICING:

1/2 pound butter

1 1/2 cups confectioners' sugar

1/3 cup unsweetened cocoa

1 cup coarsely chopped pecans

1/2 cup evaporated milk

1. Preheat the oven to 350 degrees.

2. To prepare the cake batter, combine the butter and sugar in a mixing bowl. Beat well until creamy. Add the eggs, 1 at a time, beating thoroughly after each addition.

3. Sift together the flour and cocoa. Fold this into the creamed mixture. Add the chopped nuts and the vanilla. Beat well.

4. Butter the bottom and sides of a 9 × 13-inch baking pan. Add a little flour and shake it around to coat the bottom and sides of the pan. Shake out the excess.

5. Spoon the cake batter into the pan and smooth it over. Place in the oven and bake 25 to 30 minutes. Remove from the oven and sprinkle the top with the marshmallows. Return to the oven and bake about 10 minutes, until the marshmallows are melted and starting to brown. Remove from the oven and let cool in the pan about 30 minutes.

6. Meanwhile, prepare the icing. Melt the butter in a saucepan.

7. Sift together the confectioners' sugar and cocoa. Stir this into the butter along with the nuts and milk. Spread this over the cake and let stand until thoroughly cooled.

8. Cut into slices and serve.

YIELD: **12 OR MORE SERVINGS.**

DATE AND WALNUT LOAF

³/₄ pound pitted dates
1 ½ teaspoons baking soda
1 ½ cups boiling water
1 ½ cups plus 3 tablespoons flour
¼ teaspoon freshly grated nutmeg
¼ teaspoon ground cinnamon
¼ teaspoon ground allspice
¼ teaspoon ground ginger
2 tablespoons butter, at room
*   temperature*

1 ¼ cups sugar
2 small eggs, lightly beaten
1 teaspoon pure vanilla extract
1 ½ cups coarsely chopped or broken
*   walnuts, preferably black walnuts,*
*   although English walnuts may be*
*   used, preferably toasted (see note)*

1. Preheat the oven to 350 degrees.

2. If the dates are not already chopped, chop them coarsely. There should be about 2½ cups. Put the dates in a mixing bowl.

3. Blend the baking soda and boiling water. Pour this hot mixture over the dates.

4. Sift together the flour and spices and set aside.

5. Put the butter and sugar in the bowl of an electric mixer and blend. Beat in the eggs and vanilla.

6. Start beating on low speed while alternately adding the flour mixture and the dates with their liquid. Add the walnuts and blend well.

7. Butter the inside of a standard loaf pan, measuring 9 × 5 × 2¾ inches. Pour in the batter and place in the oven. Bake about 1 hour and 10 minutes, or until a straw or thin wooden skewer inserted in the center comes out clean.

YIELD: 8 OR MORE SERVINGS.

NOTE: *To toast the walnuts, preheat the oven to 350 degrees. Scatter the nuts over a baking sheet and bake until they are crisp and lightly brown, about 10 minutes.*

NANNIE CRAIG'S FRUITCAKE

One of the recipes in the manuscript cookbook compiled for me by my mother shortly after World War II is labeled, simply, Nannie Craig's Fruitcake, and I have no idea as to her exact ancestry or relationship to my family. I have always presumed she was an aunt or other close relative. In any event, it is a great holiday cake.

½ cup chopped glacéed cherries
1 ½ cups chopped glacéed pineapple
3 cups seedless black raisins
1 ½ cups dried black currants
2 cups broken pecans
1 ½ cups chopped blanched almonds
1 cup bourbon, Cognac, or rum
2 ½ cups flour
½ pound butter
1 ¾ cups sugar
6 eggs, separated
2 teaspoons baking powder
¾ teaspoon baking soda
1 ½ teaspoons ground ginger

1 ½ teaspoons ground mace
1 tablespoon grated nutmeg
1 tablespoon cinnamon
1 cup orange juice
4 cups Grated Fresh Coconut (page 279), or 2 cups unsweetened dried coconut
1 cup Fig Preserves (page 296)
½ cup quince, apricot, or grape jelly
Quick Fondant Icing (see following recipe), optional
Candied fruits such as cherries, angelica, and so on, for decorating the cake, optional

1. Combine the glacéed cherries, pineapple, raisins, currants, pecans, and almonds in a mixing bowl and add ½ cup bourbon, Cognac, or rum. Cover with plastic wrap and let stand overnight.

2. Preheat the oven to 250 degrees.

3. Empty the fruits onto a flat surface and sprinkle with ½ cup flour. Toss to coat the fruits and nuts and set aside.

4. Put the butter into the bowl of an electric mixer. Add the sugar and start beating, first on low and then on high speed. Cream the mixture well until it is light-colored. Beat in the egg yolks, 1 at a time.

5. Meanwhile, combine the remaining 2 cups flour with the baking powder, baking soda, ginger, mace, nutmeg, and cinnamon. Sift the dry ingredients together.

6. Gradually beat the flour mixture into the butter-and-sugar mixture. Gradually beat in the orange juice, the remaining ½ cup bourbon, Cognac or rum, the coconut, fig preserves, and jelly. Fold in the floured fruit.

7. Beat the egg whites until they stand in stiff peaks. Fold them into the batter. This recipe yields about 4 quarts (16 cups) of batter.

8. Butter the baking pans well. Line them with a double layer of wax paper or a single layer of parchment paper, and grease the paper. If using Teflon-coated pans, butter the pan and line the bottom with a cutout of buttered wax paper. The batter may be portioned into pans of various sizes, but do not fill any pan full of batter, for it expands as it bakes. Always leave about 1 inch of space from the top of the pan. This recipe was most recently tested with two standard 9 × 5 × 2-inch Teflon loaf pans plus one 8½ × 4½ × 3-inch (6 cup) loaf pan (a 6-cup round tube pan could also be used).

9. Bake the cakes for 2½ hours and increase the heat to 275 degrees. Bake a total of about 3½ hours for the large loaf pans, a total of about 3 hours and 15 minutes for the smaller ones. Cooking times will vary from oven to oven. The correct internal temperature for these cakes is 160 degrees when a meat thermometer is inserted.

10. When the cakes are removed from the oven, cool them on a rack for at least 30 minutes, run a knife around the edges and, while still warm, invert them onto a rack. They should not stick on the bottom, but if they do, scrape out the stuck portion and repair the bottom with that. Frost with icing and decorate, if desired, with candied fruit.

YIELD: ONE 2¼-POUND LOAF OR 6-CUP TUBE CAKE, AND TWO 3-POUND LOAF CAKES.

NOTE: *Unsweetened dried coconut is available in health food stores. These cakes may be kept for days, weeks, and months before they are frosted. To keep them, store closely covered in a dry place. Douse them occasionally with about ¼ cup bourbon, rum, or Cognac.*

QUICK FONDANT ICING

½ cup granulated sugar
2½ tablespoons light corn syrup
¼ cup water
1½ cups confectioners' sugar

1 teaspoon egg white
1 teaspoon butter, at room temperature
Bourbon, rum, or Cognac

1. Combine the granulated sugar, corn syrup, and water in a saucepan and gradually bring to the boil, stirring until sugar is dissolved. Cook over moderate heat until the mixture registers 236 to 238 degrees on a candy thermometer.

2. Have ready a pastry brush in a cup of cold water. As the syrup cooks, run the brush around the inside of the saucepan, wiping away sugar crystals that may form above the syrup. If not removed, these will cause crystals throughout the syrup. When the syrup is ready, pour it into another saucepan and let cool.

3. Place the saucepan in a skillet or larger saucepan with water. Bring the water to the boil. Stir the syrup until it is fluid.

4. Gradually add the confectioners' sugar to the syrup, stirring constantly. Stir until well blended and lukewarm. Do not overheat.

5. Beat in the egg white and butter, and add enough bourbon, rum, or Cognac to bring the icing to a spreadable consistency.

YIELD: ENOUGH ICING FOR 2 FRUITCAKE LOAVES.

MARY ANN'S FRUITCAKE

1 pound golden seedless raisins
1 pound pecan meats, broken
3 cups sifted flour
1 teaspoon salt, if desired
1 pound butter, at room temperature

2 cups sugar
6 eggs, separated
1 teaspoon baking soda
1 tablespoon warm water
¼ cup Grand Marnier

1. Preheat the oven to 250 degrees. Butter the inside of a 10-inch, 12-cup Bundt pan. Sprinkle liberally with flour and shake out the excess. Set aside.

2. In a large mixing bowl, combine the raisins and pecan meats. Sprinkle the 3 cups flour and salt over all, and toss with the hands until thoroughly blended. Set aside.

3. Place the butter in the bowl of an electric mixer. Start beating and gradually add the sugar. Cream the mixture well and add the egg yolks, 1 at a time, beating constantly. Blend the baking soda and warm water and add it to the mixture, beating. Beat in the Grand Marnier. Pour this mixture into the fruit-and-nut mixture and blend together with the hands.

4. Beat the whites until stiff and fold them in with the hands. Continue folding until the whites are not apparent.

5. Spoon and scrape the mixture into the prepared pan, smoothing the top with a spatula. Bake 2 or 2¼ hours, or until the cake is puffed above the pan and nicely browned on top. If the cake starts to brown too soon on top, cover with aluminum foil.

6. Remove the cake from the pan shortly after it is baked. Tapping the bottom of the cake pan with a heavy knife will help loosen it. Store the cake for at least 10 days. If desired, add an occasional sprinkle of Cognac or rum to the cake as it stands. Keep it closely covered and refrigerated until ready to use.

YIELD: ONE 10-INCH CAKE.

UPSIDE-DOWN APPLE PIE

I have a good friend in New York, Gene Hovis, a professional chef, who was born in North Carolina. He came into my kitchen and demonstrated one of his mother's prized creations, a hot upside-down apple pie. It is very much "down-home," but greatly resembles the famed *tarte tatin* of France.

SHORT BUTTER CRUST:

2 cups unbleached flour
½ pound chilled butter, cut into small
    pieces
5 to 6 tablespoons ice water

THE ASSEMBLY:

8 tablespoons butter, melted
1 cup dark brown sugar
1 tablespoon grated lemon rind
2 teaspoons arrowroot

4 or 5 apples, such as Granny Smiths
    (about 2 pounds)
2 tablespoons bourbon

1. Put the flour in a mixing bowl and add the chilled butter pieces. Work the flour and butter together with the fingers or a pastry blender, until well blended.

2. Gradually sprinkle the mixture with ice water, using only enough so that the dough holds together and can be formed into a ball. Shape the dough into a ball and flatten slightly. Wrap closely in plastic wrap and refrigerate until ready to use.

3. Pour the melted butter into a dish 1½ to 2 inches deep and 12 inches in diameter (the dish might also be rectangular).

4. Sprinkle evenly with the brown sugar, grated rind, and arrowroot.

5. Peel the apples and cut away any blemishes. Quarter the apples and cut away the cores. Cut the quarters in half lengthwise. Arrange the apple pieces in neat concentric circles over the brown sugar mixture. Sprinkle the bourbon over the apples.

6. Roll out the dough on a lightly floured surface into a circle about 13 inches in diameter. Carefully place the dough on top of the apples and gently fold over the overhanging edges toward the center, pressing down lightly all around the outer rim of dough so that the apples are totally covered.

7. Cover closely with plastic wrap and refrigerate until ready to bake.

8. When ready to bake, preheat the oven to 400 degrees.

9. Place the pie in the oven and bake 1 hour. Remove to a rack and let cool briefly.

10. Run a knife around the inside rim of the pie. Place a large dish over the pie. Quickly invert the pie onto the dish. Serve hot or at room temperature.

YIELD: 12 OR MORE SERVINGS.

KENTUCKY BOURBON PIE

THE CRUST:

1 1/4 cups graham cracker crumbs
1/4 cup sugar
1/4 pound butter, melted

THE FILLING:

1/2 cup cold strong coffee
1 envelope unflavored gelatin
2/3 cup sugar
Salt to taste, if desired
3 eggs, separated

6 tablespoons bourbon
1/4 cup coffee liqueur (Kahlúa or Tia Maria)
2 cups heavy cream

1. Preheat the oven to 350 degrees.

2. To make the crust, combine the crumbs with the sugar and melted butter and rub together until the crumbs are evenly coated. Spoon the crumbs into a 9- or 10-inch pie plate and press the crumbs evenly against the bottom and sides.

3. Place the pie shell in the oven and bake 4 to 5 minutes without browning. Remove from the heat and cool thoroughly.

4. To make the filling, pour the coffee into a saucepan and sprinkle the gelatin over it. Add 1/3 cup sugar, the salt, and the egg yolks. Stir to blend thoroughly.

5. Place the saucepan over low heat and stir until the gelatin is dissolved and the mixture thickens. Do not boil.

6. Remove the mixture from the heat and add the bourbon and coffee liqueur. Chill the mixture in the refrigerator until it is cool and starts to thicken. Do not let it jell.

7. Beat the whites until stiff, gradually adding the remaining ⅓ cup sugar. Fold the whites into the gelatin mixture.

8. Whip 1 cup cream and fold it into the mixture. Turn the filling into the prepared pie plate and chill several hours or overnight.

9. Before serving, whip the remaining 1 cup cream, adding sugar to taste. Garnish with the sweetened whipped cream, and serve.

YIELD: 8 OR MORE SERVINGS.

CHESS PIE

The origin of the name "chess pie" was explained to me on a visit to Kentucky as follows: A visitor to the South went to a dining establishment. At the time for dessert, the waitress told him that pie was included. He said he would like apple pie and she replied that it was not served. "Then I'll take peach," he said. No peach either. "What kind of pie do you serve?" he asked. "Jes' pie," she told him.

When in the course of reporting recipes for publication in *The New York Times* I have mentioned the dessert known as chess pie, the response has always been impressive beyond my wildest imagination. I have been told repeatedly in each letter that I did not know how to prepare the genuine article. The following recipe came to me anonymously. It was signed "A True Southern Belle."

Pastry for a 9-inch Pie (see following
   recipe)
¼ pound butter, at room temperature
2 cups sugar
1 tablespoon flour
2 tablespoons white cornmeal
Salt to taste, if desired

4 eggs
¼ cup milk
¼ cup freshly squeezed lemon juice
2 teaspoons grated fresh lemon rind
Sweetened whipped cream for garnish,
   optional
Freshly grated nutmeg for garnish

1. Preheat the oven to 350 degrees.

2. Line a 9-inch pie plate with the pastry and flute the rim.

3. Put the butter and sugar into the bowl of an electric mixer and beat until creamy. Beat in the flour, cornmeal, and salt. Add the eggs, 1 at a time, and beat well after each addition. Beat in the milk, lemon juice, and lemon rind.

4. Pour and scrape the mixture into the pastry-lined pie plate and place on the lowest shelf of the oven. Bake 45 minutes, or until the filling is golden and firm. Let cool to room temperature.

5. Serve cut into very small wedges with, if desired, a dollop of sweetened whipped cream on each serving. Before serving, sprinkle each portion with a small amount of freshly grated nutmeg.

YIELD: 8 OR MORE SERVINGS.

PASTRY FOR A 9-INCH PIE

1 1/2 cups flour   *6 tablespoons cold butter*
1 teaspoon sugar   *3 to 4 tablespoons ice water*

1. Put the flour and sugar into the container of a food processor. Cut the butter into small bits and add to the container. Start processing and gradually add the water. Add only enough water until the dough comes away from the sides of the bowl.

2. Alternatively, place the flour and sugar in a mixing bowl. Cut the butter into small bits and add it. Cut it in with two knives or a pastry blender, until the mixture looks like coarse oatmeal. Add the water, stirring quickly with a fork.

3. Wrap the dough in wax paper and refrigerate. Let stand at room temperature for about 1 hour before rolling out.

4. If the pie shell is to be baked before filling, preheat the oven to 425 degrees. Line a 9-inch pie plate with the pastry and flute the edges. Line the pastry with aluminum foil and add enough dried beans to weight the bottom. Bake for about 10 minutes. Remove the foil and beans and bake for 2 to 5 minutes longer, until the crust is done.

YIELD: PASTRY FOR ONE 9-INCH PIE.

JEFF DAVIS PIE

I have been told (and have serious doubts) that Jefferson Davis was familiar with this confection named in his honor as president of the Confederate States during the Civil War. There are many versions of this dish and I think this is one of the best.

Pastry for two 9-inch pies (opposite)
3 eggs, separated
1 1/2 tablespoons flour
1 cup half-and-half

2 1/2 cups sugar
1/4 pound butter, melted
1 teaspoon cinnamon
1 teaspoon allspice

1. Preheat the oven to 425 degrees.
2. Line two 9-inch pie plates with the pastry and flute the rims.
3. In a bowl, mix together the egg yolks, flour, half-and-half, sugar, butter, cinnamon, and allspice.
4. Beat the egg whites until they hold stiff peaks and fold into the yolk mixture thoroughly.
5. Pour the mixture, not more than 3/4 inch deep, into the uncooked pie crusts and bake 10 minutes. Reduce the heat to 350 degrees and bake 30 to 40 minutes, preferably in the center of the oven. When done, the filling should be crystalline, not gummy.
6. Serve cold, cut into thin slices.

YIELD: ABOUT 20 SERVINGS.

BLACKSMITH PIE

I was given a recipe some years ago for an incredibly rich chocolate cake, back in the days when they first coined the name "chocoholic." This recipe for blacksmith pie was created for the Old Forge Restaurant in Miami Beach.

THE CRUST:

10 ounces (about 12) Fudge Cookies
   (see following recipe) or Oreos with
   filling scraped off and discarded

8 ounces graham crackers
1/2 pound butter, at room temperature

THE FILLING:

1/4 cup cornstarch
1 cup plus 3 tablespoons sugar
1/2 teaspoon pure vanilla extract
1 1/2 cups half-and-half, or 1 cup
   heavy cream and 1/2 cup milk
2 egg yolks

1 whole egg
3/4 pound (12 ounces) semisweet
   chocolate
3 1/2 cups heavy cream
4 egg whites

1. Using a blender or food processor, blend the fudge cookies and graham crackers until fine. There should be about 5 cups. Put the crumbs in a bowl. Cut the butter into pieces and add it, blending thoroughly.

2. Use the crumb mixture to line the bottom and sides of a 10-inch springform pan that is 3 inches deep. Chill 1 hour.

3. Meanwhile, to make the filling, combine the cornstarch, 3 tablespoons sugar, vanilla extract, and half-and-half in a saucepan. Stir with a wire whisk until blended and smooth. Put the saucepan on the stove and bring to the boil over low heat, stirring constantly with the whisk. When thickened, remove it from the heat.

4. Beat together the egg yolks and whole egg and add this to the sauce, stirring rapidly with the whisk. Return to the heat and cook, stirring, until the custard barely simmers. Pour and scrape 1 cup of the custard into a mixing bowl, and the remaining sauce into a second bowl.

5. Break up the chocolate pieces and put them in a bowl. Set this bowl in a small basin of boiling water and let stand, stirring occasionally, until melted. Add the chocolate to the 1 cup custard. Smear the bottom and sides of the chilled crumb crust with the chocolate-and-custard mixture. Chill.

6. Beat the heavy cream until partly stiff. Gradually add 1/2 cup sugar and continue beating until stiff.

7. Beat the egg whites until almost stiff, and gradually add the remaining 1/2 cup sugar, beating vigorously. Continue beating until stiff.

8. Fold the whipped cream and egg whites into the second bowl of custard. Pour and scrape this mixture inside the mold. Smooth it over. Cover with plastic wrap and chill several hours.

9. Unmold and serve cut into wedges.

YIELD: 12 OR MORE SERVINGS.

FUDGE COOKIES

¼ pound butter

*5 ounces (5 squares) unsweetened
   chocolate, grated*

¼ cup dark corn syrup

⅓ cup sugar

1 teaspoon pure vanilla extract

1 extra-large egg

1 cup sifted flour

½ teaspoon baking soda

⅛ teaspoon salt, if desired

1. Preheat the oven to 350 degrees.

2. Place the butter in a saucepan with a heavy bottom. Place the saucepan over very low heat and let stand until butter melts. Add the grated chocolate, corn syrup, sugar, and vanilla extract. Stir occasionally with a wire whisk until the chocolate melts.

3. Remove from the heat and let stand 10 minutes. Add the egg and blend well.

4. Sift together the flour, baking soda, and salt. Add the dry ingredients to the chocolate mixture and blend well. Scrape the mixture into a mixing bowl.

5. Line a baking sheet with a length of wax paper. Cover this with a sheet of aluminum foil.

6. Spoon 1 tablespoon of the mixture at 2-inch intervals over the foil and bake 10 to 15 minutes, watching carefully that the cookies do not burn on the bottom. It may be necessary to turn the baking sheet and to shift it to a higher position in the oven to prevent burning.

7. Turn off the oven heat and open the oven door. Let the cookies rest in the oven 5 minutes. Remove and transfer the cookies to a rack until cool.

YIELD: ABOUT 2 DOZEN.

SWEET POTATO PIE

Pastry for a 9-inch Pie (page 308)
1 1/2 pounds sweet potatoes
Salt, if desired
3 tablespoons butter
1/4 cup maple syrup
1/2 cup sugar

3/4 teaspoon ground cinnamon
1/4 teaspoon ground cloves
1/2 teaspoon ground nutmeg
3 eggs, separated
3/4 cup milk

1. Prepare the pastry and line a pie plate. Refrigerate until ready to use.

2. Meanwhile, place the sweet potatoes in a saucepan and add water to cover and salt to taste. If 1 potato is used, split it in half lengthwise to facilitate cooking. Simmer 15 minutes or longer, or until the potatoes are tender. Drain.

3. Preheat the oven to 350 degrees.

4. Peel the potatoes and put them through a food mill, or blend in a food processor or electric blender. Spoon and scrape the purée into a bowl and add the butter, syrup, sugar, 1/2 teaspoon salt, cinnamon, cloves, nutmeg, egg yolks, and milk. Blend well.

5. Beat the whites until stiff. Fold the potato mixture into them. Pour the filling into the prepared shell and bake 45 minutes, or until a knife inserted in the center comes out clean.

YIELD: 8 TO 12 SERVINGS.

COCONUT SWEET POTATO PIE

THE CRUST:

1 cup sifted flour
1/4 pound chilled butter, cut into small pieces

1/2 teaspoon granulated sugar
6 tablespoons ice water

THE FILLING:

2 cups mashed cooked sweet potatoes
  (approximately 1 pound fresh)
1/2 cup dark brown sugar
2 eggs, at room temperature
1 cup heavy cream, at room
  temperature
1/2 teaspoon ground ginger
1/2 teaspoon ground cloves
1/2 teaspoon ground nutmeg

1/2 teaspoon ground cinnamon
Grated rind of 1 orange
4 tablespoons butter, melted and cooled
1 teaspoon pure vanilla extract
1/4 cup dark rum
2 egg whites
1 can (3 ounces) moist shredded
  coconut

1. Place flour, chilled butter, and granulated sugar into the container of a food processor. Process, turning on and off rapidly, until butter is cut into flour and the mixture is crumbly. Add ice water and process just until the dough begins to hold together. Remove the dough from processor, gather it into a ball, and flatten it slightly. Flour it lightly. Cover with plastic wrap and refrigerate for 30 minutes.

2. Preheat the oven to 425 degrees.

3. On a lightly floured surface, roll out the chilled dough into a circle large enough to fit a 9-inch pie plate. Place the dough in the pie plate and prick the bottom and sides with the tines of a fork. Grease a piece of aluminum foil large enough to cover the bottom and sides of the pie plate. Fill the lined pie plate with weights or dried beans. Place the pie plate on rack in lowest third of oven and bake for 10 minutes. Remove the foil and weights and cook for another 7 minutes. Remove and cool.

4. Place all filling ingredients except the egg whites and shredded coconut into a food processor and process until smooth and creamy. Remove and set aside.

5. In a separate bowl, beat the egg whites until they are frothy but not at the soft-peak stage. Fold the egg whites into the sweet potato mixture. Fold in the grated coconut and mix well.

6. Mound the mixture into the baked pie shell and bake at 425 degrees for 45 minutes, or until a knife inserted in the center comes out clean. Remove from the oven and cool on a rack to room temperature.

7. Serve at room temperature or chilled with unsweetened whipped cream flavored with rum.

YIELD: 8 SERVINGS.

PUMPKIN PIE

Pastry for a 9-inch Pie (page 308)
1 1/2 cups canned pumpkin
3/4 cup sugar
1/2 teaspoon salt, if desired
1/2 teaspoon ginger, preferably freshly
  grated

1/4 teaspoon nutmeg
3 eggs
1 cup milk
1/4 cup dark rum or bourbon
3/4 cup heavy cream

1. Preheat the oven to 425 degrees.

2. Line a 9-inch pie plate with pastry.

3. In a mixing bowl, combine the pumpkin, sugar, salt, ginger, and nutmeg. Add the eggs, milk, rum, and cream and blend well.

4. Pour the mixture into the pastry-lined pie plate and bake for 15 minutes. Reduce the temperature to 350 degrees and bake 30 to 40 minutes longer, or until set. If desired, serve with whipped cream sweetened to taste and flavored with dark rum.

YIELD: 6 SERVINGS.

LEMON MERINGUE PIE

4 tablespoons cornstarch
1/4 teaspoon salt, if desired
1 cup plus 6 tablespoons sugar
1 1/2 cups water
3 eggs, separated

2 tablespoons butter
1 1/2 teaspoons grated lemon rind
5 tablespoons lemon juice
Pastry for a 9-inch Pie, baked (page
  308)

1. Preheat oven to 325 degrees.

2. Mix the cornstarch, salt, and ½ cup sugar in the top of a double boiler. Gradually add the water, stirring. Place over boiling water and cook, stirring constantly, until the mixture thickens. Cover and cook 10 minutes, stirring occasionally. Do not remove from the heat.

3. Beat the egg yolks in a mixing bowl and add ½ cup sugar. Stir a small amount of the hot mixture into the egg yolks. Immediately pour the egg yolk mixture into the remaining hot mixture over boiling water; blend thoroughly. Cook 2 minutes longer, stirring constantly. Remove from the heat and add the butter, lemon rind, and lemon juice. Cool to room temperature without stirring.

4. Turn the filling into the baked pie shell. Beat the egg whites until stiff but not dry. Gradually beat in the remaining 6 tablespoons sugar. Spread the meringue over the filling, being sure to extend it over the end of the crust.

5. Bake until delicately browned, 15 to 20 minutes. Cool to room temperature and serve.

YIELD: 6 TO 8 SERVINGS.

୭ଓ
KEY LIME PIE

If I were asked to name the greatest of all regional American desserts, my answer might very well be Key lime pie, a sweet that is difficult for most people to make authentically. The real McCoy must be made with genuine Key limes of the sort found in the Florida Keys and the surrounding territory or on most islands in the Caribbean. You can make it with the commonplace, store-bought Persian limes, but they lack the pungent, tart flavor of the Key limes. It is one of the simplest of pies to make, whatever juice you have at your disposal.

THE GRAHAM CRACKER CRUST:

1½ cups graham cracker crumbs
¼ cup sugar

¼ cup finely chopped almonds
4 tablespoons butter, melted

THE FILLING:

6 egg yolks
1 can (14 ounces) sweetened condensed
  milk (about 1 1/4 cups)

3/4 cup fresh lime juice, preferably from
  Key limes
2 teaspoons grated lime rind

THE MERINGUE (see note):

6 egg whites
1 cup sugar
1/2 teaspoon cream of tartar

1. Preheat the oven to 375 degrees.

2. To make the crust, combine the crumbs, sugar, almonds, and butter in a bowl. Blend well.

3. Use the mixture to line the bottom and sides of a 10-inch pie plate and bake 8 to 10 minutes. Remove the crust to a rack and let cool.

4. Reduce the oven heat to 350 degrees.

5. Meanwhile, prepare the filling. Beat the yolks in a mixing bowl. Pour in the condensed milk, stirring constantly. Add the lime juice and rind.

6. Pour the filling mixture into the crumb crust. Place the pie in the oven and bake 15 minutes. Transfer to a rack and let cool.

7. Make the meringue. Beat the egg whites in a mixing bowl until frothy. Gradually add the sugar and cream of tartar, beating constantly until peaks form. Continue beating until stiff.

8. Spread the meringue over the pie, being sure to cover all the way to the edge of the crust. Bake 5 to 6 minutes, or until the meringue is nicely browned. Remove to a rack to cool. After the pie cools, transfer to the refrigerator. Serve chilled.

YIELD: 6 TO 8 SERVINGS.

NOTE: *If you prefer, you may ignore the meringue and spread the pie, once baked and cooled, with a layer of sweetened whipped cream.*

DIXIE PECAN PIE

Pecans are, to my mind, the most Southern of nuts. One authority I know states that they were grown in Virginia long before George Washington was born and that the name derives from the American Indian word *pakan*. The earliest colonists in Virginia and North Carolina transliterated the word as "pagan" and as a result, the Pagan River, which flows through Smithfield, Virginia, was named for the abundance of pecan trees that grew along its shores and not for any pagans who lived nearby.

Pastry for a 9-inch Pie (page 308)	*2 cups dark corn syrup*
3 large eggs	*1 teaspoon pure vanilla extract*
2 tablespoons flour	*¼ teaspoon salt, if desired*
2 tablespoons sugar	*1 cup pecan halves*

1. Preheat the oven to 425 degrees.
2. Line a pie plate with pastry. Refrigerate.
3. Beat the eggs until light. Blend the flour and sugar and add this to the eggs. Beat well. Add the remaining ingredients, blending well.
4. Pour the mixture into the pie shell and bake 10 minutes. Reduce the oven heat to 325 degrees and continue baking about 45 minutes.

YIELD: 8 OR MORE SERVINGS.

GEORGIA PECAN PIE

Pastry for a 9-inch Pie (page 308)	*1 teaspoon pure vanilla extract*
1 cup sugar	*3 eggs, lightly beaten*
2 tablespoons butter, melted	*1½ cups coarsely chopped pecans*
1 cup dark corn syrup	

1. Line a pie plate with pastry and flute or crimp the edges.

2. Preheat the oven to 375 degrees.

3. In a saucepan, combine the sugar, butter, corn syrup, and vanilla. Bring to the simmer, stirring, until the sugar melts. Let cool briefly.

4. Add the sauce to the beaten eggs, stirring. Stir in the pecans.

5. Pour the filling into the pie shell and place in the oven. Bake 30 minutes.

6. Serve, if desired, with sweetened whipped cream.

YIELD: 6 TO 8 SERVINGS.

CHOCOLATE PECAN PIE

Pastry for a 9-inch Pie (page 308)
2 ounces (2 squares) unsweetened
  chocolate, grated
3 tablespoons butter
1 cup light corn syrup

¾ cup sugar
3 eggs, lightly beaten
1 teaspoon pure vanilla extract
1 cup coarsely chopped pecans
Sweetened whipped cream for topping

1. Preheat the oven to 350 degrees.

2. Line a 9-inch pie plate with the pastry.

3. Put the chocolate and butter in a saucepan and set the saucepan in a basin of simmering water. Cook, stirring occasionally, until the chocolate melts.

4. Combine the corn syrup and sugar and bring to the boil. Cook 2 minutes.

5. Put the beaten eggs in a mixing bowl. Combine the corn syrup and chocolate mixtures, and pour this over the eggs, stirring constantly. Stir in the vanilla and pecans. Turn this filling into the prepared pie plate.

6. Place the pie in the oven and bake 45 to 50 minutes, or until the pie is well puffed. Remove and place on a rack to cool.

7. Serve with sweetened whipped cream on top.

YIELD: 8 SERVINGS.

BOURBON PECAN PIE

5 1/2 tablespoons butter
1/2 cup dark brown sugar
3 eggs
1/4 teaspoon salt, if desired
1 cup dark corn syrup
1 tablespoon bourbon
1 cup chopped pecans
1 tablespoon flour

Pastry for a 9-inch Pie, baked (page 308)
8 to 10 whole pecans, in halves, for garnish
1/2 cup heavy cream, whipped, flavored with 2 tablespoons sugar and 2 to 3 tablespoons bourbon, optional

1. Preheat the oven to 350 degrees.

2. Cream the butter and add the brown sugar slowly, beating constantly until all is absorbed and the mixture is fluffy. Add the eggs, 1 at a time, beating continuously after each addition; then add the salt, corn syrup, and bourbon. Toss the pecans in the flour, then fold them into the filling. Pour filling into the crust.

3. Place in the oven and bake for 35 minutes, or until the filling is firm. Decorate the top by making a border of pecan halves and bake for 5 minutes more.

4. If desired, garnish the pie with whipped cream flavored with sugar and bourbon.

YIELD: 8 SERVINGS.

FRESH COCONUT CREAM PIE

Pastry for a 9-inch Pie (page 308)
3 eggs
9 tablespoons sugar
Salt to taste, if desired
1/4 teaspoon grated nutmeg

2 cups milk
1 teaspoon pure vanilla extract
1 1/2 cups grated fresh coconut (page
    279)

1. Prepare the pastry and line a pie plate. Refrigerate until ready to use.
2. Preheat the oven to 425 degrees.
3. Beat the eggs until well blended. Add the sugar, salt, nutmeg, milk, and vanilla and beat until smooth. Add the grated coconut.
4. Pour the custard mixture into the prepared shell and bake 15 minutes. Reduce the temperature to 350 degrees and bake 30 minutes longer, or until a knife inserted an inch from the pastry edge comes out clean.

YIELD: 8 TO 12 SERVINGS.

MINCEMEAT PIE

Pastry for two 9-inch pies (page 308)
3 to 4 cups Mincemeat (see following
    recipe)

1. Preheat the oven to 450 degrees.
2. Roll out the pastry into 2 circles. Line a 9-inch pie plate with 1 of them. Fill it with 3 to 4 cups mincemeat. Cover the pie with the other crust and flute the rim. Prick several holes in the top crust to let steam escape.
3. Bake the pie for about 30 minutes. Serve warm.

YIELD: ABOUT 8 SERVINGS.

MINCEMEAT

The texture of mincemeat is a question of personal taste. Some like it fine, some medium, and some coarse. If you want it coarse, the various fruits and meats should be chopped or cubed by hand. If you want it medium or fine, use a food processor or, more tediously, an electric blender, and process or blend to the desired texture. Some sources recommend grinding the mincemeat; others recommend grinding half the ingredients and chopping the rest. Take your choice.

This mincemeat is not destined to be cooked until it is made into pies. Let it age for at least 3 weeks and preferably a month before using.

1/2 pound cooked beef
1/2 pound cooked beef tongue
1 pound black currants
1 1/2 pound black raisins
2 ounces chopped candied lemon peel
2 ounces chopped candied orange peel
1/2 cup chopped diced candied citron
1/2 cup chopped glacéed cherries
1/2 cup chopped glacéed pineapple
3/4 pound finely chopped or ground suet
2 cups peeled, cored, and finely diced apple

2 cups brown sugar
Grated rind of 1 lemon
Grated rind of 1 orange
1/4 cup lemon juice
1 teaspoon ground nutmeg
1/2 teaspoon ground cloves
1/2 teaspoon ground allspice
1 teaspoon ground cinnamon
2 cups Cognac or other brandy
1/2 cup dry sherry
1/2 teaspoon salt, if desired

1. Cube or chop the beef, beef tongue, currants, raisins, lemon peel, orange peel, candied citron, cherries, pineapple, and suet. Pour this mixture into a bowl.

2. Add the remaining ingredients and mix well with the hands. There should be about 12 cups. Spoon the mixture into fruit jars and seal tightly. Store in a cool place to age.

YIELD: 12 CUPS.

JELLY ROLL WITH RASPBERRY FILLING

In my home, as in many Southern homes, we enjoyed many fancy desserts that were considered as Southern as cotton blossoms and cape jasmine. In later years, I discovered that they were really of French origin and they included charlottes (generally charlotte russe) and blancmanges. One of my favorite desserts was jelly roll, a traditional Southern sweet that goes by the name of *biscuit roulé* in French.

5 eggs, separated	2 tablespoons butter
1/3 cup plus 7 teaspoons sugar	1 1/2 cups raspberry jelly
1/2 cup plus 3 tablespoons flour	

1. Preheat the oven to 450 degrees.

2. Grease a jelly-roll pan with butter. Cover with a rectangle of buttered wax paper or parchment cut to size. Set aside.

3. Put the yolks in a mixing bowl and add all but 1 teaspoon sugar. Beat until light, lemon-colored, and thick, at least 5 minutes.

4. Sift the flour, a little at a time, over the yolk mixture, folding it in slowly with a rubber spatula.

5. Heat the butter over low heat just until it melts.

6. Beat the egg whites. When they are almost but not quite stiff, add the remaining 1 teaspoon sugar. Continue beating until stiff.

7. Spoon and scrape the egg whites into the mixing bowl with the egg yolk mixture. At the same time add the melted butter, and fold the butter and whites immediately into the egg yolk mixture.

8. Pour and scrape the mixture onto the prepared baking sheet. Use a spatula to smooth it over left to right, top to bottom. Place in the oven and bake 7 minutes.

9. Line a flat surface with wax paper. Turn the cake out quickly but carefully onto the wax paper. Pull off the wax paper or parchment on which the cake was baked. Turn the cake top side up.

10. Spoon the jelly onto the cake. Roll the cake sidewise for a short, thick roll, or lengthwise for a long, thin roll.

YIELD: 12 OR MORE SERVINGS.

HUGUENOT TORTE

I am persuaded that one of the finest desserts of Southern origin is known as a Huguenot torte. I am also persuaded that it has been perpetuated with greatest emphasis because it is included in a softcover volume titled *Charleston Receipts,* first published in 1950 by The Junior League of Charleston, South Carolina. The following version of the dessert was adapted from the book and given to me by a young master chef, Bill Neal of Crook's Corner Restaurant in Chapel Hill, North Carolina.

6 ounces pecan meats (about 1 1/2 cups)
1/2 cup flour
Salt to taste, if desired
2 teaspoons baking powder
2 apples (about 3/4 pound)

3 large eggs
1 cup plus 1 tablespoon sugar
1 teaspoon pure vanilla extract
2/3 cup heavy cream
8 crisp, toasted, browned pecans

1. Preheat the oven to 325 degrees.
2. Butter the bottom and sides of two 9-inch cake pans. Cut 2 rounds of wax paper to fit inside the bottom of the pans. Place rounds in the pans and butter lightly. Sprinkle the paper with flour; shake out the excess.
3. Process the pecan meats in a food processor or electric blender until fine but not a paste.
4. Put the processed pecans in a mixing bowl and add 1/2 cup flour, the salt, and baking powder. Blend well.
5. Peel the apples and cut them into quarters. Cut away the cores. Cut each quarter into thin slices, and the slices into thin strips. Cut the strips into very small cubes. There should be about 2 cups. Add the apples to the pecan mixture and stir to blend well.

6. Beat the eggs with a whisk or electric mixer, about 2 minutes. Continue beating while gradually adding 1 cup sugar, a little at a time, about 5 minutes. Beat in the vanilla. Gradually fold in the apple mixture.

7. Pour an equal portion of the batter into each of the prepared pans and smooth over the tops. Place the pans on the center shelf of the oven and bake 35 minutes, or until a cake tester inserted in the center comes out clean.

8. Transfer the cake pans to a rack and let stand 10 minutes.

9. Run a knife around the rim of each cake and unmold. Let stand on a rack until the layers are cool.

10. Put the cream in a mixing bowl and start beating. Gradually add the remaining 1 tablespoon sugar and continue beating until the cream is stiff.

11. Spread 1 cake layer with slightly more than half the whipped cream. Top with the second layer.

12. Spoon the remaining whipped cream into a pastry bag outfitted with a No. 5 star tube. Pipe 8 rosettes of whipped cream on top of the cake.

13. Chill the cake briefly. Top each rosette with a pecan.

YIELD: 8 SERVINGS.

STRAWBERRY SHORTCAKE

THE BISCUITS:

2 1/2 cups unbleached flour
2 tablespoons baking powder
2 tablespoons granulated sugar
12 tablespoons butter, cut into small
    pieces

1 cup sour cream
2 large eggs, lightly beaten
1 teaspoon pure vanilla extract

THE ASSEMBLY:

4 pints strawberries
2 tablespoons fresh lemon juice

1/2 cup superfine sugar
2 cups heavy cream

1. Preheat the oven to 450 degrees.

2. Put the flour, baking powder, and granulated sugar into a sifter. Sift the mixture into a mixing bowl.

3. Add the butter and work with the fingers until well blended. Make a well in the center and add the sour cream, eggs, and vanilla. Blend well with the fingers.

4. Turn the dough out onto a lightly floured board and knead briefly.

5. Roll the dough out on a lightly floured surface into a circle about 12 inches in diameter and about ½ inch thick. Using a biscuit cutter about 3 inches in diameter, cut the dough into rounds. As the rounds are cut, arrange them on an ungreased baking sheet an inch or so apart. Gather up the remaining scraps of dough and roll out. Cut out more rounds. Continue rolling and cutting until all the dough is used. There should be 12 to 16 rounds.

6. Place in the oven and bake 15 minutes.

7. Meanwhile, pick over the strawberries. Pick out 12 to 16 perfect, unstemmed berries and set them aside. Remove and discard the stems from the remaining berries, and cut them in half. There should be about 4½ cups. Put the berries in a bowl.

8. Add the lemon juice and superfine sugar and blend well. Cover and refrigerate.

9. Split the biscuits in half. Arrange half of them on a serving dish.

10. Whip the heavy cream.

11. Using a pastry bag and star tube, pipe stars of whipped cream around the inside rim of each biscuit half. Fill the inside of the ring with the sweetened strawberry halves. Top each serving with the remaining biscuit halves. Pipe whipped cream around the inside rim of each. Fill the centers with more of the sweetened strawberries. Garnish each serving with 1 of the reserved whole strawberries.

YIELD: 6 TO 8 SERVINGS.

CHARLOTTE RUSSE WITH BOURBON

I have often wondered why a dessert so traditional in French pastry making should be considered so decidedly Southern. But that is the case with a charlotte russe. I was weaned on it and it remains to this day one of my favorite creations.

8 egg yolks
1 cup granulated sugar plus more to
  taste
2 cups milk
¾ cup coffee
2 envelopes unflavored gelatin

12 to 18 ladyfingers
¼ cup water
2 tablespoons bourbon
1½ cups heavy cream
1 tablespoon confectioners' sugar

1. Place the egg yolks in a saucepan and add 1 cup granulated sugar. Beat vigorously with a whisk until light and lemon-colored.

2. Bring the milk to the boil in a saucepan, and add it gradually to the yolk mixture, stirring constantly. Add ½ cup coffee and cook, stirring, until the sauce coats a wooden spoon. Turn off the heat but continue stirring. Blend the gelatin with the remaining ¼ cup coffee and add it to the hot custard, stirring to dissolve. Strain the mixture through a fine sieve. Let cool.

3. While the custard is cooling, lightly oil the bottom and sides of a round mold. Line the mold with the ladyfingers. To do this, start by placing a small round of ladyfinger in the center. Cover the bottom with a daisy-petal pattern, using the small round as a focal point. Stand ladyfingers side by side upright and close together around the sides. Blend the water and bourbon and brush the ladyfingers with it.

4. When the custard is cool and still unset, whip 1 cup cream in a large mixing bowl. Pour in the custard and fold it in to blend well. Pour the mixture into the ladyfinger-lined mold. Refrigerate several hours, or until set.

5. Unmold the charlotte onto a round serving platter. Whip the remaining ½ cup cream and add sugar to taste. Spread this over the top and sides of the charlotte.

YIELD: 8 TO 10 SERVINGS.

PERSIMMON PUDDING

¼ pound butter, at room temperature
1 cup sugar
5 large persimmons
2 eggs, beaten
¼ cup sifted flour
1 teaspoon baking powder
½ teaspoon cinnamon

¼ teaspoon ground cloves or allspice
¼ teaspoon salt, if desired
¼ cup white cornmeal
1½ cups milk
1 cup grated raw sweet potato
1 teaspoon vanilla

1. Preheat the oven to 350 degrees.
2. Work the butter and sugar together with a wooden spoon until creamy.
3. Force enough persimmons through a food mill to yield 3 cups of pulp.
4. Add the pulp to the butter and sugar along with the eggs, beating well.
5. Sift together the flour, baking powder, cinnamon, cloves or allspice, and salt. Stir in the cornmeal.
6. Add the dry ingredients alternately with the milk to the persimmon mixture. Add the sweet potatoes and vanilla.
7. Turn into a greased 2-quart casserole and bake 1 hour, stirring thoroughly four times as the mixture bakes.
8. Serve warm with whipped cream, if desired.

YIELD: 12 SERVINGS.

EGGNOG MOUSSE

4 cups milk
1 vanilla bean, split, if available, or
   1 1/2 teaspoons pure vanilla extract
8 egg yolks
1 cup sugar
3 envelopes unflavored gelatin

1/3 cup water
1/4 cup bourbon
2 cups heavy cream
Apricot Sauce (see following recipe)
Whipped cream, optional

1. Bring the milk with the split vanilla bean to the boil. Do not boil further. If the bean is not to be used, add the vanilla extract later. Remove the vanilla bean, if used, rinse it off, dry it, and reserve for subsequent use.

2. Place the yolks in a saucepan and add the sugar. Beat with a wire whisk until thick and lemon-colored.

3. Gradually add the milk to the yolk mixture, beating constantly. Use a wooden spoon and stir constantly, this way and that, making certain that the spoon touches all over the bottom of the saucepan. Cook until the mixture has a custardlike consistency and coats the sides of the spoon. Do not let the sauce boil, or it will curdle. Add the vanilla extract, if used.

4. Soften the gelatin in the water and add it to the sauce, stirring to dissolve. Add the bourbon and strain the mixture into a bowl. Let cool.

5. Whip the heavy cream until stiff and fold it into the mixture.

6. Rinse out a 10- to 12-cup ring mold without drying. Sprinkle the inside with sugar and shake out the excess. Pour in the custard mixture and place in the refrigerator. Chill several hours or overnight, until the custard is set.

7. When ready to serve, dip the mold into hot water and remove immediately. Wipe off and unmold. A damp, hot cloth could also be used on the mold to help loosen the mousse. Serve with apricot sauce and, if desired, whipped cream.

YIELD: 12 OR MORE SERVINGS.

APRICOT SAUCE

1 1/2 cups apricot preserves
1 tablespoon water

2 tablespoons rum, Mirabelle, or other
liqueur

Combine the preserves with the water in a saucepan and cook over low heat, stirring, until smooth and melted. Stir in the rum and serve.

YIELD: ABOUT 1½ CUPS.

BASIC VANILLA ICE CREAM

6 egg yolks
1 cup sugar
4 cups milk

1 cup heavy cream
1 vanilla bean, or 2 teaspoons pure
vanilla extract

1. Put the yolks and sugar in a heavy saucepan. Beat with a wire whisk until pale yellow.

2. In another saucepan combine the milk and cream. If the vanilla bean is used, split it down 1 side and add it. Bring just to the boil.

3. Add about ½ cup of the hot mixture to the egg yolk mixture and beat rapidly. Add the remaining hot mixture, stirring rapidly. Scrape the tiny black seeds from the center of the vanilla bean into the custard. Heat slowly, stirring and scraping all around the bottom with a wooden spoon. Bring the mixture almost, but not quite, to the boil. The correct temperature is 180 degrees. This cooking will rid the custard of the raw taste of the yolks.

4. Pour the mixture into a cold mixing bowl to prevent it from cooking further. Let stand until cool or at room temperature. If the vanilla bean is not used, add the vanilla extract at this point.

5. Pour the mixture into the container of an electric or hand-cranked ice cream freezer and freeze according to the manufacturer's instructions.

YIELD: 8 TO 12 SERVINGS.

FRESH PEACH ICE CREAM

1 cup heavy cream
2 cups milk
4 egg yolks
1 cup sugar

Salt to taste, if desired
1 teaspoon pure vanilla extract
1 cup peeled, pitted, and crushed
  ripe peaches

1. In a saucepan with a heavy bottom, combine the cream, milk, egg yolks, ½ cup sugar, salt, and vanilla. Cook over low heat or in a double boiler, stirring constantly with a wooden spoon all around the bottom to make sure the custard does not stick.

2. Continue cooking and stirring until custard is as thick as heavy cream (180 degrees). This cooking will rid the custard of the raw taste of the yolks. Remove the custard from the heat at once, stirring constantly for a minute or so. Let cool.

3. To the peaches add the remaining ½ cup sugar. Stir to dissolve. Add this to the custard.

4. Pour the mixture into the container of an electric or hand-cranked ice cream freezer and freeze according to the manufacturer's instructions.

YIELD: 8 TO 10 SERVINGS.

CARAMEL PECAN ICE CREAM

6 egg yolks
1 ¼ cups sugar
4 cups milk
1 cup heavy cream

1 vanilla bean, or 2 teaspoons pure
  vanilla extract
2 tablespoons water
1 ½ cups pecans, coarsely broken

1. Preheat the oven to 350 degrees.

2. Put the egg yolks and ¾ cup sugar in a heavy casserole. Beat with a wire whisk until pale yellow.

3. Combine the milk and cream in a saucepan. Bring just to the boil.

4. Add about ½ cup of the hot mixture to the egg yolk mixture and beat rapidly. Add the remaining hot mixture, stirring rapidly. Scrape the tiny black seeds from the center of the vanilla bean into the custard. If vanilla extract is used, it will be added later. Heat slowly, stirring and scraping all around the bottom of the pan with a wooden spoon. Bring the mixture almost but not quite to the boil. The correct temperature is 180 degrees. This cooking will rid the custard of the raw taste of the yolks.

5. As the custard heats, combine the remaining ½ cup sugar with the water. Heat slowly. Cook gently, stirring, until the sugar becomes golden brown. Continue cooking until the sugar is a dark amber. Take extreme care that the sugar does not burn; if it burns, it will be bitter.

6. Add about 1 cup of the custard to the caramel, stirring. Return this caramel mixture to the custard, stirring.

7. Pour the mixture into a cold mixing bowl to prevent it from cooking further. Let stand until cool or at room temperature. If the vanilla bean is not used, add the vanilla extract at this point.

8. Meanwhile, put the pecans in a pan and place in the oven. Bake 10 minutes, or until crisp and nicely toasted. Let cool.

9. Pour the custard mixture into the container of an electric or hand-cranked ice cream maker. Partly freeze according to the manufacturer's instructions.

10. Add the pecans and continue freezing until the ice cream is solid.

YIELD: 8 TO 12 SERVINGS.

COCONUT ICE CREAM

5 cups grated fresh coconut (page
   279)
1 cup sugar

3 cups milk
5 egg yolks

1. Put the grated coconut in a saucepan and add the sugar and milk. Bring to the boil and cook about 5 minutes. Let cool.

2. Strain the liquid through a piece of cheesecloth and squeeze the coconut meat to extract as much liquid as possible. Reserve 2 cups of the grated meat and discard the rest or put it to another use.

3. Put the egg yolks in a mixing bowl and beat with a whisk. Beat in the sweetened liquid and scrape the mixture into a saucepan and heat. Use a wooden spoon and stir constantly, this way and that, making certain that the spoon touches all over the bottom of the saucepan. Cook until the mixture has a custardlike consistency and coats the sides of the spoon (180 degrees). Do not let the sauce boil, or it will curdle. This cooking will rid the custard of the raw taste of the yolks.

4. Immediately remove the sauce from the heat and continue stirring. Set the saucepan in a basin of cold water to reduce the temperature. Let the sauce cool to room temperature.

5. Pour the custard into the container of an electric or hand-cranked ice cream maker. Partly freeze according to the manufacturer's instructions. Add the reserved 2 cups coconut pulp and continue freezing until solid.

YIELD: 12 OR MORE SERVINGS.

STRAWBERRY ICE CREAM

4 egg yolks	*1 cup water*
2 cups plus 1 tablespoon sugar	*2 pints strawberries, hulled and rinsed*
4 cups milk	*1 cup heavy cream*

1. Place the yolks in a large saucepan and add 1 cup sugar. Beat with a wire whisk until light and lemon-colored.

2. Meanwhile, bring the milk almost but not quite to the boil.

3. Gradually add the milk to the yolk mixture, beating constantly. Use a wooden spoon and stir constantly, this way and that, making certain that the spoon touches all over the bottom of the saucepan. If a thermometer is available, cook to 180 degrees and remove from the heat. If a thermometer is not available, cook the sauce until it becomes like a very thin custard. This cooking will rid the custard of the raw taste of the yolks. Immediately pour and scrape the sauce into a mixing bowl to prevent further cooking. Let cool.

4. Meanwhile, put the water in a saucepan and add 1 cup sugar. Stir and bring to the boil. Simmer 10 minutes and remove from the heat. Let cool.

5. Put the strawberries into the container of a food processor or an electric blender and blend thoroughly. Combine the strawberries with the sugar syrup and the custard.

6. Whip the cream and before it is stiff beat in the remaining 1 tablespoon sugar. Fold the cream into the strawberry mixture. Pour the mixture into the container of an electric or hand-cranked ice cream freezer and freeze according to the manufacturer's instructions.

YIELD: 12 TO 16 SERVINGS.

BUTTER PECAN ICE CREAM

Pecans were introduced to the East Coast (perhaps from Texas) by Thomas Jefferson, who moved a few trees from the Mississippi Valley to Monticello, Virginia. He, in turn, gave a few trees to George Washington, who planted them at Mount Vernon. Three of those original trees are said to remain in existence.

I have a special fondness for butter pecan ice cream, and one of the finest recipes I have ever sampled is that of Patrick O'Connell, chef and co-owner of The Inn at Little Washington, a splendid establishment with elegant food in Washington, Virginia.

2½ cups heavy cream	9 egg yolks
1 cup milk	1 cup sugar
¼ pound butter	1 teaspoon pure vanilla extract
1½ cups whole pecans	Caramel Sauce (see following recipe)

1. Combine 1 cup cream with the milk in a saucepan and bring to the boil. Pour the mixture into another container and chill thoroughly. A film will form on top when the mixture is chilled. Remove this film.

2. Heat the butter in a heavy skillet and add the pecans. Cook, shaking the skillet and stirring, until the pecans begin to brown. Strain but reserve both the butter and pecans.

3. Put the yolks in a mixing bowl and add ½ cup sugar. Beat thoroughly.

4. Bring the remaining 1½ cups cream and ½ cup sugar to the boil in a heavy saucepan. Slowly pour half this mixture into the egg mixture, beating constantly. Return this mixture to the saucepan with the remaining cream-and-sugar mixture and heat gently without boiling, or the egg might curdle. Stir in the reserved butter in which the pecans were cooked, and add the vanilla. Pour and scrape the mixture into a mixing bowl and add the chilled cream mixture. Add the pecans and pour and scrape the mixture into the container of a hand-cranked or electric ice cream freezer. Freeze according to manufacturer's instructions.

5. Serve with caramel sauce.

YIELD: 8 OR MORE SERVINGS.

CARAMEL SAUCE

1½ cups heavy cream	⅓ cup water
1⅓ cups sugar	1 teaspoon pure vanilla extract

1. Put the cream in a saucepan and bring to the boil. Set aside.

2. Combine the sugar and water in a saucepan and bring to the boil. Use a brush dipped in cold water and brush the inside of the saucepan, brushing just about the level of the simmering sauce. Cook over high heat until the mixture is golden brown.

3. Remove from the heat and slowly whisk in the reserved cream. Return to the boil and cook over low heat for 2 to 3 minutes. Stir in the vanilla.

YIELD: ABOUT 2 CUPS.

PERSIMMON ICE CREAM

3 cups heavy cream
7 egg yolks
½ cup honey
6 to 8 soft, ripe, unblemished
  persimmons (about 1½ pounds)

Pecan Sauce (see following recipe),
  optional
Whole pecans for garnish, optional

1. Bring the cream to the boil and set aside briefly.
2. Combine the egg yolks and honey in a heatproof mixing bowl and blend well. Set the bowl inside a skillet and add water to the skillet. Bring water to the boil and, using a wire whisk, beat the honey and yolks until quite thick, about 5 minutes.
3. Add about ½ cup of the hot cream to the yolk mixture, beating rapidly. Add the remaining cream, stirring vigorously.
4. Bring the custard mixture almost to the boil, but do not let it boil or it will curdle. Cook, stirring constantly, about 10 minutes. The correct temperature is 180 degrees. This cooking will rid the custard of the raw taste of the yolks. Put the mixture through a fine sieve and let it cool.
5. Meanwhile, peel the persimmons and remove the seeds. There should be about 2 cups of pulp. Put the pulp into the container of a food processor or electric blender and blend as fine as possible.
6. Add the persimmon pulp to the cream mixture. Pour the mixture into the container of an ice cream freezer and freeze according to the manufacturer's instructions.
7. If desired, serve the ice cream with pecan sauce. To serve, spoon the sauce onto a dessert plate. Add a scoop of ice cream to the center. Surround each scoop of ice cream with pecan halves arranged symmetrically, if desired.

YIELD: 8 OR MORE SERVINGS.

PECAN SAUCE

1 cup whole or broken pecan halves	*¼ cup sugar*
(about ¼ pound)	*2 tablespoons water*
¼ pound butter, at room temperature	*¾ cup heavy cream*

1. Put the pecan meats in the container of a food processor or electric blender. Blend as fine as possible.

2. Add the butter and blend thoroughly.

3. Combine the sugar and water in a heavy saucepan. Bring to the boil and let cook, stirring often with a wire whisk, until the mixture turns amber. Continue cooking, stirring, until the sugar mixture becomes the color of dark caramel.

4. Immediately add ½ cup of the pecan butter, stirring, and stir in the heavy cream. Bring to the boil and remove from the heat. Add the remaining pecan butter and stir to blend.

5. Pour the mixture into a mixing bowl. Let cool. Serve at room temperature.

YIELD: ABOUT 2½ CUPS.

NOTE: *The sauce will harden if refrigerated. To restore, set the bowl containing the sauce in a basin of hot water until it softens.*

BURNT-SUGAR ICE CREAM WITH BUTTERSCOTCH SAUCE

THE ICE CREAM:

2 cups milk	*1½ tablespoons finely grated*
1 large egg	*orange rind*
¼ cup flour	*1 cup heavy cream*
1 cup sugar	

THE BUTTERSCOTCH SAUCE:

1 1/2 cups sugar

1 1/2 cups light corn syrup

4 tablespoons butter

2/3 cup heavy cream

1/4 cup bourbon whiskey

1. Bring the milk to the simmer.

2. Combine the egg, flour, and 1/2 cup sugar in the bowl of an electric mixer. Start beating the mixture until it is thoroughly blended, then pour in the hot milk. Pour and scrape the sauce into a saucepan and start beating over moderate heat. Cook until the mixture is thickened and smooth.

3. Put the remaining 1/2 cup sugar in a small nonstick skillet and cook, stirring, until the sugar is melted and starts to take on a light caramel color. Immediately add the orange rind and blend, stirring constantly. Remove from the heat and add the caramel-orange mixture to the sauce. Blend well.

4. Line a mixing bowl with a sieve and pour the sauce into it, pressing all around with the sides of a rubber spatula to extract as much flavor as possible from the orange rind. Discard the rind.

5. Add 1 cup heavy cream and stir. Let cool. Pour the mixture into the container of a hand-cranked or electric ice cream maker and freeze according to the manufacturer's instructions.

6. Meanwhile, make the sauce. Put the sugar in a 12-inch nonstick skillet and cook, stirring, until the sugar is melted and becomes dark caramel in color. Add the corn syrup, stir to blend, and remove from the heat. Stir in the butter to blend. Stir in the 2/3 cup cream and the bourbon. Serve with the ice cream.

YIELD: 6 TO 8 SERVINGS.

PECAN SUGAR COOKIES

2 cups unbleached flour
1 ½ teaspoons baking powder
½ cup sugar
8 tablespoons butter

2 eggs, lightly beaten
½ teaspoon lemon extract
2 teaspoons pure vanilla extract
¾ cup chopped pecans

1. Sift the flour, baking powder, and sugar together into a mixing bowl. Add the butter, eggs, lemon extract, vanilla, and pecans. Blend thoroughly with the hands.

2. Shape the dough into 2 rolls, each about 1½ inches thick. Wrap each roll neatly in wax paper. Chill for 30 minutes or longer.

3. Preheat the oven to 350 degrees.

4. Lightly flour a baking sheet, shaking off the excess flour.

5. Slice each roll crosswise into rounds, each about ½ inch thick, or slightly less. Arrange rounds on the baking sheet. Place in the oven and bake 25 to 30 minutes, or until golden brown. Remove and let cool.

YIELD: ABOUT 3 DOZEN.

SOUTHERN AMBROSIA

4 large, heavy, sweet seedless oranges
1 cup freshly grated coconut (page 279)

⅓ cup confectioners' sugar, more or less to taste

1. Peel the oranges. Slice them or section them with a knife. Put them in a crystal bowl.

2. Add the coconut and mix gently.

3. Sprinkle with confectioners' sugar and chill until ready to serve.

YIELD: 6 SERVINGS.

NOTE: *Some people add cubed bananas to the ambrosia; others add pineapple cubes, and some add a final garnish of whipped cream, but this last step is not appropriate.*

CREOLE PRALINES

Like a great deal of French cooking that was "borrowed" by the residents of Louisiana many years ago, pralines, Creole style, underwent a sea-change in preparation from one country to the other. The classic praline of the French kitchen is made by cooking almonds, preferably whole, with sugar, until the sugar becomes liquid and then becomes caramel-colored. The mass is spooned onto a greased board and allowed to cool. When it cools it becomes brittle and can be cracked easily. The Creole version of this confection is made with pecan halves cooked with brown sugar and butter to the soft-ball stage. It is then spooned onto a flat surface. When it is cooled it is fairly soft to the bite; it is not brittle.

2 cups granulated sugar
1 cup dark brown sugar
1/4 pound butter

1 cup milk
2 tablespoons dark corn syrup
4 cups pecan halves

1. Combine all the ingredients except the pecans in a heavy 3-quart saucepan. Cook 20 minutes, stirring constantly, after the boil is reached.

2. Add the pecans and continue cooking until the mixture reaches a temperature of 236 degrees on a candy thermometer, or forms a soft ball when dropped into cold water.

3. Arrange several sheets of wax paper over layers of newspapers.

4. Stir the praline mixture well. Drop it by tablespoons onto the sheets of wax paper. Let cool. When cool, stack the pralines in an airtight container, with wax paper between the layers.

YIELD: 30 TO 36 PRALINES.

SUGARED PECANS

Do not attempt this recipe on a rainy or damp day; the sugar will not harden.

½ cup sugar	⅛ teaspoon salt, if desired
½ cup heavy cream	1 tablespoon butter
1 tablespoon light corn syrup	2 cups whole pecans
Grated rind of 1 orange	

1. In a small heavy skillet, combine the sugar, cream, corn syrup, grated orange rind, salt, and butter. Bring to the boil and cook, stirring constantly, until the mixture reaches a temperature of 240 degrees on a candy thermometer, or when dropped into very cold water forms a soft ball that flattens on removal.

2. Remove from the heat, beating with a whisk. Pour and scrape the mixture into a mixing bowl. Beat with the whisk until cool.

3. Add the pecans and continue beating until they are coated. Separate the pecans and put them on a rack. Let them stand in a cool, dry place until the sugar coating firms up. This may take several hours, depending on the humidity. Store in an airtight container.

YIELD: ABOUT 2 CUPS.

PECAN BRITTLE

2 cups sugar	½ teaspoon baking soda
1 tablespoon butter	2 cups whole or broken pecans

1. Lightly oil the surface of a jelly-roll pan.

2. Put the sugar in a very heavy skillet and cook, stirring constantly, until the sugar turns golden brown. Continue cooking and stirring until the sugar turns amber-colored. Take care that the sugar does not burn; if it burns, it will taste bitter.

3. Immediately add the butter, baking soda, and pecans. When the baking soda is added, the mixture will foam up.

4. Turn the mixture out onto the prepared pan. Smooth it over with a spatula. Let cool. When hard, break up into bite-size pieces, and store in an airtight container.

YIELD: ABOUT 1¼ POUNDS.

CHOCOLATE FUDGE

2 ounces (2 squares) semisweet
  chocolate
2 cups superfine sugar
⅔ cup heavy cream or milk

2 tablespoons light corn syrup
2 tablespoons butter
1 teaspoon pure vanilla extract

1. Cut the chocolate into small bits so that it will melt more rapidly.

2. Combine the chocolate, sugar, cream or milk, and corn syrup in a saucepan and let simmer until the sugar is dissolved. Continue cooking, stirring frequently from the bottom, until the syrup reaches a temperature of 236 degrees on a candy thermometer. This is the soft-ball stage, which is to say that a little of the syrup dropped into a basin of very cold water will form a soft ball that will flatten on removal.

3. Remove the saucepan from the heat and add the butter, without stirring. Let the candy cool to lukewarm (100 degrees) and add the vanilla. Beat with a wooden spoon until the fudge loses its satiny look and a small amount spooned onto a plate will hold its shape. Pour the candy into lightly buttered pans.

4. Let cool to room temperature and cut into squares.

YIELD: ABOUT 3 DOZEN 1-INCH SQUARES.

PEANUT MOLASSES BRITTLE

2 cups sugar
1/2 cup molasses
1/2 cup water

5 1/2 tablespoons butter
1 teaspoon baking soda
2 cups blanched, roasted peanuts

1. Combine the sugar, molasses, and water in a saucepan and cook, stirring, until the sugar dissolves. Continue cooking over low heat until the temperature of 300 degrees is reached on a candy thermometer. Or test a few drops of syrup in cold water. It should be very brittle.

2. Remove the saucepan from the heat. Stir in the butter and beat in the baking soda. Add the peanuts and mix well. If the peanuts have been salted, remove the excess salt before adding them to the mixture.

3. Pour the mixture out onto a well-buttered slab or baking sheet. Smooth it over with a spatula. Mark the candy in squares, if desired. In any case, loosen the candy from the baking sheet while it is still warm. When cold, break it into squares or into irregular pieces. Store in an airtight container.

YIELD: ABOUT 1¾ POUNDS.

DIVINITY

3 cups sugar
2/3 cup water
1/2 teaspoon salt, if desired

3 egg whites
1 cup dark corn syrup

1. Combine the sugar, water, and salt in a saucepan and bring to the boil. Cook until a few drops crackle when added to cold water.

2. Have the corn syrup ready to heat in another saucepan.

3. Beat the egg whites until stiff, and when the sugar syrup is ready, remove it from the heat and place the corn syrup on to boil.

4. Immediately start adding the sugar syrup gradually to the egg whites while beating constantly. Scrape the mixture into the bowl of an electric mixer. Start beating.

5. Test the corn syrup. Heat until it spins a thread, that is to say when the syrup spins a 2-inch thread when dribbled from a fork or spoon. Start adding this syrup to the meringue, beating constantly on high speed.

6. Use 2 teaspoons to shape the candy into individual servings. If the mixture gets too thick to work with, add a few drops of water.

YIELD: 3 TO 4 DOZEN, DEPENDING ON SIZE.

CANDIED GRAPEFRUIT PEEL

I cannot fathom why candied grapefruit stands out in my mind as a great Southern specialty. I presume it is part of the American culture, nationwide, but it was very much a part of my life at home. Then again, my mother was a great candy maker.

8 large grapefruit	1 1/2 cups sugar, plus more for coating
1 1/2 cups water	the rind

1. Using a potato peeler, shave the rind off the grapefruit, in pieces as large but as thin as possible. Then cut the peel into thin strips. Cover with water, bring to the boil, and drain. Repeat the boiling process three times. The fourth time, cook the peel for 15 minutes after it comes to the boil. Drain thoroughly.

2. Combine 1½ cups sugar with 1½ cups water. Add the peel and cook over low heat, about 45 minutes, until the syrup has almost evaporated. Keep an eye out while the syrup cooks so the peel doesn't stick to the pan and scorch.

3. Sprinkle a large tray with lots of sugar. Add the drained peel and mix until every piece is thickly coated. Dry on a wire rack. This will take a day (in dry weather).

YIELD: ABOUT 1½ CUPS.

NOTE: *You can substitute 12 large lemons or 8 large navel oranges for the grapefruit.*

WHISKEY BALLS

This confection—or at least a version of it—was an early Southern version of those chocolate truffles that became the rage for chocolate lovers during the 1980s in this country. The whiskey balls are made, of course, with cocoa rather than chocolate.

3 cups vanilla wafer crumbs
½ cup finely chopped pecans
½ cup unsweetened cocoa
2 cups confectioners' sugar

½ cup bourbon
3 tablespoons light corn syrup
Salt, if desired

1. Blend together the crumbs, nuts, cocoa, 1 cup confectioners' sugar, bourbon, corn syrup, and a dash of salt. Form into small balls the size of walnuts.
2. Roll each ball in the remaining 1 cup confectioners' sugar and place on a cookie sheet. Chill in the refrigerator for several hours or overnight.

YIELD: ABOUT 3 DOZEN.

NOTE: *It is traditional in the South to use bourbon, but rye may also be used.*

MISSISSIPPI DELTA EGGNOG

I was raised in a home where alcohol was permitted only once a year, and that was at Christmas. My mother was famous for her eggnog and no wonder—it was heavily spiked with bourbon. Because she was a dedicated Southerner, no other whiskey, or anything as alien as rum or Cognac, would do. I remember Christmas as a very special time when almost everyone in the house (except my father, who was a lifelong teetotaler) became a trifle giddy.

8 large eggs, separated　　　　*½ cup heavy cream*
¾ cup sugar　　　　　　　　　*Nutmeg*
1 cup bourbon

1. Put the egg yolks and sugar into the bowl of an electric mixer and beat until light and lemon-colored.
2. Gradually add the bourbon, beating on low speed.
3. Whip the cream until stiff and fold it into the egg yolk mixture.
4. Whip the egg whites until stiff peaks form and fold them into the eggnog.
5. Serve in goblets or mugs with a sprinkling of nutmeg on top.

YIELD: 8 SERVINGS.

KENTUCKY EGGNOG

12 eggs, separated　　　　　*2 cups milk*
4½ cups sugar　　　　　　　*6 cups heavy cream*
1 quart bourbon　　　　　　*2 cups Cognac*
2 cups dark rum

1. Beat the egg yolks until they are light and frothy, and continue beating while adding the sugar.

2. Slowly stir in the bourbon and rum. Stir in the milk and cream, and then the Cognac.

3. Beat the egg whites until stiff and fold in.

YIELD: ABOUT 20 CUPS.

EGGNOG FOR ONE

For those who do not want to make a nog in such volume, here is a recipe for an individual eggnog.

1 egg
3 tablespoons bourbon, rum, sherry,
   Cognac, or applejack

1 teaspoon sugar
½ cup milk
Nutmeg

1. Combine all the ingredients in a cocktail shaker and add 1 cup cracked ice. Shake vigorously, and strain into a tall glass.

2. Sprinkle with nutmeg and serve.

YIELD: ABOUT 1 CUP.

PLAIN EGGNOG

Although spirits are generally used in making eggnog, the drink is also delicious flavored only with a dash of nutmeg or coconut. Here is such an eggnog, especially recommended for the children who come to call during the holiday season.

6 eggs, separated
1/2 cup sugar
4 cups milk, scalded
1/4 teaspoon salt, if desired

2 cups heavy cream, whipped
2 teaspoons pure vanilla extract
Nutmeg or shaved coconut

1. Beat the egg yolks until light and frothy and add 1/4 cup sugar, still beating. Slowly stir in the hot milk. Cook over hot water, stirring constantly, until the mixture coats a spoon. Chill.

2. Add salt to the egg whites and beat until stiff. Add the remaining 1/4 cup sugar gradually, still beating.

3. Fold the egg whites and then the whipped cream into the mixture separately. Add the vanilla and chill for several hours.

4. Pour into cups and sprinkle with nutmeg or coconut.

YIELD: ABOUT TWENTY 1/2-CUP PORTIONS.

Index